14 JUN 1957

HORATIO BOTTOMLEY

1913.

HORATIO
BOTTOMLEY

A BIOGRAPHY BY

JULIAN SYMONS

LONDON

THE CRESSET PRESS

1955

First published in 1955
by the Cresset Press Ltd., 11 *Fitzroy Square, London, W*.1
Printed in Great Britain by Western Printing Services Ltd.
Bristol

ACKNOWLEDGMENTS

MANY people have helped me to write this book by giving me information or suggesting useful lines of approach. Among them I must thank particularly the Earl of Birkenhead, Mr. C. Bradlaugh Bonner, Mr. J. Crocker, Mr. Norman Edwards, Mr. W. J. Gage, Mr. Daniel George, Mr. John Hingeley, Viscount Rothermere, Mrs. Vera Stewart and Rear-Admiral Sir Murray F. Sueter. Mr. Philip Fothergill and the Liberal Party Organisation have answered queries most patiently. Mr. Roy Fuller has read the manuscript and helped to correct my ignorance in legal matters. I owe a particular debt, finally, to Mr. C. H. Norman, who has given me much helpful advice and has eliminated some errors of fact and interpretation.

J.S.

IN MEMORY OF
COLIN YOUNG

CONTENTS

ILLUSTRATIONS

Chapter I

THE YOUNG HORATIO

'The result of our investigations as to "the condition and prospects of the Company" is to show that its condition is insolvent and its prospect is liquidation.'— *Report by the Committee of Shareholders of the Anglo-Austrian Printing and Publishing Union Ltd., March 1891.*

THE CITY FINANCIER Osborne O'Hagan was not a man who wasted his time. From the moment he arrived at his office at ten o'clock in the morning he was busy dictating letters, elaborating ideas that had occurred to him at the opera or the card table the night before, using the telephone, or talking to the several people who were waiting to see him, either by appointment or simply because they had an urgently important business operation to propose, the success of which depended on O'Hagan's financial blessing.

Such is perhaps the normal life of a business man, although there are few financiers who can say with O'Hagan's assurance that they do not call on other people, because 'there is a certain rule in the City, and people were content to call on me'. But other things were going on in O'Hagan's offices that required his frequent attention. In his boardrooms directors of the many companies in which he was interested, were meeting almost every day. He looked in on most of these meetings for a short time, and then returned to his own office to give his lawyers and

B   1

accountants instructions for the preparation of contracts and investigation of accounts in connection with the new businesses in which he had been asked to take an interest. At five o'clock O'Hagan took an hour's rest, dictated until seven and then often went home for an evening of business negotiations conducted over a good dinner, succeeded by two or three hours' work before going to bed. In bed, no matter what the time, he spent an hour in meditation. 'I reviewed in my mind all I had done during the day, both in business and socially, and I was never lenient with myself for my faults and failings, whether of commission or omission.'

Such a life had brought this son of a Northern Irish civil engineer, who was known for his smiling face and his good stories, into a powerful position in the City in the eighteen-eighties, before he was thirty years old. At the age of eighteen he had tried to develop an ingenious scheme for a 'Reinsurance Company' which was to afford a free cover to the insurer against the failure of his chosen company (a danger much greater then than now); the profit was to come from the substantial commissions paid by insurance companies on the introduction of a policy. The scheme failed to obtain sufficient backing, but a man with such ideas could not be long in making his fortune. O'Hagan turned successfully to tramways, collieries, breweries and cement companies. His dealings were usually on a large scale, and it can only have been his invariable smiling courtesy, and a regard for his principle that a man should never be allowed to feel a sense of injury against him, that led him one day in 1886 to see a young man named Horatio Bottomley, who called upon him with a letter of introduction.

The young man was short, bulky, clean-shaven, with an open and friendly face and a manner of engaging frankness. Like most of the people who came to O'Hagan's office he wanted financial backing, in this case for a small company which he owned, called the Catherine Street Publishing Association. O'Hagan listened patiently to the young man, and then said that the business was too small for him. Had it been a printing business, he added, he might have been interested, because the firm could then have handled all the printing work for his various companies.

Bottomley went away. He came back a couple of days later, bringing with him a rough and downright Scotsman named Douglas MacRae, who owned a printing works which was working much below its full capacity. This time O'Hagan, as he had promised, was interested. He agreed to form a company which would take over MacRae's printing firm, Bottomley's Catherine Street Publishing Company, and another small firm of advertising agents and newspaper publishers named Curtice and Company. This company had a capital of £100,000 in one pound shares, of which half was underwritten by O'Hagan and his friends. A prospectus was issued and the shares offered for sale, but only 231 of them were taken up. Horatio Bottomley, who was then twenty-six years old, was appointed chairman of this company.

After MacRae, Curtice had been running for twelve months, with the benefit of O'Hagan's printing work, the firm rather surprisingly declared a dividend of 12 per cent; and, more surprisingly, although the shares had apparently still not been taken up, the capital of the company was increased by £20,000. Three company meetings were held, and at these the power of young Bottomley's oratory was for the first time made evident. There is no record of what he said on these occasions, what words he used to dazzle the indifferent and to convert enemies into friends. As a result of his persuasive powers, however, supported no doubt by some dexterous financial manipulation on the part of O'Hagan, the formerly unsaleable shares were sold

3

at a large profit. The price of these shares rose to thirty shillings, then to two pounds. Those who bought them at this price had, as O'Hagan demurely puts it, 'apparently secured a very desirable investment'.

Young Bottomley was not satisfied to be simply a persuasive chairman. MacRae, Curtice owned and published a number of small trade papers; they published also the *Financial Times*, which was at this time an unsuccessful rival to the *Financial News*, and the *Draper's Record*; and by his own account, written some years later, Bottomley suggested to MacRae that the two should divide their energies, one of them handling the printing and the other the newspapers. 'MacRae was a bit angry, and thought I was desirous of elbowing him out of the journal, so, with Quixotic impulse, I gave him the choice. He was a printer and I was a journalist—but he took the paper and left me the printing works.'

Such was Bottomley's story: which was true at least in the essentials that MacRae left the partnership, taking with him the *Financial Times*, which operated for years at a financial loss, and the well-established and prosperous *Draper's Record*. Left with the printing company Bottomley again approached Osborne O'Hagan and asked for his support. He had obtained options on a number of firms engaged in the printing and publishing trades. They were important firms; among them were Wymans, Clement Smith (who had at that time almost a monopoly in pictorial posters), a firm of newspaper publishers and a firm engaged in photographic reproduction. The idea behind such an amalgamation as Bottomley proposed was the revolutionary one of offering to newspaper proprietors and others the chance of having all their work handled by one large firm, instead of depending on several agents who operated independently of each other, as was customary. Last, and most important, Bottomley revealed to O'Hagan that he

4

had obtained an option on the printing of the Hansard reports of Parliamentary debates.

O'Hagan should have been impressed, and perhaps he was; but he refused to back the scheme. He liked Bottomley as a man, but had come to the conclusion that he was 'wanting in ballast' and 'unsuited to the paths of finance'. Bottomley managed without O'Hagan's backing. Within a few months the Hansard Publishing Union Limited was founded with a capital of £500,000. The directors of the company, besides Bottomley, were Sir Henry Isaacs, who had been Lord Mayor of London, Coleridge Kennard, who was the proprietor of the *Evening News*, a well-known Orientalist named A. P. Sinnett, and Sir Roper Lethbridge, who had been Press Commissioner to the Government of India. A month or two later the Anglo-Austrian Printing and Publishing Union Limited was founded, again with a capital of £500,000, and with the same directors, to whom must be added Lord Teynham and a Liberal Member of Parliament named Agg-Gardner.

Was the young Horatio unsuited to the paths of finance? That depends on what direction one expects those paths to take. If the prime purpose of high finance is to provide oneself with a comfortable living at the expense of others, the history of the Anglo-Austrian Printing and Publishing Union suggests that Bottomley was, at an uncommonly early age, well equipped to be a financier.

The company was designed to be a kind of companion to the Hansard Union. The Hansard Union was to be a printing federation for England, and the Anglo-Austrian Union was to extend this federation abroad by the purchase of various foreign printing and publishing businesses. The final pattern, had it been completed, would have been of a vast international trading organization which could have gained control of the printing industry by undercutting all

5

opposition when necessary: a pattern familiar today, but novel in the eighteen-eighties. With this end in view Bottomley went to Vienna. He was ignorant of any language but English, and the only person he knew in Austria was a retired officer, who augmented his pension by earning commissions as a patent and general agent. This ignorance of language and people proved no bar to his success. He was taken to the Grand Hotel and installed there in the apartments occupied by the Prince of Wales on his visits to Vienna; the entire male staff of the hotel waited in the courtyard to receive him. This reception had been arranged by the agent, who came to the hotel every morning with a few friends to join Bottomley in drinking champagne and eating caviar. The agent accompanied Bottomley to various printing firms and there acted as his interpreter; he introduced the visitor to Dr. Kunwald, an English-speaking Austrian lawyer, and to several journalists who spread news of the vast purchasing scheme in the wind. The agent obtained interviews with the Home Secretary, the Minister of Commerce, and even, on the morning before Bottomley's departure, with the Austrian Prime Minister, Count Taaffe.

Bottomley's Austrian friends waited on him to accompany him on this visit. With surprise he saw that they were wearing evening dress, with distress remembered that he had sent his own baggage forward, and had no clothes except those he stood up in. It was unthinkable, his friends said, that he should be presented to Count Taaffe in anything but evening dress, and a suit was borrowed from a man who was, like Bottomley, stout and stumpy. Too stout and stumpy, in fact, so that the visitor was compelled to pad up to meet the Prime Minister. The interview was successful. Before Bottomley left for home he had obtained options on thirteen Austrian printing and publishing firms, and there is no doubt that his project, as *The Times* correspondent said, 'had the goodwill of the Austrian Government'.

Back in England, Bottomley told his fellow directors that he could obtain the thirteen companies for £600,000, and showed them a telegram from the Austrian committee which had been formed to carry out the transfers of the various firms. He stressed further that he must have £75,000 of this money at once to avoid forfeiture of the contracts. The directors obligingly gave Bottomley the money, a handsome gesture on their part since the total subscription of shares came to only a little more than £90,000. There is some confusion about what happened afterwards. Bottomley obtained three prolongations of the Austrian options, but how much money he paid for doing so is not known. Several board meetings of the Union were held during the latter part of 1890. At these the directors, with the exception of Agg-Gardner, who had become dissatisfied with the way the company was being conducted, cheerfully voted themselves the customary fees; just as cheerfully they paid out further cheques to Bottomley of £10,000, £2,500 and £1,000, all of them described on the cheque counterfoils as for 'additional working capital'; and they even, with what must surely seem to the most euphoric financier an excess of optimism, declared a dividend of 8 per cent on the preference shares and 15 per cent on the ordinary shares. At these meetings no statement of account was presented, no reports were read, and no money except the original capital had been received.

Such a situation could hardly endure, and early in 1891 a committee of shareholders was appointed. They held several meetings, interviewed the directors, and issued the following simple and instructive statement of accounts:

	£	s.	d.		£	s.	d.
Receipts from Shares and Debentures	93,022	0	0	Cash—to Mr. Bottomley	88,500	0	0
				Three quarters' Debenture Interest	1,024	16	6
				Dividend-Preference	690	2	9
				Dividend-Ordinary	1,456	4	1
				Office Expenses	150	0	0
				Directors' Fees and Remuneration	1,116	11	0
				Stamp Duty and Bank Charges	58	0	8
				Balance at Bank	26	5	0
	£93,022	0	0		£93,022	0	0

'The Company has acquired no business in Vienna or elsewhere, has no property whatever, and its whole capital appears to be lost', reported the committee. They added of the £26 cash balance shown: 'The balance in hand was then about to be reduced, and there are not sufficient funds to pay the expenses of printing this Report.'

The history of the Hansard Publishing Union was less dramatic. Here the original £500,000 capital was all subscribed, so that there was a good deal of money to play with. At the end of the first year's business a dividend of 12 per cent was declared on the ordinary shares (the same dividend, it may be remembered, that was declared by MacRae, Curtice); and what may be called in the light of later events typically Bottomleyesque plans for expansion were made. Paper mills and country printing works were actually bought, and plans were made to purchase a variety of important printing, bookbinding and other firms. Henry Burt, an authoritative figure in the printing trade, who had been unequivocally opposed to the Union, was shown over the works already established and at a meeting of the shareholders expressed himself as astonished and deeply impressed by the immense possibilities of the organization. The Stock Exchange, which had at first refused to allow any dealings in the shares, granted them an official quotation. The expansion involved the doubling of the share capital to a million pounds. Mr. Burt told the shareholders that after the expansion had been completed the Union in its powers and possibilities would be superior to any organization of its kind in the country; and he readily accepted the post of general manager in the expanded company. In Bottomley's own words, however, 'wild rumours were floating about the City', rumours perhaps connected with the fate of the Anglo-Austrian Printing Union, and the second half-million was not by any means fully subscribed. The interest due to a Debenture Corporation which had underwritten a debenture issue of £250,000 remained unpaid; and this Corporation suddenly put in a receiver.

Why should the Debenture Corporation have done this, when the Hansard Union was moving from accomplished prosperity to a vision of riches? Bottomley indignantly asked, and it was a question he went on asking for years. He warned the shareholders that they were being tricked, and he excommunicated the treacherous Burt, who at the first sign of trouble became the ally of the Debenture Corporation. He hinted at a deliberate wrecking action by the proprietors of the businesses taken over, those who 'wear faultless frock coats and scrupulously correct hats and gloves—and tell their friends how greatly they have suffered by their unfortunate connection with the wicked Bottomley'.

All this was in vain. In vain, too, did he urge the appointment of a committee which should 'apply itself assiduously to the task of Reconstruction' with himself the principal reconstructor. In vain he attacked the liquidators and asserted that they were merely the tools of the Debenture Corporation. In vain he issued a tremendous 12,000

9

word 'Manifesto to the Hansard Shareholders' stressing
the solvency of the Union and attacking vigorously the
receiver, the owners of the various companies purchased,
the Debenture Corporation, and above all Burt, 'whose
enthusiasm for our Union a few months ago knew no
bounds, and who has received £40,000, in cash, of our
money'; a manifesto delayed in circulation because 'the
Debenture Corporation's Receiver has during my absence
locked up my Offices and denied me access to my papers,
including the set of envelopes I had prepared'. Unhappily
in vain all this. On the 1st of May 1891, Horatio Bottomley
filed his first petition in bankruptcy.

Chapter II

THE SECRET WORLD

Q. Has he the full use of his faculties?
A. Undoubtedly.
From the application made on 30 November 1869 for the admission of Horatio William Bottomley to Sir Josiah Mason's Orphanage, Birmingham.

THE PROMISING FINANCIAL career thus sharply checked began on the 23rd of March 1860, when Horatio William Bottomley was born in St. Peter Street, just off the Hackney Road in London. He was the second child of a tailor's cutter named William King Bottomley and his wife Elizabeth; they already had a two-year-old girl named Grace Madeline. Bottomley's father and mother both died while they were still in their thirties, before he was five years old, his father of tuberculosis and his mother of 'congestion of the brain'. The children were separated, Grace being adopted by a reasonably prosperous engineer, and Horatio William being sent to board in Battersea. His mother's maiden name had been Holyoake, and she was a sister of George Jacob Holyoake, the radical agitator and secularist who played a large part in founding the Co-operative movement. Holyoake had several children of his own, and he was a poor man, but he made a small weekly contribution to young Bottomley's support, and took some interest in him. He made application to Sir Josiah Mason's Orphanage and, thanks to a personal acquaintance with Mason, and to the fact that he was himself a native of

Birmingham, was successful. Horatio William went to the orphanage when he was just ten years old, and left at the customary age of fourteen. On the application form he is described as 'a healthy, promising child, likely to turn out clever and, no doubt, grateful'. The boy, Holyoake said, had been less than eight years old when his friends had attempted to procure his admission to a London institution, and he was 'suffering morally for want of training'.

There are few people alive today who remember the boy at the orphanage, but the shadowy picture that does come through is in general what might be expected. Young Bottomley was a short, thick-set boy with a large head, quiet and fond of reading, with no taste for schoolboy games and with few friends. It is said that he once raided the girls' quarters at night, was caught and sentenced to a severe thrashing and a week's bread and water in the clock tower of the orphanage. If that escapade is true, it is the only one associated with his name. He was above the average in ability, and extremely well behaved. Good behaviour was powerfully enforced. Sir Josiah Mason's Orphanage was no worse, perhaps better, than other mid-Victorian institutions of its kind: which means that the food was scanty and the discipline strict. 'I have not many happy recollections of our school days,' writes an old man who was at the orphanage with Bottomley. 'Life in fact was hardly worth living. It is not many of the "Old Boys" of my time who would admit ever being in the school.' One fragmentary letter of the time, written by young Bottomley to his uncle George Jacob Holyoake, tells him: 'You are allowed to send presents at any time, but they must be books, toys or fruit, but nothing in the shape of pudding or anything of the kind is allowed to come. . . .'

Bottomley does not seem to have been especially unhappy at the school, nor was he ashamed of having been a pupil there. When he left it he lived for a short time with

an aunt and uncle at Edgbaston, and worked as office boy
to a Birmingham builder. Then he came to London and
stayed with various members of the Holyoake family in
turn; among them his uncle William Holyoake, who was
an artist of sorts, and Mrs. Austin Holyoake who some years
later had considerable success as an actress in Ibsen's plays.
He fell ill, was sent for a short time to Brighton, and then
settled down in lodgings with a widow at Battersea. Here
he paid five shillings a week for his share of a bedroom,
and bought food which his landlady cooked for him. He
stayed in Battersea for two years, until he was married at
the age of twenty.

During these years after he left school the boy did a
variety of jobs. There was no one to help him, no one to
look after him; the Holyoakes, whether through lack of
money or for other reasons, gave him only a temporary
habitation. At Brighton he worked in a jeweller's shop
during his convalescence from illness; in London he was
office boy and general clerk in an ironworks, revised proofs
and did odd jobs for George Jacob Holyoake on *The
Secularist* and later on the *National Reformer*, and carried
round samples for a haberdasher. He also worked in a
City solicitor's office where the managing clerk for years
levied and collected a fictitious 'County Rate' upon many
firms in the City of London, actually taking offices from
which the usual Demand Notes and Final Notices were
issued. Here Bottomley mastered the procedure of the
Lord Mayor's Court, and learned to serve a writ and swear
an affidavit. When two policemen called one day and asked
the ingenious managing clerk to go with them to the
Guildhall, he moved on to another and more respectable
solicitor's office. Among the records kept for many years
by this solicitor is said to have been an engrossment in
which the word 'share' had been omitted by the copyist
and later inserted in Bottomley's unmistakable hand-

writing; an incident which has its own pleasant symbolism in the light of his later career.

In this office he learned shorthand and at the age of twenty joined Walpole's, a firm of shorthand writers attached to the law courts, in whose service he was enrolled as a Member of the Institute of Shorthand-Writers Practising in the High Court. Before long the name of the firm was changed to *Walpole and Bottomley*, and for some three years Bottomley attended the law courts as an official shorthand writer. What he learned there of argument and dicta, of the ingenuities and intricacies and loopholes of the law, marked his career for life. In 1880 he was married at the New Wesleyan Chapel in London Road, Wandsworth, to a young woman named Eliza Norton, and on the marriage certificate his profession is given as 'shorthand writer'.

All children live, more or less, within a secret world in which the details and shapes of their experiences appear in forms that must seem to adults strangely distorted. If we could enter that world completely all aberrations might be explained, though hardly all talents. There is a sense in which every biographer's task is the interpretation of his subject's childhood, the elucidation of tangled threads that can never be carried through quite to their origins in the conservatory or the woodshed, the double bed or the quarrel in the next room, the neglectful mother or the beautiful aunt. In Bottomley's life these years are a blank, in the sense that we know almost nothing of his thoughts, longings or fears during this formative time: yet a pattern may be suggested which has its significance, even though much in it remains ambiguous.

A small mist of ambiguity surrounds his birth. There is no substantial doubt that he was the son of William King Bottomley and Elizabeth Holyoake; yet the mist, although

14

so unsubstantial that it should be possible to blow it away with one good puff, is never quite dispersible. Bottomley bore a marked resemblance to Charles Bradlaugh, that determined secularist who provoked the greatest parliamentary storm of the nineteenth century when he insisted on merely assenting instead of taking the oath in full, when elected as Radical Member of Parliament for Northampton. The two faces are of a cast quite strikingly similar, although Bottomley's expression has a ruthlessness that is missing in Bradlaugh's. Bottomley professed an intense admiration for the famous freethinker, and for many years kept photographs and busts of Bradlaugh in his home and his offices, placed side by side with photographs of himself. He would draw the attention of visitors to the resemblance between the two faces, and would hint that he was Bradlaugh's illegitimate son. When hints were insufficient to arouse interest he resorted at times to direct statement. In an interview he gave shortly before his death to that most soulfully prurient of journalists James Douglas, Bottomley was asked ' Do you believe in life beyond the grave?'

'I am no religionist,' he replied. ' You know that Bradlaugh was my father. My mother was a beautiful woman. She died when I was four.'

The rash deduction has been made from these hints that he was the child of Bradlaugh and Annie Besant, an idea simply disproved by the fact that in the year of his birth Annie Besant was twelve years old. Is it possible that he was the illegitimate son of Bradlaugh and some other 'beautiful woman'—perhaps Elizabeth Holyoake, or some other member of the Holyoake family? The suggestion will outrage devout Bradlaughites, yet it is not absolutely impossible. Acceptance of it involves the assumption of a degree of complaisance on the part of the Holyoake family, and a very discreditable indifference to his illegitimate son on the part of Bradlaugh. Bottomley had some slight contact with Bradlaugh during the months that he worked in the secularist movement, but so far from taking a particular interest in the youth Bradlaugh is said to have expressed the opinion that he would come to no good end.

Behind the youthful shorthand writer there lay, in any case, years which must certainly have had their share of misery. In later life he made no attempt to hide the fact that he had been at the orphanage, and had worked for his living from the age of fourteen; and he bore no resentment against anybody connected with his youth. He returned each year to the orphanage, gave away presents, made speeches and paid for a great tea or outing for all the children; he attended the Holyoake family conferences, gave financial help when it was needed, and interested himself even in remote members of the family. The brass surface was that of the self-made man who proudly asserts his humble origin; beneath it lay who can tell what agonies, what spiritual defeats and personal humiliations?

We only know that defeats and humiliations were inevitable in the course of things: for the boy was not only an orphan but a child for whom there was nobody particularly to care, not only an intelligent boy but one whose ambition was stimulated by frequent contact with the high-minded Holyoakes, a family poor in worldly goods but within their own radical and free-thinking circle highly influential. He reacted sharply away from the Holyoakes and from Bradlaugh, and later referred often with contempt to the dull days spent reading Darwin, Huxley, Adam Smith and John Stuart Mill; yet he felt respect for them too, and a kind of yearning for the integrity of mind and conduct he rejected. Bradlaugh was now, and for years afterwards, his exemplar; and it should be realized that to profess oneself a follower of Bradlaugh in the eighteen-eighties was not a way to popularity. The personality that emerged from the secret world of childhood into adult life had still some adolescent features. Horatio Bottomley had an unprincipled generosity, a desire to dazzle others with the magnificence of his giving; a personal greediness for the things he had been denied in childhood, good food and drink, easy living; the wish to be famous rather than to be a great man. His assets were a mind wonderfully quick, light and limber, lacking in depth or subtlety; a self-deceiving egotism that was able to blend immediate generosity with a genuine deep insensibility to suffering; a fine natural vulgarity; and the peculiar sense of publicity methods likely to appeal to mass audiences which is often joined, as it was in him, with a tongue that can charm the banknotes out of men's pockets.

The fragmentary personal anecdotes that come through to us of his life in Battersea show a youth groping towards ideas and ways of life that will later become habits. He is often unable to pay the rent but always goes round to see the Shaftesbury estate manager in person, and obtains credit; is fond of using hansom cabs, for which he sometimes has to borrow the fare from his landlady; tells this landlady stories that he will inherit property when he is twenty-one; is kind and generous to the landlady's son; has to postpone his wedding because he is unable to pay for a wedding cake he has ordered. The girl he married, Eliza Norton, was the daughter of a collector at a local vinegar brewery. She worked as counter assistant in a dressmaker's, and was far from Bottomley's equal in intellect. It is likely that had he waited two or three years he would have realized the unwisdom of such a marriage on the part of a man who wished to make his way in the world. As it was, Eliza Bottomley played a very small part in her husband's life. She gave him a daughter named Florence, she made a home for him in these early days, she worried about keeping up the hire purchase payments on the furniture, she slapped his face when he bought a small dog with the money that

C 17

should have been used for a payment on the piano, she found it hard to get more than a pound a week from her husband as housekeeping money. 'Oh, 'Orace, do give me some', she cried one day when as the result of some deal he brought home fifty sovereigns: but the money was all apportioned to friends or dedicated for various purposes, and she got only two of the sovereigns for herself.

During the early eighteen-eighties a large number of debating societies were founded in London, conducted on the lines of the House of Commons, with government and opposition parties. These societies, some of which still exist today, were called Local Parliaments. Bottomley had the idea of reporting the proceedings of the Local Parliaments, and founded a small paper called the *Hackney Hansard* to report the Local Parliament in Hackney. When other societies asked for reports of their proceedings he blended them all in a weekly journal called *The Debater*. Some of the societies, Bottomley casually observes, granted *The Debater* small subsidies from their funds, 'receiving in return special attention from our reporting staff', which consisted of Bottomley and a fellow shorthand writer.

This publication was the germ of the Catherine Street Publishing Association, founded in 1885, which handled with more or less unsuccess a number of magazines and periodicals. Among them was *Youth*, a boys' paper notable only for the fact that Bottomley's sub-editor on it was a pale young man named Alfred Harmsworth; *The Municipal Review*, which specialized in publishing lengthy biographical notices of mayors in several boroughs, on the understanding that a large number of copies of the *Review* would be ordered for local distribution; the *Daily Recorder of Commerce*, which later (after Bottomley had sold it) became a commercial supplement to the *Financial News*, later still the *Evening Post*, and eventually was amalgamated with the *Evening News*; *The Mercantile Shipping Register*, *The Furniture Gazette*, and *Baby*, or *The Mother's Magazine*; with the *Draper's Record* and *Financial Times* already mentioned. Most of these periodicals were in Bottomley's possession when he first went to see Osborne O'Hagan. He did some kind of jobbing journalism for them all, writing leaders or gossip paragraphs, puffing the goods mentioned in the advertisement columns or the shares which his friends in the City wanted to sell. A little later he was engaged in an unsuccessful attempt to found an English daily paper published in Paris, which was to embody a modernized version of the current *Galignani's Messenger*.

The young man had also political aspirations. The roots of them lay partly in his association with Bradlaugh and Holyoake, partly in an urgent desire for personal publicity, and partly in the feeling that politics might one day provide him with a rich living. At the age of twenty-seven he met the Candidate Committee of the Hornsey Liberal Association, and was invited by them to stand as candidate for a vacancy caused by the elevation of the Tory member to the peerage. Hornsey was an impregnable Tory constituency, but in a lively campaign against H. C. Stephens (of Stephens' Ink) Bottomley succeeded in reducing a 3,000 majority to 1,800. Perhaps more remarkable is the fact that he induced Stephens to lend him money to fight the campaign, by offering him a series of bills which were afterwards allowed to go by default. After the election he received a complimentary note from Gladstone, and the local Liberal and Radical Association presented him with a silver tea and coffee service, accompanied by a tribute to political valour which had exceeded the line of duty:

> In the face of the most formidable difficulties, and without being animated by the hope of success, you entered on the contest with courage and energy, and conducted it with a

degree of vigour and of ability, as well as with a courtesy, which excited the admiration, and earned the gratitude, of your supporters.

He was invited to stand for the adjoining constituency of North Islington, which at the last election had returned a Conservative member with a majority of 1,500. By his own account he was a little reluctant to take on another forlorn hope, but once he had agreed to do so he nursed the constituency assiduously, in ways which would hardly be acceptable today. He opened soup kitchens as well as bazaars, and gave parties every Christmas for hundreds of children as well as addressing meetings very willingly on almost every possible occasion. During these years he perfected the particular blend of humorous egotism, moral sentiment and patriotic rhetoric which characterized him as a speaker; he developed the man-to-man approach which had such a powerful effect upon all kinds of audience, a combination of bulldog equalitarianism with the most evident and shameless snobbery. 'I have often observed that the most popular form of democracy is that which gives us the right to fraternize upon terms of equality with our social *superiors*,' he remarked. Speaking to the Liberal and near-Radical electors of North Islington no man was more Radical and nonconformistly equalitarian than he; and no man, at the same time, could confess more amiably his own weaknesses, his liking for a glass of champagne or a game of billiards or a flutter at the races, his eye for a pretty woman. His assertion is probably true, that when he filed his petition in bankruptcy and resigned as parliamentary candidate he had the constituency in his pocket. In these financial and commercial enterprises, now and throughout most of his life, he had helpers: and they were assistants of no ordinary kind, for these men were attached to him by personal as well as commercial bonds. They were at once bodyguards, confidential friends, boon

companions and errand boys; they could be employed upon
the most dubious financial missions or in the most delicate
emotional affairs; they lived on the pickings from his financial table and upon the money he gave them. Some of these
men were intelligent, all were audacious and unscrupulous, and all felt a respect that was almost worship for the
personality of their leader, who was already beginning to
be known as the Chief, the Governor, or H.B.

Chief of these helpers was a quick-witted minnow of a
man invariably known as Tommy Cox, although his
Christian names were Alfred Locke. Young Cox was a
medical student when he first met Bottomley and was fascinated by his eloquence and the rich warmth of his personality. Right from the beginning of Bottomley's career
as financier and company promoter, which has been seen
so far in its very earliest stages, Tommy Cox assisted him in
many capacities. Most notably he was a director or officer
of many companies, of the Catherine Street Publishing
Association and the Anglo-Austrian Printing and Publishing Union and later of dozens, almost of hundreds, of companies bearing such various names as the West Australian
Loan and General Finance Corporation, Nil Desperandum
Gold Mines and the John Bull Investment Trust and
Agency. The name of Alfred Locke Cox was to be found on
so many pieces of company literature, circulars, prospec-
tuses and even cheques, that he became known as 'Bottomley' rubber stamp'.

Although Tommy Cox idolized Bottomley he was in personality by no means a mere rubber stamp. He was a man
hardly more than five feet tall; a great drinker, with un-
alterably alcoholic breath; a great womanizer, with an un-
ending fund of dirty stories. A little ingenious wriggling
man, clever in his way, with his nose in everybody's business and his ear at every keyhole, all in his master's service. He will be found, now and hereafter, organizing those

parties for children and old people—and obtaining most of the food or gifts for nothing from local tradesmen; using a version of the modern advertising whispering campaign by 'dropping' Bottomley stories for circulation among publicans, barbers, shoeblacks and small shopkeepers; obtaining names of children in hospitals, sending them gifts in Bottomley's name and publicizing the incidents through local papers; addressing political meetings; furthering Bottomley's theatrical speculations, which as yet have reached no further than the backing of an unsuccessful piece called *The Bungalow*; organizing a claque who will be paid a shilling or two a head to cheer Bottomley as he enters the law courts or appears at political or company shareholders' meetings, the claque containing a few tough figures who will be very ready to shout down or even throw out any intransigent heckler or shareholder. A merry little grig, Tommy Cox, who loved his master and the world he lived in, and showed that love by his perpetual happy grin.

It was Tommy Cox who discovered a raucous good-natured leather-lunged orator who preferred the name of Perkins to his given name of John Harrison, and enlisted him into what Bottomley was later to call his stable. This Perkins is a professional orator, or ranter, who will speak in support of any sect or party if paid to do so. He speaks thunderously, and effectively, for Bottomley, and becomes known as 'the People's Perkins' in reference to his insistence that he is a man of the people, a true democrat. There are others, an Austrian Jew named Saul Cooper, a furrier, who makes himself generally useful in the City, and will lend such prestige as his name possesses to many a Bottomley enterprise; another furrier, Charles Dollman, Bottomley's relative by marriage; and others now forgotten in all but name.

The Bottomley stable is small as yet, but the whole of it has been engaged in one form or another of his enterprises, financial, journalistic or political. Now these enterprises grind slowly to a stop with the examination in bankruptcy conducted on behalf of the Official Receiver. There are awkward questions about books and papers, it is said that they have been slackly kept or not kept at all. Bottomley complains, Bottomley is indignant, finds himself unable to answer exactly the questions that are asked, but is indignant nevertheless.

'I am sorry to trouble you, not to answer the question; but I did not keep the books. Though I do not keep the books, indirectly I was manager of the company. I wish to give you a direct answer, if you think that I personally kept the books. I personally never kept a book in my life.' This he says in relation to the Hansard Union, but there are unpleasant remarks about the Anglo-Austrian Union as well. The upshot of it all is that the Board of Trade sanctions a prosecution, on the charge of conspiring to obtain money from shareholders of these companies. Bottomley appears at Bow Street, with Sir Henry Isaacs, Joseph Isaacs and Charles Dollman, and after a long, very long, investigation, is committed for trial by the magistrate, Sir John Bridge. Mysteriously, the case seems to be dropped. Nothing happens for months; until, in fact, Bottomley is in the witness box in relation to another case, and is asked during cross-examination: 'I believe you are awaiting trial on a criminal charge?'

'I really can't say,' he replied. 'I *was* committed many months ago, but the prosecution seems to have forgotten it.'

This is enough, and indeed too much. The evening newspapers come out with bills asking: 'What About Bottomley?' A day is fixed for the trial to be taken by Mr. Justice Hawkins.

Bottomley is not by any means dismayed by the prospect of the trial. He hurriedly produces in book form, probably with the help of Tommy Cox, a privately-printed self-justification called *Horatio Bottomley, Hys Booke*. The book's dedication is sufficiently remarkable:

DEDICATED
(*without permission*)
TO
SIR JOHN BRIDGE, KNIGHT,
Chief Magistrate of the Metropolis
*In Grateful Acknowledgement
Of the Opportunity He Has Given Me, Through The
Medium of an Impending Trial, To Vindicate
Myself Before the World.*

In a short preface the author considers the disaster that has come upon him:

> In the year 1890 I occupied a fairly respectable position in society—and enjoyed all the surroundings of unobtrusive prosperity. True, I did not keep race horses or coursing dogs, and was not a personal friend of the Prince, but I endeavoured to give good dinners and to tell good stories, and was therefore looked upon as one of the coming men. . . . In my presence I was spoken of as a great financier—in my absence, as a successful Company Promoter. At any rate, I was known to be connected with certain large undertakings, and also to be a candidate for parliamentary life—so my social credentials were complete; and I was quietly settling down to an admitted place amongst the Upper Nine.
>
> In 1891 my companies had come to grief, my affairs were in the Bankruptcy Court, I had ceased to be a candidate for Parliament—all was ruin and desolation around me!

The preface ends upon a swelling organ-note of righteous Victorian morality:

> Until the day of vindication arrives, I must wait patiently on, borne up by the hope that when these dark days are over, I may emerge, riper in experience, and with name unsullied,

yet to do something in the world to erase the blot, and perchance to relieve some of the suffering of a great catastrophe,
the moral responsibility for which, before God, I disclaim.

Even more characteristic, however, is a letter included
among the several pages of advertisements, for financial
periodicals and share dealers and corporations, at the end
of the book. The letter is contained in the advertisement of
Messrs. Fewings and Co., Public Accountants and Trustees
in Bankruptcy:

TO MESSRS. FEWINGS AND CO.
Dear Sirs,
I have much pleasure in certifying that you have been of
very great assistance to me in connection with my affairs, and
I shall certainly advise all my friends, as they become bank-
rupt, to avail themselves of your services.
Yours faithfully,
HORATIO BOTTOMLEY.

Chapter III

FIRST TRIUMPH: THE HANSARD UNION

'Your conduct of the defence was remarkable in its ability and completeness, and your future career should be one of distinction and high repute.'—Letter from Sir Edward Clarke, Q.C. to Horatio Bottomley after the Hansard Union case.

THE CASE OF Regina *v.* Bottomley and Others came on before Mr. Justice Hawkins and a special jury in the High Court of Justice on the 30th of January 1893. It ran continuously until the 17th of February, and had then to be postponed until the 17th of April, because a juryman was suffering from severe influenza and was unable to attend. The case ended on the 25th of April.

There were many odd, and even comic, features in the case, which worked in Bottomley's favour; he was strangely lucky in many of his law cases. The proceedings were instituted by Sir Edward Clarke, Q.C., Solicitor-General in the Unionist Government; and Sir Henry Isaacs retained for his defence Sir Charles Russell, Q.C., perhaps the leading figure at the Bar, and a professing Liberal. But before the case was heard the Unionist Government was replaced by a Liberal one, in which Sir Charles Russell was appointed Attorney-General. It throws a pleasant light upon the tolerant ethic of the legal profession that Sir Charles, as Attorney-General, now led for the prosecution (Sir Henry Isaacs having obligingly agreed that he should be prosecuted by his own counsel); while Sir Edward Clarke was

26

now retained by Isaacs for his defence. Besides Russell, the Crown was represented by the Solicitor-General, Sir John Rigby, Mr. Charles Mathews, Mr. C. F. Gill and Mr. Sutton—these last three all destined for various degrees of legal eminence. Sir Edward Clarke led for Sir Henry Isaacs, and Mr. Lawson Walton (later to be Attorney-General) for Bottomley's brother-in-law Charles Dollman.

Bottomley conducted his own defence, inspired, as he said, by the example of Bradlaugh, who had defended himself so skilfully on various occasions in the law courts. This was a risky thing to do and yet, for a man like Bottomley with considerable legal knowledge, natural astuteness, and high oratorical ability, it has great advantages. A certain effect is produced on a jury by a man conducting his own case ably. He appears to be one with the lawyers arguing in the well of the court, and there is a trifle of absurdity in his departure from there to the witness box or the dock. Yet at the same time the jury are impressed by the man's cleverness and courage—he seems almost one of themselves, a beanstalk Jack cunningly evading the clutches of the assembled legal ogres; and this effect is naturally enhanced if the litigant's appearance and manner are pleasing. The way in which Bottomley was able to exert the charm of his personality in court is indicated by this pen picture of him in action:

> Mr. Bottomley was on his feet making his opening statement. His appearance at once arrested attention. Short and stout in person, he is relieved from insignificance by a massive head, a masterful power, and a certain geniality about the eyes and brow. . . . It is the face of a strong, determined man. It is capable of softness and tenderness to friends and relatives; it is the face of a man with an active conscience; but it can also be stark and stern and even pitiless at times. Mr. Bottomley represents the solid stuff out of which England's greatness has been woven.

The voice is one of singular charm and power. Low, melodious, strong, it is an admirable instrument for an advocate. For five hours on end Mr. Bottomley addressed the jury. For the most part his tone was conversational; now and again the low voice would rise to indignant heights; ever and anon, as the litigant appealed to the noblest instincts of the jury, or declaimed in accents of scathing reproach and scorn against the flimsiness and inadequacy of the case he had to meet, his voice would be hushed almost to a whisper which only the startled silence of the Court made audible.

In general it is true that a judge is inclined to grant more latitude to an accused man conducting his own case than to counsel handling it for him; and Bottomley was fortunate, again, in his judge. Mr. Justice Hawkins, known popularly as 'Hanging Hawkins', was not markedly merciful, and in the Jabez Balfour case he had recently sentenced Balfour to twelve years' imprisonment for fraud: but he had a marked vein of eccentric humour, and there were few things he enjoyed more than exposing the ignorance or inadequacy of the counsel who pleaded before him. This trait in Hawkins was to serve Bottomley very well before the case was over.

Nevertheless, although Bottomley said that he preserved his confidence after Russell's opening speech, there must have been many, in court and out of it, to whom the prosecution's case seemed overwhelmingly strong. What Bottomley was accused of was, in essence, the simplest of frauds. He had approached the directors of the Union ('men of good name and of commercial experience' as Sir Charles put it) and had told them of the companies he was able to buy. With the faith that men of commercial experience so often showed in Bottomley they had paid him £325,000 for the purchase of these companies. In the meantime the companies had been bought by one James Phillips for £238,000 and Phillips sold them to the Hansard Union at the higher figure. Phillips, then, had made a

profit of £87,000, and in addition had made another
£15,000 which was supposed to cover the stock and book
debts of one of the companies. Who was James Phillips?
It was not denied that he was merely a clerk in Bottomley's
employ, a dummy purchaser, and that Bottomley had
received the money. 'If the other directors did not know
what Bottomley did, they were guilty of a very grave
neglect of duty. If they knew, so much the worse for them,'
said Sir Charles.

This was not all. It will be remembered that the original undertaking had been extended by the purchase of
paper mills and country printing works. These consisted of
a works at Redhill which Bottomley bought for £7,500,
and of some paper mills at Cullompton in Devonshire belonging to a firm named Hall and West. These Cullompton
mills had cost Hall and West £4,500 in 1885 and they had
lost money ever since. Bottomley and Joseph Isaacs got
wind of them at the same time. Bottomley withdrew from
the negotiations and Joseph Isaacs bought the mills for just
over £15,000, transferring them to Bottomley's brother-
in-law, Charles Dollman, who was an undischarged bankrupt. The Hansard Union directors then received an offer
of the Cullompton mills from Dollman at a figure of
£102,000 which was to include 'improvements' estimated
at £50,000. The Hansard Union sent down an accountant
named Dalton Eason, another member of Bottomley's
stable, who reported that the Cullompton mill was worth
the money. Dollman agreed to take £70,000 cash, and
shares for the rest of the money, and this sum was paid him
in a series of cheques which were simply endorsed with his
name and paid into Bottomley's account. When the winding-up order was made, Russell said dramatically, it was
found that some £600,000 of the Hansard Union's money
had 'disappeared'. Bottomley had also prepared an arrangement by which, had the proposed future extension gone

through, he would have made another £100,000 profit on the purchase of more businesses, using another of his clerks as dummy buyer.

It seems to the amateur a strong case, yet somehow its strength was slowly dissipated as the days went by. The prosecution failed, for some never-explained reason, to bring any evidence to show the actual worth of the Cullompton mills; they were unable to show that Sir Henry Isaacs had intended to make any profit out of the affair at all, and although Joseph Isaacs agreed that he had expected to make £5,000 out of the sale of the mills he asserted that this was perfectly legitimate commission—and besides, that because of the Union's collapse he had never received the money. Sir Roper Lethbridge and Mr. Kegan Paul, two directors who were quite free of any involvement in the purchase, were only two of the important witnesses who for some reason were not called by the prosecution. As for Bottomley, he stoutly maintained that it was the invariable custom of company promoters to use dummy purchasers and vendors. He admitted that the original group of companies had been sold to the Hansard Union at a 'gross advance' of £87,000 but denied that most, or even much, of this was profit. His expenses had been enormous, and he calculated that he had made at most £15,000. Would any shareholder have been worried, he asked, by learning that he was making a little money out of this deal, or that he was using Phillips as a medium for buying these various printing and publishing concerns. He would have been concerned, no doubt, had they been anything but what they were—first-class business propositions which, but for the iniquitous Debenture Corporation and the prejudiced Official Receiver, would have been welded into an immensely powerful and profitable organization. With regard to Cullompton Mill, was there any indication that he had exerted any pressure on the other directors to buy it? On the contrary. When Mr. Kegan Paul said that he had heard of this mill and thought it a poor investment, Bottomley had said immediately that they had better not buy it; and only when Mr. Kegan Paul had discovered that his doubts referred in fact to some quite different paper mill in Devon had negotiations been reopened. He dismissed scornfully the point stressed by the prosecution, that when he had accompanied the Isaacs brothers to Cullompton he had used the name of Williams. This was an elementary business subterfuge—had he revealed himself to the mill owner, Mr. Hall, as Bottomley of the Hansard Union the price asked would have gone up immediately. After the business discussion, he said, they 'had a very pleasant evening as provincial evenings go— music and singing. Sir Henry Isaacs sang and Mr. Hall prayed'.

'Should that not be "played"?' asked the judge.

'No,' Bottomley replied. '"Prayed" is correct.'

Hawkins showed, quite early in the case, that levity which is often combined with severity on the bench. When the prosecution put in Bottomley's diary as evidence, he read one or two extracts. '"The Reverend J. MacNeil preached"—has this anything to do with it?' There was dutiful laughter. When Bottomley, in his opening speech, referred to the indictment and said that although not of advanced years he had apparently found time to commit twenty-one pages of crime, Hawkins interposed.

'That is nothing. I remember an indictment with ninety-nine counts.'

'That must have been for some older criminal,' Bottomley smoothly responded.

Relations between judge and accused were thus pleasantly established, and Hawkins allowed Bottomley considerable latitude in examining the Official Receiver, Mr. C. J. Stewart. Bottomley had suggested in his book that

31

Stewart was a tool in the hands of the Debenture Corporation's Receiver Mr. John Annan, and that the members of the Corporation never met without 'taking a glass of wine, and having a good laugh at the expense of Mr. C. J. Stewart, the *Official* Receiver'. Now, with Stewart in the witness box, Bottomley accused him of a strong personal feeling in the case, of having neglected to bring out points that might help the defence, and of having said to a solicitor that if he could bring about a prosecution of Bottomley and Sir Henry Isaacs it would be a feather in his cap. Stung by Bottomley's continual questioning Stewart cried: 'I can give you no idea what wages were paid by the company, nor what the turnover was. All I know is there was a great deal of fraud in it.' Five minutes later, however, he had to admit that charges of fraud he had made in connection with the Anglo-Austrian Union had been unreservedly withdrawn. Bottomley then called a solicitor who testified that Stewart's remark about the feather in his cap had been made to him.

The case had reached a critical point, with the powerful effect of Russell's opening balanced against the frequently damaging cross-examinations made by Bottomley and Sir Edward Clarke, when the juryman was taken ill: it was resumed two months later in an altogether different atmosphere. Sir Charles Russell had accepted an invitation to serve on the Behring Sea Commission. The prosecution case was thus left in the hands of the Solicitor-General, Sir John Rigby, an eminent equity lawyer who was wholly unused to dealing with a jury. Bottomley and Sir Edward Clarke took full advantage of Rigby's uncertain approach; and Mr. Justice Hawkins took evident pleasure in the opportunities given him for correcting the errors of a Solicitor-General. Rigby's juniors were either amused or appalled by the floundering of their leader; and each day that passed, with its quota of interruptions and inter-

BOTTOMLEY AT THE AGE OF 33, JUST BEFORE HE STOOD
HIS TRIAL IN THE HANSARD PROSECUTION.

From his own pencil drawing

BOTTOMLEY AS SERGEANT BUZFUZ IN A PERFORMANCE OF
Pickwick Papers

jections, weakened the prosecution case and turned the whole affair to comedy. Bottomley submitted that there was no case to answer on two of the counts. Rigby replied at great length, addressing the jury. 'Is the Solicitor-General supposed to be addressing your Lordship or the jury?' Bottomley asked. 'I haven't the remotest idea,' Hawkins said, and threw out the two counts. Sir Edward Clarke then submitted that there was no evidence for a criminal charge against Sir Henry Isaacs. Rigby said that he had always thought that if a defendant called evidence the case must go to a jury. 'Good sense would show it was not so,' Hawkins observed with relish. Constantly interrupted by the judge, Bottomley, and Sir Edward Clarke, the Solicitor-General tried at great length to justify the case for conspiracy. He referred to the low price the mills had fetched when sold, and Hawkins, who had frequently asked for some independent evidence of their value, commented that the price the mills fetched was about the weakest evidence of their value that could be imagined. The judge attacked the way in which the indictment had been drawn up, calling it 'a novel form' and saying that some parts of it were meaningless. Then he ruled that there was no case to go to the jury in relation to Sir Henry Isaacs. Shortly afterwards he made a similar ruling about Joseph Isaacs. The despairing Rigby complained that he had not been heard. 'I heard you for a whole day,' Hawkins retorted, and said that he had made up his mind.

Bottomley's final address to the jury included a powerful, and typical, attack on the Official Receiver. 'Was there ever a more degraded exhibition than that of Mr. Stewart in the witness box? He is the real prosecution. He made the appalling, the astounding admission that it was by his suggestion that certain available witnesses were kept out of the box. I ask you to disbelieve Mr. Stewart's evidence.' Immediately afterwards he said virtuously: 'I am not going to vilify my opponents instead of answering the case.' There was applause at the end of his lengthy speech.

Rigby's speech for the prosecution was also long. The judge contented himself, by way of interruption, with saying that part of it was bad pleading, but he sent down a note to another counsel during the speech:

PATIENCE COMPETITION

FIRST PRIZE: Henry Hawkins.
HONOURABLE MENTION: Job.

When Rigby had finished, Hawkins said that it was rather late for him to begin summing up. The foreman asked if the jury could rely on the summing up being finished on the next day. 'Oh! can't you?' Hawkins responded. 'Oh, yes, beyond all question.' He added the by now unnecessary injunction that the jury should keep their minds open.

The summing up was almost wholly in the defendants' favour. Hawkins began by congratulating the Solicitor-General on his maiden speech to a jury, but that was the only matter on which he congratulated Sir John Rigby. He ruled that only four of the original twelve counts remained for consideration, and said that the evidence of conspiracy against Bottomley was about as unsatisfactory as it could be. He emphasized that the conduct of the directors had been scandalously careless and neglectful, but said that such neglect was far from conspiracy. He said that he thought the Official Receiver showed animus against Bottomley, and animus was a thing he hated to see. 'A constable who arrests a man ought to be fair. He should have it in mind to help the defence as much as the prosecution. Everything ought to be fair.' He said also that a defendant ought not merely to be given the benefit of the doubt. 'He has a right to say "I claim the right to be acquitted if you are satisfied"; that is the right every

34

Englishman has.' With these fine words ringing in their ears the jury went out. They came back twenty-five minutes later to say that they found the defendants, Bottomley and Dollman, not guilty. 'And that is the verdict of you all?' Hawkins asked. The foreman replied that it was. 'In that case there are thirteen of us,' the judge remarked. As the twelve jurymen left the box they filed in front of Bottomley, who sat in the well of the court, to shake hands with him.

By Bottomley's story Mr. Justice Hawkins sent for him afterwards, congratulated him on his conduct of the case, and advised him to go to the Bar. Bottomley did not act on the advice; but the judge did not hold this against him and when they met one day in a dining car asked for Bottomley's address. A few days later Hawkins's clerk presented himself at Bottomley's office carrying a brown paper parcel which he placed upon the table. 'This', he said, 'is from Sir Henry Hawkins. He wishes you to have it. It contains the wig he wore during the whole time he was on the Bench, and his original notes made during the Hansard trial. You are to keep them as a memento of the case, but you are not to make use of the notes at any time during his life.'

The story is unsupported: but certainly Bottomley had the wig and the notes, and they were shown to friends at his Pall Mall flat before the judge's death. After that they were put into a glass case, with a large volume containing the minutes of evidence in the case, and placed—as it were—on public exhibition.

Whether or not the story is true, there can be no doubt of the completeness of Bottomley's triumph, and of its importance to him. He had clashed with the most powerful forces the Crown could put against him, and had gained a decisive victory. His success served as a tonic to other company promoters, and as a kind of immunity licence for Bottomley himself. He must have felt that he was not likely to be subjected to an official prosecution again, unless a verdict against him seemed certain: he had only to exercise reasonable caution and a blind eye would be turned to his activities. Success gave him also a love of the law for its own sake, so that he welcomed the opportunities for the display of his own eloquence and ingenuity given by the dozens of court cases in which he was involved during the next few years. More important still was the effect of the Hansard Union case in establishing him as a public character. The little man doggedly defending himself, the amateur teaching professionals their business, the speculator justified as a truly honourable man—all these aspects of the case were warmly appreciated by readers of the newspapers which did so much to further Bottomley's career. Although everybody connected with the Hansard Union had in fact lost money, a feeling was somehow engendered in the mind of the public (which means, in this connexion, the share-buying public) that any enterprise in which Horatio Bottomley engaged was bound to be successful. He was so very evidently a clever and eloquent man: and he convinced almost everybody who met him that he was a sincere and honest man as well.

Chapter IV

THE GOOD LIFE

Sing first that sweet remote Cockagne
Where whiskey-rivers run,
And every gorgeous number may
Be laid by anyone.

W. H. AUDEN

DURING THE YEARS that followed the Hansard Union prosecution Horatio Bottomley turned from a mere financier into a public character. His stocky smiling figure, warmed always with the sun of money, appeared in dozens of places where he had been formerly unknown: in Tattersall's, at Romano's, at first nights; at dinners attended by the respectable as well as the rich; at lavish parties as well as obscure political gatherings; at country houses and at shareholders' meetings. He had a luxurious flat in Pall Mall and more than one 'little country retreat', as he modestly put it.

The most notable of these was a small cottage at Upper Dicker near Eastbourne, which he enlarged gradually year by year, until it became a vast rambling hideously ugly mansion where half a dozen, then a dozen, then twenty or thirty week-end guests might be accommodated. The villagers noted with surprise that instead of using the original cottage as a lodge and building a house behind it, he was determined to enlarge the original property. He did this constantly, so that a kitchen turned into a billiards room, and a sitting-room became an unnecessary hall, and

37

architects and builders tried despairingly to give shape and style to his wandering fancies. At The Dicker, as it was called, Mrs. Bottomley lived with the pretty and likeable Florence; here over the years Bottomley built modern cottages for the villagers to replace their generally insanitary homes, employed the villagers as gardeners (the grounds and tennis court at The Dicker called for eight full-time gardeners) or as workers for him in one way or another, direct or indirect. Sometimes, strolling through the village, he would find a man out of work; then he would call for the rent book, rule out the arrears, and give the man a job. At the suggestion of the local vicar he had trees planted at the four corners of the village recreation ground; he presented to the church a lectern and a Bible that had won a prize at the 1851 Exhibition; he paid heavily for wonderful feasts at the Diamond Jubilee, and later at King Edward VII's Coronation; he invited everybody to use his telephone, which was the only one in the village; trains invariably stopped to pick him up at the Dicker Halt. He patted the heads of schoolchildren, bought them sweets, remembered their names, gave them pony rides, and was never in so much of a hurry that he could not talk to them. He attained a mystical eminence in the minds of young people at Dicker; so that when a Sunday school teacher asked if anybody could be greater than God, she was told: 'Yes, Mr. Bottomley.'

At Dicker, then, Bottomley was respected, was almost worshipped even; but he was not quite liked. It is very difficult for a stranger to make himself liked in an English village. The villagers noted that although he had given a Bible and a lectern he never entered the church; they observed too that these new cottages built for them, although no doubt much better than the old ones, were twice as costly to rent. And they did not care for the way in which he ran their celebrations. Bottomley did not

understand that villagers like to conduct their own quarrels on their own committees, and ask nothing more of a rich interloper than a large cheque. They prefer to organize celebrations themselves in their own haphazard, quarrelsome and inefficient way; when Bottomley organized them on their behalf, much more grandly than they could have done, they took what was given but criticized gift and giver when his back was turned. They noted also that the sheafs of betting telegrams sent down to the owner of the village shop, a man thoroughly opposed to all forms of gambling, were never accompanied by money to pay for them.

This reluctance actually to pay money, as distinct from promising it, was noticed unfavourably rather higher in the social scale, when Bottomley's five-guinea subscription to the local cricket club became due. Those who played tennis and billiards at The Dicker, also, were amused or annoyed according to their temperaments to discover that these games presented certain unusual complications with Bottomley as opponent. Because of his girth, Bottomley found it difficult to run about, and the tennis court had been made with very little space at the back and sides so that certain shots, at which he had become adept were almost impossible to return. This natural advantage he supplemented by calling 'fault' or 'out' to his opponent's shots on any occasion when such a call seemed even faintly plausible; and many opponents found very welcome the bottle of dry champagne opened at the end of each set. Bottomley would play tennis all the morning and billiards all the evening; and at the latter game also, his use of the score board needed careful watching.

Move one step higher still up the social scale and the squire of Dicker (as he regarded himself) was very coldly regarded. Mrs. Bottomley was quite wonderfully vulgar in dress and appearance and was apt to alternate between bursts of grandiose boasting and a plaintive regret that

'Orace had not stayed in the happy near-poverty of their youth; and an odour of ill-repute clung to Bottomley himself, or at least was discovered by the sniffing upturned noses of the local gentry, in spite of all his attempts to remove it. The wife of a neighbouring clergyman refused to let her children come to play on the vicarage lawn at Dicker, for fear that they might meet the terrible Mr. Bottomley there. Few local people came to the big garden-parties given at the constantly-expanding house, few accepted invitations to dinner. One big garden party was attended only by a number of personal friends staying at Eastbourne and a few people from the vicarage; the great lawns were three-quarters empty. The guests made little impression upon the tables laden with food for tea and supper, the band brought down specially from London played in vain. At last Bottomley understood that he was not socially acceptable to country society, and the parties at The Dicker were restricted to his friends from London, and one or two friends he had in the neighbourhood. He was a man not easily dispirited or hurt, and he may have reflected that the people from London who accepted his invitations were much more distinguished and important than the local people who refused them.

Week-ends only were spent at The Dicker. During the week he was to be found in his handsome and expensive Pall Mall flat. Here he breakfasted, usually on kippers and champagne, sometimes on champagne alone. For prefer-ence the champagne was Pommery, and it must be dry; but he would drink other champagne, and even drink sweet champagne, rather than not drink it at all. He drank it at breakfast, and regularly at eleven o'clock; with lunch, and instead of tea at tea-time; and, of course, in the evening. The arrival of a friend or a prospective client would always be marked by the opening of a bottle, and cham-pagne was Bottomley's cure, also, for any moment of nervous tension. The stable, which had now grown to include a valet and a driver, a racehorse trainer and various obscure solicitors' clerks and dubious accountants, shared in the champagne if they were in Bottomley's company. He must have drunk, or helped to drink, several bottles of champagne every day.

Champagne was drunk a great deal at the races. At race meetings Bottomley obeyed the poetic injunction of Kipling, and met both triumph and disaster by drinking champagne. He became a race-horse owner in 1898, with the object of winning both the Derby and the Grand National. To fulfil the former purpose he bought a promising two-year-old named Hawfinch for 5,000 guineas, and bought as a potential Grand National winner a mare named Gentle Ida. He talked about Hawfinch so much, and backed him so freely during the winter, that the colt became Derby favourite in the ante-post betting. In the Two Thousand Guineas, however, Hawfinch ran unplaced. There was some doubt of his fitness for the Derby, but Bottomley announced that the public must have a run for their money. The Bottomley colours, a vermilion and black jacket with white sleeves and cap could not be seen when the field came round Tattenham Corner, and Hawfinch finished ninth. Gentle Ida started favourite for the Grand National, but fell at the first fence.

It is an odd feature of Bottomley's career that no breath of scandal was ever connected with the running of his race-horses. On the contrary, bookmakers welcomed his arrival on the course and vendors of horses regarded him as a pigeon to be plucked. His betting was wild, heavy and untouched by the shrewdness that marked his other financial dealings. His wins were even more spectacular than his losses, although they were less frequent. Within an hour of Hawfinch's Derby failure he had recouped his losses with a heavy bet on one of his horses named Splendour, which won a selling plate; in the year of Gentle Ida's Grand National failure he had one of the biggest wins of his career when Northern Farmer, wearing his colours, won the Stewards' Cup at Goodwood by a neck. Bottomley backed the horse from 50 to 1 down to less than half that price, and was said to have won nearly £70,000 on the race. Within a few years his horses won the Cesarewitch, the Crawfurd Plate, the London Cup, the Earl Spencer's Plate, and dozens of lesser races. Some of his gambles were legendary; and no doubt, like most legends, they had a basis of truth. It was said that he made £80,000 when his horse Wargrave won the Cesarewitch; and the victory of one of his horses, Le Blizon, when matched against Jack Joel's Sundridge at Hurst Park, won him some £15,000. He had little understanding of what made a good or a bad horse, or of how horses should be treated. Hawfinch was said to have failed in the Derby partly because Bottomley wanted to see a Derby trial every time he went to the training ground; and to the disgust of his trainer Batho he insisted on running Wargrave in another race the day after he had won the Cesarewitch. Yet, though he knew surprisingly little about horses, Bottomley was passionately fond of them, not merely as potential money-makers, and was most reluctant ever to part with any of them. The lesser lights in his stable were constantly winning selling plates (so called because after the race the winner is put up for auction, half of the purchase price going to the owner of the horse placed second and half to the Jockey Club), and Bottomley would always buy them in, often at ridiculously high prices. Adansi, which won him twenty races, most of them selling plates, cost him a fortune at auctions. The stables of his trainer, Batho, were conveniently placed near Dicker, at Alfriston, and Bottomley was a constant visitor to them.

At race meetings and elsewhere his fondness for pretty

girls was made very evident. These might be blonde, brunette or red-headed, large or small (although his preference was for small women, with auburn hair), but almost all of them were recruited from a low social level and very many came from the casts of musical comedies popular at the time. One of Bottomley's own stories suggests why he confined his amorous attentions to his own class in society. The manner of its telling shows him at his worst:

It was the day of the Oaks, and I was at Epsom with a party in a box. Amongst the guests were a Scotch ex-member of Parliament, his wife, and their very sweet daughter—a typical lassie of about nineteen. Everyone was buzzing round her—like bees round a honeypot—and saying sweet things—so I thought I might as well buzz, too. . . . Near our box was one in which there sat the late Sir Burdett Maple, wreathed in smiles, and preparing, mentally, to lead in the winner—for his filly, Nun Nicer, was a raging favourite, and, in the language of the 'heads', could not possibly 'get beat'. Here, then, was my chance—and I went for it bald-headed. 'Tell me, sweet maiden,' said I, 'why, when this race is over, the name of the winner will remind everybody of you?' She smiled vacantly and 'gave it up'—for she was not yet versed in gee-gees and their odds! . . . I kept near the little charmer, and as the race progressed got nearer and nearer, in order the more effectually to whisper in her dainty ear 'Because its name is Nun Nicer.'

Great heavens and Great Scott! What was that cry that went up to the skies? 'Blime, she's beat— 'ere, ten to one the fav'rite.' I edged gently a few paces from the Amazon— still hoping for the best, but little anticipating the worst. The race was over. Nun Nicer was beaten! Up went the number of the winner, and I scanned my card for its name, praying that even now the Fates had not deserted me. 'Well, what has won?' said a still, small voice. 'Why, an outsider, Airs and Graces—*an old cast-off of the Duke of Portland's,*' said a sporting member of our party!

Bottomley's personality attracted women of all classes; but his reputation as a persistent and successful amorist was confined to waitresses, woman journalists and chorus girls. It was partly in pursuit of sexual ends—but partly, again, from a genuine childish delight in theatrical glamour—that he backed plays, revues and musical comedies. These ranged from such oddities as a play about Nelson and Lady Hamilton which was not saved even by the appearance of Forbes Robertson and Mrs. Patrick Campbell in leading parts, to the very successful Forbes Robertson *Hamlet* at the Lyceum, and included many musical comedies and revues which were backed by Bottomley because of his personal and intimate interest in some more or less important member of the cast. Everything was done handsomely on such occasions. The claque, organized by Tommy Cox, was there to ensure at least an enthusiastic first night; and afterwards the whole company would be entertained to supper after the show. In a certain sense Bottomley was faithful to his lady friends; his interest extended from the girl herself to her whole family, and it was not at all uncommon for him to visit the family home of a girl friend, heralding his arrival by a messenger who brought a couple of bottles of champagne. When the family had been won to adoration of this remarkable man, one or more of them might be employed for a while in the Bottomley stable, which always had need of confidential clerks and secretaries with flexible memories. The girl herself, if she was a musical comedy actress on tour, or if Bottomley himself for one reason or another had to be away from her, would receive daily an affectionate telegram signed with one of those pet names like 'Skipper', 'Botty', or 'Horace' by which he was known to women. Even when the affair was over, Bottomley did not lose interest in the girl's career.

He was unusually faithful then; but he was unusually

44

unfaithful also, in the sense that he very often conducted three or four such affairs at once. The more fortunate, or more important, ladies would be installed in flats found by Tommy Cox; the less important would be visited in hotels or at their homes. All were expected to be accommodating enough not to show signs of jealousy or to demand a position in Bottomley's life which he was unable to give them; all were well treated in the sense that they received money and gifts.

Such were Horatio Bottomley's recreations; such was the routine of his life, away from his business and political dealings. This pattern of mistresses, champagne, gambling and entertaining was fixed in the eighteen-nineties, and it remained unchanged for a quarter of a century. The mistresses changed, the horses changed, there were times when it was difficult for him to gamble; but in essentials the pattern did not change. There was no reason why Bottomley should have changed it, indeed, for this was his own private version of the good life. He had discovered the good life, the ideal life, and he lived it.

The basic reason for Bottomley's immense popularity with poor working-class people was their realization that he had fulfilled in his own life the unattainable earthly Paradise of which they had dreamed idly and vaguely in their poverty-stricken youth and miserable age. To have an endless variety of women available, and to stay emotionally independent of them; to breakfast on kippers and champagne; to lead in a winner at Epsom; to gamble as if you had a private mint of money: all this is the poor man's dream come true. It is a vulgar conception, undoubtedly, this earthly Paradise without responsibilities or dishonoured cheques, but it is one that has a powerful and enduring fascination. By providing an incarnation of this dream in his own stout person, Bottomley took on the nature of a mythical fetish. Men and women willingly lost money in order that such a man should live the good life; it is customary to pay tribute to an idol. For hundreds of thousands of men and women Horatio Bottomley became a symbol of something desirable, something essentially good. Their faith in the symbol was to survive many trials, exposures, revelations; survive the loss of their savings; survive even the idol's imprisonment and death. A biographer writing twenty years after this death still receives many letters expressing faith in a great man. *We trusted him with our money*, the letters say. *The money is lost. We would trust him with it again for he was truly an honest man. He did not mean to do wrong.* Such letters are not supported by facts; there are no facts to support them. They are an expression simply of the worshippers' faith in a man who seems to fulfil in his own life certain archetypal desires of a particular class in a particular time.

Chapter V

A MAN OF MILLIONS

'The good life's founded upon £. s. d.'
BERT BRECHT, *trans. Christopher Isherwood.*

A T THE END of the Hansard Union case Bottomley was
still faced with the problem of his bankruptcy. His
lengthy public examination was concluded in August
1893, and during it he put forward one of those schemes
which were to be repeated more than once in his career.
He would deposit all of his property for distribution among
the creditors; he would also bind himself to go to Vienna,
collect the assets which he positively stated to be there,
ready to hand, for the Anglo-Austrian Printing and Publishing Union. This scheme was adopted by the majority
of the creditors, but opposed by the Official Receiver. In
later years it was Bottomley's practice to send agents to
buy up the book debts which he professed himself unable
to pay. The agent would present himself to the unhappy
creditor and say: 'Bottomley owes you £1,000. (Or £100
or £10,000.) You have no prospect of getting more than a
tiny fraction of this money from him. I represent a syndicate which is trying to come to an arrangement with
Bottomley, and I am prepared to offer you £250 for your
£1,000 debt.' A sufficient number of creditors would agree
to these terms to ensure a majority of votes at the shareholders' meeting, which, with a certain amount of voci-
ferous opposition, would then accept any scheme for the
settlement of his affairs put forward by Bottomley.

47

In this first bankruptcy, however, such tactics were not necessary. The principal creditors were the Hansard Union and the Anglo-Austrian Union; and the directors of these firms, in friendship or innocence, had full belief in Bottomley's integrity. The Official Receiver accused Bottomley of rash speculation and fraudulent breach of trust, and asserted that the assets finally recovered could never amount to more than a few shillings in the pound. These were serious charges: but Bottomley was fresh from his Hansard Union triumph, and the public examination had been going on for two long years. Mr. Justice Vaughan Williams agreed to Bottomley's scheme of composition, and the Receiving Order was rescinded.

The subsequent developments also serve as a pattern, with some variation, for Bottomley's later career. He paid a visit to Vienna, but came back with none of the contracts which his imagination had foreseen. His creditors took in settlement shares in the West Australian Loan and General Finance Corporation, or in Associated Gold Mines of West Australia. These companies were founded in 1894, with capitals of £250,000 and £375,000 respectively. During the next few years these and several other companies backed by Bottomley were 'reconstructed'—the Lake View South Gold Mines, Nil Desperandum Gold Mines Limited, Waitekauri United Gold Mining Company Limited are three of many companies formed between 1894 and 1900. Most of them were devoted to the idea of obtaining the gold believed to lie beneath the ground of Western Australia, although there were a few like the Rubber Exploration Company Limited which extended their optimism into different fields. Every year one or more of these companies went into voluntary liquidation and was reconstructed, in a slightly different form or under another name. After the reconstruction had been agreed to at a meeting packed with Bottomley supporters, the public shareholders would receive a letter which told them that West Australian Joint Stock Founders (let us say) had been reconstructed and enlarged. The board had voted to double the holdings of every shareholder at half the original outlay so that on receipt of a cheque for only £25 an original holding of £50 would be transferred as a holding of £100 in the reconstructed company.

That was the general form of reconstruction, which could be presented optimistically or pessimistically according to the feeling of the promoter. Always, however, shareholders were faced with the fact that the existing company had lost a great deal of money, which had in fact been used by Bottomley in return for his multifold services; always it was represented to them that the company could be saved by the provision of a little more money; always the acceptance of this money by Bottomley was made to appear almost a favour to the provider of it. The shareholder who refused to play this game, and asked for his money back, might be treated in several different ways. If he was a small shareholder his letters would receive no answer. He would call at the company's offices, and be met there with vague promises that something should be done; and then nothing would be done. If he persisted long enough, if he threatened legal action, he might get his money back: but more likely he would give up the quest for his few pounds in despair, or send a little more money for shares in the reconstructed company. Large shareholders got different treatment. They were admitted to the Bottomley presence, they heard one end of spectacular telephone calls involving hundreds of thousands of shares; they emerged, soaked with champagne, and radiantly happy that they had been given the privilege of buying a few thousand shares in an entirely new Bottomley company.

Behind all these activities there was little capital, and

E   49

little serious knowledge of City affairs, or of company promotion. Bottomley began his career in the City with the help of £2,000 borrowed from Osborne O'Hagan (to O'Hagan's surprise all his acceptances were met), and perhaps an equal amount obtained from other friends and acquaintances. A keenly intelligent opportunism made Western Australia the scene of his activities. In 1892 the Coolgardie gold field was discovered, and Kalgoorlie was found in the following year. The rewards of the 'Golden Mile' were immense, and in the hope of finding equally rich mines elsewhere hundreds of fields were opened up almost simultaneously by wildcat and other prospectors. When they found a promising field they came to London for money with which to develop it. They found money— or at least they found Bottomley, who was not very ready with money, but was prepared to float a company. Perhaps there was gold worth mining, perhaps not. The costs of development were generally too great to be undertaken.

Such were the circumstances in which Bottomley began his promotion of gold mining companies. During a period of less than ten years he launched companies with a nominal capital of some £25,000,000. Some of this capital was not taken up, much was duplicated in the various reconstructions, but the actual cash that came into Bottomley's hands during these years must have amounted to some millions of pounds. It is natural to ask how all this money was spent. Part of it was paid out in dividends—when you are paying dividends out of capital it is possible for a short time to do something rather handsome for your shareholders. Some went into the hands of the staunch directors who faithfully followed Bottomley's star. Some went to the tame accountants, solicitors, stockbrokers and hangers-on who made up the 'stable', a good deal to the trainer of horses in that other stable to which he was so devoted. Women and champagne accounted for much more. But when all has been said the mystery remains unresolved, and Bottomley appears to be a man who had perfected an opposite art to that for which the ancient alchemists strove. He had discovered the secret of turning gold into base metal.

It may seem that such a snowball, or chain letter, method of finance could not continue for long; but in fact it lasted without being seriously questioned for several years. When in 1897 the *Financial Times* published a pictorial supplement called 'Men of Millions' it showed Bottomley as one of a dozen financiers. Some of them suffered fates as unhappy as his own. Woolf Joel was shot dead in his Johannesburg office; Barney Barnato committed suicide; Colonel North dropped dead in an apoplectic fit just before the collapse of his companies; Ernest Terah Hooley and Whitaker Wright, like Bottomley, received prison sentences. In the same year the great financier took a step to put right his reputation with people who felt that some cloying, undesirable publicity still attached to him in relation to the Hansard affair. An advertisement was published inviting all Hansard shareholders to attend a meeting at Cannon Street Hotel. There, on Hansard Day, as he called it, a smiling but basically serious Bottomley appeared on the platform. Flanking him were some of those respectable men whose names are by now becoming well known to us; Sir Henry Isaacs and Sir Roper Lethbridge, Mr. A. P. Sinnett and Mr. Agg-Gardner; with the solicitor, the auditor, the secretary and the manager of the Hansard Union. An unsuccessful attempt had been made to get Sir Henry Hawkins to act as chairman; his place was taken by George Wreford, the bankruptcy official who had dealt with Bottomley's petition.

The walls were placarded with judicial tributes to Bottomley's honest intentions: the shareholders, critical but attentive, heard Mr. Wreford associate himself with those

51

tributes. The accountant Dalton Eason certified that Bottomley had already disbursed more than £30,000 among the Hansard shareholders and creditors. Then came the master stroke. Bottomley announced that he had always been unhappy about the position of the Hansard Union shareholders; now, in these days of his success, he was in the happy position of being able to present them with the sum of £250,000. No wonder that the 'loud and prolonged cheers' which greeted the announcement were extended also to the peroration in which he said that the crime which wrecked the Hansard Union was 'written, I believe, in the Books of God in letters as black as any you will find in all the Calendars of Newgate'. Mr. Wreford agreed to act as trustee, Mr. Sinnett and Sir Henry Isaacs moved votes of thanks, another speaker called Bottomley a Napoleon of finance and said that, like Napoleon, he had never been so great as after disaster. It was a magnificent gesture and one that cost its maker very little in money; for the amount paid was not in hard cash, but in West Australian gold mine shares. Rather more than £100,000 of shares, by Bottomley's own account, were distributed to shareholders; and the rash critic who called the Hansard Relief Union 'a swindle from inception' was made to pay heavily for his presumption.

The Great Hall of Cannon Street Hotel was the scene of many triumphs for Bottomley as orator and money-charmer. In a certain sense his task was uncommonly difficult, for generally he had nothing tangible to sell. There was gold, no doubt about it there was a great deal of gold, in the fields of Coolgardie and Kalgoorlie. There were surveyors and assessors who sent reports on such properties. But West Australia was thousands of miles away, and of necessity there could be no proof that the land held by this or that company was gold-bearing. It was all a matter of doubt, a matter of speculation, and Bottomley was always

very genially frank about the whole thing. 'We are not in
any sense a mining company,' he told the shareholders of
the West Australian Market Trust. 'We own no mines,
we do not go mining; and speaking for myself personally
I do not profess to understand very much about mining.'
He understood enough, however, to know that they were
all going to become very rich.

> We found in one of our mines—one of those privately
> floated—there was practically in sight something like
> £4,000,000 worth of gold. To show that we were not ready to
> accept everything that our own independent investigator
> said, we telegraphed: 'Is there not some mistake in this?
> Verify your investigations and report again.' We received not
> only a reply to that from the person to whom we addressed
> it, but also from others who had previously occupied the
> position, and were then occupying positions of trust, all of
> them agreeing and concurring in this.

The West Australian Market Trust was a company of
considerable importance to Bottomley. He founded it with
a capital of £2,500,000, taking advantage of the favourable
publicity he gained through the Hansard Relief Fund. The
Trust acted as a holding company for the purpose of
buying up various more or less worthless gold mining properties. This statement about the four millions in gold bol-
stered the market position of the shares for only a short
time. Within a year the pound shares were being quoted at
one and sixpence. It was then made clear that Bottomley's
words, although persuasive, were not necessarily official
currency. An awkward shareholder at a meeting of the
subsidiary Northern Territories Goldfields asked the chairman whether in fact there were four millions of gold laid
open in the Howley Mine.

CHAIRMAN: Are you quoting a speech of someone?
SHAREHOLDER: It is Mr. Bottomley.

CHAIRMAN: Then I think it is only fair to state that which Mr. Bottomley explained in making those remarks.

SHAREHOLDER: I have done so.

CHAIRMAN: Excuse me, you have not done so. He stated that he made those statements on his own authority. He had private advices from the Northern Territories, and that was the source from which he got his information.

SHAREHOLDER: I will read what he says. 'There is four millions of gold laid open in the Howley Mine.' Now, is it?

CHAIRMAN: I think if you want to get a direct answer—

SHAREHOLDER: Where is it?

CHAIRMAN: Ask Mr. Bottomley. (Laughter.)

SHAREHOLDER: Mr. Bottomley is not here. I cannot ask him.

A little later, however, somebody says: 'A gentleman here wishes to speak.' There are cries of 'Bottomley, Bottomley,' and the short, sturdy figure comes forward to make a statement. What about the gold? He is very positive:

> I say to you again today, and I say in the presence of your Board, and defy their own managers to contradict me—that in the Howley Mine you have four millions of gold—(hear hear)—for all practical purposes in sight.

The chairman is just as positive, however, to slightly different effect:

> Gentlemen, I have just one remark to make in connection with what Mr. Bottomley has said, in case any shareholder should be under misapprehension. I am not sure that I caught what Mr. Bottomley said, but I have only to state that the Board have no report from their manager that there is four millions of gold in sight in the Howley Mine. Mr. Bottomley may have a report, but we have not.

So the shareholders were left, happy or unhappy according to their beliefs and temperaments; and the board of Northern Territories was certainly not committed to the statement made by optimistic Mr. Bottomley. It remains to be said that the gold which was 'for all practical purposes in sight' was never in hand or in bank. There was, for all practical purposes, no gold in Howley Mine.

In the course of things one or other of Bottomley's companies was, at some time or another, almost bound to strike gold. This happened in a curious way. He had been caught more than once on the Stock Exchange by jobbers and brokers who sold shares of his companies at a premium, forcing him to buy them up if he wanted to maintain the price. These premium shares were sold before allotment, and the speculators would apply for an allotment of shares to cover those they had sold. If the issue went badly they would withdraw their applications, if it went well they would deliver the shares they had bought at par and already sold at a premium. This is the kind of simple, and almost foolproof, operation which made cynics speak of Stock Exchange operations as legalized robbery. (Dealings in shares before allocation are not permitted today.) On one occasion the pressure on Bottomley had been so great that he had been compelled to withdraw a company altogether, with a heavy loss, rather than go on buying its shares as they were offered.

When Bottomley brought out the Waitekauri Gold Mining Company in 1896 the 'stags' adopted their usual tactic and sold them at a premium in advance of allotment. It has been said that this tactic is almost foolproof: but it is not quite foolproof, for if the shares are heavily over-subscribed the 'stags' may receive no allotment at all and they are then (as it were) on the horns of a dilemma. This is what happened in the case of Waitekauri. All the shares offered were bought; and when allotment day came not a single share was allotted to the speculators who had sold them. They began a frantic effort to get out by buying shares so that they could fulfil their obligations on settling day: when the £1 Waitekauri shares were quoted at £10 the speculators realized that they were the victims of a Bottomley *coup*, and that he might, if he wished, put the shares up to £100 a piece since it was thought that he controlled them all. The indignant speculators asked their solicitors to deal with the matter and tried to induce the Lord Mayor to issue a summons against Bottomley for conspiracy, which he refused to do. The speculators then asked Osborne O'Hagan to arbitrate, and decide a price at which the speculators should be let out of their bargains. While O'Hagan was drawing up the agreement for arbitration Bottomley came to see him and said that he wanted nothing out of the affair. O'Hagan was, very naturally, surprised, and asked his reason. Bottomley replied that he knew O'Hagan did not approve of what he had done. 'I have always avoided doing anything when you have told me it was wrong, and I am sure you disapprove of what I have done, so I don't want to go on with the matter.'

At this O'Hagan was even more surprised, and no doubt flattered. Was this Bottomley's real reason? At any rate he took O'Hagan's advice to wind up the company so that all contracts for buying and selling shares became invalid. It was not until some time later that O'Hagan discovered that Bottomley had received a cablegram at the time he was ready to sign the arbitration agreement, telling him that a big lode had been found on the property, showing several ounces of gold to the ton. He had kept the property, instead of selling it to the company, and made a great deal of money out of it. O'Hagan's final comment is of some interest, and throws a pleasant illumination on his own ethics:

> So that was his secret, and the reason he abandoned his claim against the 'stags'. But Bottomley had not been clever; he might have gone on with the Arbitration, recovered substantial moneys from the 'stags', and still kept all the shares of the Company and wound it up at his own sweet will. Strange that never occurred to him.

56

The Waitekauri Gold Mine was the kind of exception that it is almost shocking to read about. In general the course of Bottomley's flotations was smooth and simple. Subscription; Stock Exchange quotations, with the price artifically pushed up for a short time; issue of a 20 per cent dividend; slow or speedy decline of the stock; liquidation or reconstruction. It is a foolproof operation, given a small army of professional shysters to carry out the essential work of deception; given, also, a public of extreme gullibility. The gullibility of almost all the people with whom Bottomley came into contact gives his progress through life something of the hard brightness of Jonsonian comedy. It is impossible to feel anything for these people, they are so foolish, so greedy, so happy to be deceived. Bottomley himself developed a contempt for his gulls, and could hardly be bothered to invent plausible deceptions. A note supposed to have been written to a friend at this time may be apocryphal, but the casualness of it has a ring of truth:

> What on earth have you done with our nugget?—the one we used to show our shareholders in the old days? I've got hold of a promising client: all he wants is a sight of the stuff.

He employed the same indifferent vagueness in dealing with shareholders, quoting unsupported figures, and shrugging his shoulders when some pettifogging complainant objected that no accounts had been issued. What was the reason for so many liquidations and reconstructions? It was simple. 'We feel that it would be robbing you to sell our shares at the present absurd prices.' If they left things to him, if they did not inquire too closely into the mechanics of the way it was done, they would all get rich. His listeners half-believed what he told them; the operations of the Stock Exchange appear fascinatingly wicked to many English minds infected by the miasma of Nonconformism.

Under the spell of Bottomley's oratory, they regarded investments in gold mine shares as a perfectly legal form of gambling in which they were almost certain to win. Each indication of his carelessness in money matters was a fresh proof that there must be a great deal of money about or no man could speak so neglectfully of it. When he told shareholders of the Westralian Market Trust that their companies were worth £3,000,000 and then suggested that they should 'write off an odd million of it if you like' in case of errors and disappointments he was met with applause, not criticism. He answered questions about a disparity of some £700,000 with engagingly audacious frankness:

> He was appealed to by Mr. Snow as to where the £700,000 had gone. He could only say, in all sincerity and honesty, he had not the remotest idea. (Laughter.) He knew he had not had it, and he presumed that the books would show what had become of it. That also answered Mr. Snow's question as to the books. . . . He supposed the £700,000 had disappeared by virtue of the fact of many of the securities by which it was represented having dropped from perhaps a high premium on the Stock Exchange to a considerable discount. He would think that was probably the explanation. (Hear, hear.)

Such an attitude could not be maintained for ever; there comes a point at which the most ingenious reconstruction seems implausible or distasteful to the most innocent shareholder. In 1903 the shareholders of the Associated Financial Corporation, which had passed through a series of eight reconstructions, rebelled vigorously and insisted on the appointment of a committee to examine the situation. Bottomley was always very ready to agree to the formation of a committee, and it was rarely that any committee reported adversely on his handling of affairs. The chairman of the present committee was Godfrey Isaacs, brother of Rufus Isaacs. It will be remembered from the Hansard

Union case that Bottomley had friendly relations with other members of the family. Sure enough this committee, although it called the directors ignorant and incompetent, exempted Bottomley from such criticisms. ('We have all had sufficient indication of his ability as financier.') The directors were discarded. Bottomley was retained. There was one more reconstruction, involving the formation of two new companies, the Selected Gold Mines of Australia and the Joint Stock Trust and Finance Corporation. We shall hear more of the latter company; the point to be noted here is that the Selected Gold Mines was the last of its kind. Whitaker Wright had fled from England after the collapse of his London and Globe Finance Corporation; had been extradited from the United States and most reluctantly prosecuted—for it was thought that he had not broken the very elastic company law of the time; had been sentenced to seven years' imprisonment, and taken cyanide on leaving the dock. Nobody spoke of prosecuting Bottomley, but the West Australian fields were, from the financial point of view, exhausted. The wonderful spree, which had lasted nearly ten years and which had brought Bottomley perhaps three million pounds, was over.

The path of the company promoter during this decade was not always an easy one. A pamphlet was issued by a man named Taylor, which called Bottomley an expert dividend dodger, and an associate of notorious bucket-shop keepers. It accused him of packing meetings with his friends, and said that they put forward bogus resolutions. It asserted that the Hansard Union Relief Fund was a swindle. The pamphlet was called 'Horatio Bottomley, Politician, Philanthropist, Financier and Labour Candidate' and below this heading was the question: 'Oh, where and oh, where has the public money gone?' Bottomley brought a libel action which was settled when Taylor saw

59

he receipts of the fund, professed himself satisfied of Bottomley's honesty and withdrew the pamphlet.

More serious was the attack made by Henry Hess, who ran a financial paper called *The Critic*, in which he made savage remarks about many companies and individuals. Financial journals did not show then the impartiality and probity which, doubtless, distinguishes them now. *The Critic* was one of a half-dozen papers which existed for the purposes of puffing certain companies, in return for a consideration, and violently attacking others. Bottomley had his own paper, *The Joint Stock Circular*, which he used in this way, and he was for some reason at odds with Hess. The remarks which appeared in *The Critic's* 'Black Book' added something to Taylor's accusations and said also that Bottomley's case against Taylor was 'a bogus one'. The things Hess said could hardly be ignored:

> Since the day when this barefaced swindler had the luck to escape conviction over the Hansard Company's frauds, he has engineered one imposition after another upon the credulous public. . . . His West Australian Market Trust (reconstructed twice), his Howley, his Northern Territories, his Joint Stock Institute, and his Associated Finance Corporation, have been deliberately planned schemes to rob the public, and they have succeeded all too well, with the result that many of his victims are now in the workhouse, and he without thinking of their ruin is bribing with their money the unwashed of South Hackney to send him to Parliament. His place is at the Old Bailey, not at Westminster.

The trial of Hess for libel, which lasted five days, was another victory for Bottomley, who conducted his own case. His opening speech lasted nearly two days, and he produced the satisfied Taylor as a witness of prime importance. Subsequently the evidence of Sir Charles Turner, the retired Indian judge who was administering the Relief Fund, made it clear that Taylor was easily satisfied, for

Turner told the court that Bottomley had paid £15,000
down in cash, and had then suggested to the trustees that
they should use Market Trust shares. The judge showed no
friendliness to Bottomley, commenting ironically in his
summing up that Mr. Bottomley always appeared to win
whilst the shareholders lost, although of course there
might not be any dishonesty involved in the matter. Hess,
however, was a poor witness and made no attempt to justify
his statements factually, relying chiefly on his own long
statement to the jury. Bottomley's cross-examination of
Hess was ruthless in demonstrating the defendant's failure
to buttress his allegations with facts. His last question
amused the judge, the jury, and Mr. Asquith, who looked
in near the end of the cross-examination and said afterwards (according to Bottomley) 'That is destined to become
a "locus classicus".'

B. Now, Mr. Hess, do you still persist, after all you have
learnt in the course of this trial, in these charges against
me?
H. Yes, in all of them.
B. And you say you are worth £7,500?

The jury did not take this hint, but within half an hour
they found a verdict for Bottomley and gave him £1,000
damages.

In 1903 Bottomley moved back into journalism with the
purchase of a London evening newspaper named the *Sun*.
The need for public approval, and the desire for self-justification, were marked features of his career, and from this
time onwards he was hardly ever without some periodical
for the expression of his opinions, which could be used
also for publicizing his current schemes. The *Sun* contained
four large pages, printed usually on pink but occasionally
on vivid green paper. It gave much space to criminal cases,

in particular those involving the massage establishments popular at that time; carried on a campaign of sniping against the Unionist Government and its conduct of the Boer War; and gave generous space to all of Bottomley's speeches and public appearances. These were mostly made to the Liberal, Radical and Labour organizations in South Hackney and contained many roundhouse swings at popular targets. He blamed goldfield magnates and 'the bloated millionaire' Kruger for the South African War, and at the same time attacked the government for unpreparedness and for the inferior equipment supplied to the troops. He warned Hackney trade unionists against using their powers in the attempt to enforce demands which were not consonant with reason, justice and fair play, but expressed his general support for the Labour movement. In the November 1900 general election the bills asked Hackney voters to return 'Horatio Bottomley, the working man's friend'. He was active in the constituency, which had of course been nursed carefully for years by Perkins and other members of his stable. He was an excellent speaker and he had a good organization. This was a 'Khaki Election', in which Unionist candidates almost everywhere were returned with greatly increased majorities, yet Bottomley lost by only 338 votes. His defeat in the end was perhaps attributable to the publication of Hess's violent attack, which was distributed free in the streets of Hackney.

Bottomley was not in any sense an academic journalist. He fully justified the claim that whatever else might be said of the *Sun* under his ownership, nobody could say that it was dull. He brought down as editor a journalist named Theodore Dahle who had been editor of the *Leeds Daily News*, and who was established as a Bottomley henchman for more than a quarter of a century. Dahle, according to Bottomley, 'stoked the fires to white heat. Be our sensation for the day what it might, we taught our readers

62

to expect another one tomorrow. From being utterly ignored, we were everywhere quoted.' The *Sun* published what purported to be the confession of a murderer named Dougal, in a facsimile of his handwriting, on the morning he was hanged. The paper raised a defence fund for a Sunday school superintendent named William Gardiner, when it seemed that he was to be put upon trial for murder a third time, after two juries had disagreed. At last the prosecution was withdrawn and the *Sun* claimed all, and perhaps more than, the credit that was its due. In a famous murder case of the time, the murder of a woman on Yarmouth beach by her husband, a man named Bennett, the *Sun* ran a campaign against the tentative appointment of Mr. Justice Ridley to try the case, and claimed a 'Big Score' when the Lord Chief Justice decided to try it in person. Then the paper made an appeal for money on behalf of Bennett's two-year-old daughter and obtained enough to provide for her education.

Bennett was defended by Edward Marshall Hall, K.C., who was convinced of his innocence, and was one of the subscribers to the fund for his daughter. Marshall Hall had already become a firm friend of Bottomley. He had appeared as defence counsel when Bottomley was sued as the guarantor of a Stock Exchange account, and had protested warmly when Mr. Justice Ridley, who was trying the case, said 'I cannot believe this man's evidence.' Bottomley later published in the *Sun* an Open Letter to Ridley in which he said that if the letter made him guilty of contempt of court, that was precisely the attitude with which he regarded Mr. Justice Ridley's court.

There can be no doubt that Marshall Hall, like many other lawyers and politicians, admired Bottomley and found pleasure in his company. Audacity, radiant good humour, ready unpretentious vulgarity, immediate generosity: all of these qualities combined to make him an

63

immensely likeable personality to many people who had
no interest in his dubious financial enterprises. His shame-
lessness was so complete that it was difficult not to be
charmed by it. There are many stories dealing with this
side of his character which deserve record. Typical is that
which tells of an indignant shareholder's visit to his Pall
Mall flat: when, after listening to a furious tirade against
his moral and financial character, Bottomley hoisted the
tails of his frock coat and invited the shareholder to lift
his boot. And equally typical, in a slightly different way, is
his defence of an office boy in one of his companies, caught
stealing stamps. 'You'd better given him another chance.
We've all got to start in a small way.'

It was during the period in which Bottomley owned the
Sun that he developed with Marshall Hall's aid a plan of
campaign which was used for several years with great
success. One of the novelties associated with the *Sun* was
the 'Sunspots' contained in certain copies, which brought
prizes to the reader buying those copies. The prosecution
maintained that this constituted a lottery, and Marshall
Hall told Bottomley that only one counsel in England could
do him justice in the case. 'Who is that?' Bottomley asked.
'Yourself.' Marshall Hall therefore appeared for the pub-
lisher of the *Sun*, and Bottomley conducted his own case.
In the case of the Sunspots he escaped with a £25 fine, and on
many future occasions the team of Bottomley and Marshall
Hall worked together wonderfully well, with Bottomley
taking full advantage of the licence traditionally allowed
to a defendant conducting his own defence, and Marshall
Hall adding his skill and knowledge to Bottomley's and
beginning his address to the jury: 'Following as I do after
my unlearned leader . . .'

The Sunspots were only one of the *Sun's* eccentricities.
Bottomley contributed to it a column called 'The World,
the Flesh—and the Devil', full of knowing personal refer-

ences to famous men. He would refer to 'my dear old friend Lord Brampton' (as Mr. Justice Hawkins had become), and would casually mention that his 'esteemed uncle Mr. George Jacob Holyoake' had said that his column had no rival in the Press for interest and instruction. A new invention, like that of the engineer who planned to win the South African War by the use of portable armoured cars made with revolving steel shutters or the man who had invented a combined protective screen, battle shield and ambulance, was always front page news. And for one or two weeks in each year editorship of the paper was handed over to a notable figure of the period. A special cricket issue was edited by Prince Ranjitsinhji. George Jacob Holyoake edited the paper for a week, during which he wrote twenty-nine articles and 'was paid ten times as much as I have ever received before' so that he thought himself in 'a paradise of journalism'. Ben Tillett and Dan Leno were also editors for a week, and so was Doctor Joseph Parker, the famous preacher of the City Temple. Doctor Parker sent a brisk response to Bottomley's invitation to act as editor.

Dear Mr. Bottomley,

No betting.
No gambling.
No speculative finance.

during my editorship.

I wish I could see you. Do you ever pass the City Temple about *one* on a Thursday? Best wishes,

Yours faithfully,

JOSEPH PARKER.

Parker had his way. The paper appeared in a deeper shade of pink than usual, racing tips and City news were suppressed. The stop press news said: 'The Wages of Sin is Death.' Parker himself referred to the week in which the paper was in his charge as 'a great and perhaps perilous experiment': and certainly Bottomley was imperilled by it. Such teasing questions as 'Will London accept a religious daily paper' had been appearing for several days before Parker's editorship. At the end of it Bottomley considered the paper's declining circulation and knew that the answer was 'No'.

A successful newspaper does not indulge the whims of the proprietor in such unprofitable ways; and the *Sun* always cost money. Bottomley sold the paper when the gold mining boom was over, and it was three years before he obtained control of another newspaper. Then the experience rather expensively gained during the time in which he had controlled the *Sun* was put to use for *John Bull*.

Chapter VI

THE MEMBER FOR SOUTH HACKNEY

'Mr. Bottomley was a hopeless candidate. No man with such a name as Horatio Bottomley could possibly win an election. To be laughed at is to be lost, and the mere mention of the above remarkable conjunction of names is quite enough to create mirth.'—*St. Stephen's Review, July 1887.*

IF ONE WERE looking for a consistent thread in Horatio Bottomley's life and actions, it might at first sight be found in his unwearying determination to be a Member of Parliament. The practical benefits of entering the House of Commons were indirect but considerable for him. Membership afforded him opportunities of meeting all kinds of men who would have been very dubious of Bottomley the financier, but were amused or impressed by Bottomley the orator. It allowed him to put his finger into new and freshly-flavoured pies; it provided a desirable, though very thin, coating of respectability for his financial transactions; it offered an additional source of publicity. Yet something more than that seems to have been involved. It would be an overstatement to say that Bottomley had any political convictions at all. He was drawn to a radical liberalism by the circumstances of his early life, by the examples of Bradlaugh and Holyoake, and most of all by his awareness that only as a Liberal would he have full play for his demagogic oratory. He was never trusted by any Liberal leader and the passing years showed him not as a Liberal, even of

the most independent variety, but simply as a Bottomleyite:
convinced, in the end to the point of megalomania and self-
destruction, of his mission to act as a political leader.

The election of 1905 found the Bottomley organization
in South Hackney, headed by Tommy Cox, Perkins, and
Bottomley's election agent William Cornish, ready for
battle. In the years after his narrow defeat at the 'Khaki
Election' Bottomley had addressed dozens of meetings in
Victoria Park and at Hackney Town Hall. He lunched in
the Hackney pubs, paying corkage on the bottles of champagne he took in with him. He attended smoking concerts
and opened bazaars, made speeches at dances, religious
meetings and trade union rallies. His Christmas parties for
the children grew larger every year, and he would appear
in the midst of them, a stumpy Santa Claus, the embodi-
ment of benevolent cheerfulness. Everywhere he went the
faithful following cheered him. He was cheered at the
entrance to bazaars and when he stepped from his motor-
car to enter a pub; when an opponent held a meeting to
expose his commercial morality, Bottomley supporters
attended in such large numbers that the threatened exposure was abandoned.

His opponents at this election were the sitting Unionist
member T. H. Robertson, and a local Nonconformist
minister named Riley, who stood as an Independent
Liberal. It is an indication of the disfavour with which
Bottomley was viewed by orthodox Liberals that the *Daily
News*, *Chronicle* and *Star* advised all South Hackney
Liberals to vote for Riley. The *Daily News*, indeed, expressed itself in such terms that a writ for libel was issued
against them, which was afterwards compromised by the
paper paying £150 to local charities. But neither Riley,
who issued a handbill asking 'How would Jesus vote?', nor
Robertson, was any match for Bottomley. When Robertson's supporters put up a poster advising electors to 'Vote

68

for Robertson, your old and tried Member' the word 'tried' was changed overnight to 'tired'; and another poster reading 'Vote for Robertson and Reputation' was pasted over to read 'Robertson and Repetition'. Bottomley's own approach is indicated by the following piece of election propaganda:

LATEST SPORTING INTELLIGENCE

South Hackney Stakes

RUNNERS:

Mr. John Bull's HORATIO (*dark horse, by Vox Populi out of Fairplay*).

Mrs. Robertson's HERBERT (*gray horse, by Clap-trap out of South Hackney*).

Mrs. Grundy's RILEY (*H.b., by Crank, out of His Mind*).

Horatio, the favourite, continues to go strong. He is daily doing some excellent gallops, and yesterday went the full course of the constituency, pulling up sound and well. His party are very confident.

Herbert on the other hand, travels badly. All sorts of sinister rumours are afloat. It is said that his fiscal ligament is very dicky, and yesterday he was confined to gentle exercise round the Chinese compound. Certainly his recent outings in public are not calculated to inspire confidence. Apart from a marked disinclination to face the crowd, he has more than once shown a strong desire to bolt. He is probably stale, and requires rest. Every effort will, however, be made to get him to the post. After which he will probably be sent back to Ireland.

Riley, the outsider, was not mentioned.

CLOSING PRICES:

    20 to 1 on Horatio.

    20 to 1 against Herbert (offered freely).

    1,000 to 1 Riley (offered).

Two thousand people were in the Morley Hall at Bottomley's first meeting, and thousands more waited in the rain outside; his eve of poll meeting packed out Hackney Baths. When the result was announced the figures were:

H. Bottomley (L)	6,736
T. H. Robertson (U)	3,257
Rev. W. Riley (Ind.)	804

At last he was in Parliament. It was nearly twenty years since he had been invited to become the Liberal candidate for Hackney. His majority was the largest achieved by any Metropolitan Liberal member. Like Bradlaugh he chose to affirm allegiance rather than take the oath.

His reception in the House of Commons was chilling. He was viewed contemptuously by the Unionist opposition and regarded as an embarrassment by most members of his own party. C. F. G. Masterman, later Chancellor of the Duchy of Lancaster in the Liberal Government of 1914, and a man pursued by Bottomley with unrelenting virulence in later years, has left a vivid impression of the general hostility to him:

> I heard his first speech in the House of Commons. It was perhaps the most unpleasant afternoon I have ever spent there—far worse than being shouted down. . . . as a House of men of property there is one crime which damns a politician for ever there. That is the suspicion of financial dishonesty. . . . He spoke through icy silence: a silence cold and contemptuous, which could be felt. He made his little jokes and no one laughed. He made his eloquent periods and no one cheered. He had to march up to the Speaker's table to present his Bill: with all eyes fixed on him and yet no word of praise, and only frozen contempt. One could not help feeling pity for the man in such an ordeal, profoundly glad when it was over.

This maiden speech was made in the debate on the King's Speech. Bottomley talked about Chinese labour in

the Transvaal, about religious teaching in schools, about
old age pensions and income tax. He struck the critical
and personal note which was to be characteristic of his
approach to debate, in the peroration, when he said that
he was only voicing the aspirations of a democratic constituency, that he was pledged to give his loyal support
to the Ministry if they carried out the reforms in their
election programme, and that the interests of the poor
and lowly were his first concern. He was not ostracized for
long. Good humour, geniality of presence and ingenuity
of mind will always make friends; and the unblushing
frankness of his approach melted many hearts that would
have remained hardened to an emotional appeal. 'As the
Chancellor would probably call me', he remarked, 'his
more or less honourable friend,' and Masterman noted with
surprise that he told his friends he was a rogue and 'was
more pleased at being a rogue than if he had been an
honest man'. Roguish, in another sense, was his habit of
proposing measures, and introducing Bills, that had not the
slightest chance of becoming law, but were of such a nature
that they obtained a good deal of attention in the newspapers. Such were his suggested Bill to compel every bookmaker to take out an annual license, thus supplying state
recognition of betting; his objection to Sunday closing of
public houses, and tabling of a Saturday Closing Bill on
the ground that 'Saturday is the big drinking day'; his
Bill authorizing the wives of men sentenced to long terms
of imprisonment to marry again; his advocacy   five
shillings a week old age pension for all in need
also, was his attempt to induce the House t
Derby Day. He put down a question askir
Wednesday next is the anniversary of
Festival' the Prime Minister would co
rising on that day. When Sir Henry (
innocently said that he knew of no

date, Bottomley was ready for him. 'Isn't the right honourable gentleman aware,' he asked 'that Wednesday next is the anniversary not only of peace with the Boers, but also of the birth of Mr. Alfred Austin, the Poet Laureate?' These wayward suggestions were marked by an ingenuity that compelled attention, and even the *Daily Chronicle* noted the intentness with which Mr. Asquith, Mr. Lloyd George and other members of the front bench listened to his suggestions on the Budget debate of 1908 in which he proposed an Employers' Tax of a penny in the pound on all wages paid, a super tax on Foreign Investments, a stamp duty on Share Certificates, the taxation of advertisements and high-priced theatre tickets and—once again—a tax on betting. Some of his speeches at this time, in particular those opposing the Licensing Bill and Sunday closing seem nowadays marked with evident good sense, and still make excellent reading: but of course the fact that there was not the slightest prospect of his suggestions being adopted gave him a freedom of which he made full use. During the course of the debate on the Licensing Bill, Lloyd George sent him a note: 'When the Savoy is acquired by the State it is proposed to convert it into an ABC and put it under the control of Sir Thomas Whitaker. I trust this arrangement meets the view of the Hon. Member.'

The flattering attention which Mr. Asquith and Mr. Lloyd George paid to Bottomley's speeches was not translated into any improvement of his position within the Liberal party. He had founded *John Bull*, a paper which in its expressed view that all parties were organized hypocrisies, and in its promise to write about the remarkable people in the House of Commons, 'some doing their country's work; some doing their own; most of them doing nothing', was not exactly reassuring. He had referred to Asquith as 'this perky little lawyer—without soul, without humour, without enthusiasm, without magnetism'. But

72

above all it was the rumours that there was something quite painfully wrong with Bottomley's financial operations that alarmed the Liberal leaders: of whom Lloyd George, at least, seems to have respected his quick wit and liked his impudence. In 1906 the Joint Stock Trust and Finance Company went into liquidation. The voting strength displayed on this occasion aroused the attention of the Official Receiver, for out of a total issue of two million shares over one million eight hundred thousand votes were cast. This percentage was so very much higher than usual that the Receiver and his solicitor decided to inspect the company's transfer and share registers. They put in a day's work putting the transfers in order—and found them all thoroughly disarranged on the following morning. This procedure was repeated on two or three days following. Great confusion was created: not so great, however, but that some striking irregularities were apparent. An application was made for the compulsory winding up of the company, instead of the voluntary liquidation originally planned; and this application was granted.

Thereafter a long battle went on, for the most part subterranean; but every now and again with strange and disturbing appearances above the surface. There was protest after protest from Bottomley. Thinly-veiled threats had been made against the company's officials, he said; its secretary had been advised to 'make a clean breast of everything'; reports of fraud were flying about the City. As a public man and a Member of Parliament he demanded an examination of the company's directors. Bottomley complained to Lloyd George, at that time President of the Board of Trade, to the Attorney-General, and to the Solicitor-General. Lloyd George wrote a stonewalling letter, the law officers politely expressed their slightly incredulous sympathy. For a time things were quiet, but then quite

73

positively there were rumours about the official prepara-
tion of a case involving the duplication of many thousands
of shares. Bottomley protested again, most strongly, to
Lloyd George, telling him that the operations of the official
winding-up branch were 'a screaming farce'. In reply,
Lloyd George smoothly and soothingly suggested that Mr.
Bottomley would no doubt wish to assist the Official
Receiver in every possible way.

Bottomley denounced the Public Trustee (now that Mr.
Stewart who had been the Official Receiver in the Hansard
case); he denounced the Official Receiver, H. de. Vaux
Brougham. He had long conversations with the Attorney-
General, Sir John Lawson Walton (who had also been involved in the Hansard case, as counsel for Charles Dollman).
He published editorials in *John Bull* referring vaguely
to a coming exposure of 'the whole conspiracy' against
him, saying that he was giving the Public Trustee and the
Official Receiver a little rope, that was all, and hinting that
he was being persecuted for his opposition to the Licensing
Bill. Everything that man could do, he did; but on the 20th
of November 1908 it was officially announced that he had
been charged with conspiracy to defraud and was to appear
at the Guildhall on December the 1st. Bottomley issued his
own notice, in moving terms. 'Readers, Friends, Constituents,' it said, 'I am a strong man, accustomed to
battle; but my heart, though I hope still brave, is very full
and I sorely need your trust.'

Chapter VII

JOHN BULL

The world is a bundle of hay
Mankind are the asses who pull;
Each tugs it a different way,
And the greatest of all is John Bull.

BYRON

THE NEWS THAT Bottomley was again to be prosecuted for conspiracy to defraud gained a great deal of its interest from the reputation he had established as editor of *John Bull*.

There are many stories about the original conception of *John Bull*; at this distance of time it is impossible to distinguish the true from the apocryphal. It is said that the germ of the paper came from Bottomley's discovery one day of Theodore Hook's short-lived and scandalous journal of that name; it is said again that the paper's original title was *Man* and that the name *John Bull* was suggested by one or another of his friends. It is said that half the money needed to start *John Bull* was provided by Bottomley's friend and fellow financier Ernest Terah Hooley. There are stories that Bottomley tried for months to induce various friends and acquaintances, among them Lord Northcliffe (who had been his sub-editor on the paper *Youth* some twenty years before), Henry Dalziel, Alfred Butt, Alfred Drage and F. E. Smith, K.C., to give him their financial support. He approached also several of the money-lenders with whom he had intricate and costly dealings during most of his life. Not until he had been refused backing from any other source did he turn, in desperation and at third hand, to an expanding but still only medium-sized firm of printers named Odhams Press.

The moving spirit of Odhams was an ambitious young man named Julius Salter Elias, who had come to the firm twelve years before as an office boy. Bottomley asked Elias to come and see him in his Pall Mall flat. Elias found him, at half past eleven in the morning, wearing a dressing gown and carpet slippers and breakfasting on kippers and champagne. Elias refused a glass of champagne, but listened carefully while Bottomley explained the scope and appeal of the projected magazine. He looked at the twenty-four page dummy Bottomley had to show him and heard without surprise that the first print order was to be 50,000 copies, and that this no doubt would soon be greatly increased. He made tentative inquiries about payment and received vague reassurances. Then he agreed to print *John Bull*. The agreement was sealed by the opening of another bottle of champagne, Bottomley's third that morning. This time Elias accepted a glass and took a few sips from it.

A compact could hardly have been concluded between two men more dissimilar. Elias was a dapper, thrifty Jew, in personal affairs punctiliously honest and polite. He was shy and his tastes were simple. He ate frugally, drank hardly at all, and disliked all forms of gambling; he read the Bible every morning in his bedroom. In small matters he was a nervously cautious man: yet a powerful ambition led him two or three times to take chances that to most people would have seemed foolhardy. This blend of caution and risk-taking in the course of years turned the obscure Julius Salter Elias into Viscount Southwood, managing director of Odhams Press and the directing force behind the *Daily Herald* in the days when it too climbed from obscurity to win the race for a daily circulation of two million readers.

The biggest chance that Elias took in his life was undoubtedly the printing of *John Bull*. To undertake the work Odhams had to engage fresh staff, buy new machines, and altogether enlarge their scale of operation. Had the paper failed, particularly in the early years, Odhams might have failed too. That it succeeded was due in large part to the harmonious relations between Elias and Bottomley, and the strict division of work and authority between them. The first few issues were edited and assembled in the Pall Mall flat, but later on Odhams provided accommodation for the periodical in Long Acre. Within two or three years, however, they had the difficulty in obtaining payment that Elias must have expected. This was solved by Odhams taking over the management of the paper and handling all receipts from sales and advertisements. They then deducted their own charges and handed the remainder to Bottomley. *John Bull*, from this time onward, consisted of two separate organizations housed in the same building. All editorial affairs were handled by Bottomley and his staff; Elias was responsible for the circulation and advertising departments, and had as little connexion as possible with the editorial side. That ebullient literary and financial buccaneer Frank Harris played a large part in planning the make-up and contents of the paper; he was also for some time its literary and dramatic critic, a fact which has remained unnoticed by his biographers. The first issue appeared on the 12th of May 1906, some five months after Bottomley had entered Parliament. The cover showed a burly John Bull, stick under arm, with a rather melancholy-looking bulldog for companion. The verse from Byron used as heading for this chapter was also on the cover, and below the masthead inside where the paper's mottoes: 'Politics without Party—Criticism without Cant;

Without Fear or Favour—Rancour or Rant.' The price was one penny. Bottomley removed his 'The World, the Flesh, and the Devil' column from the *Sun*, and took over also a slogan which the years were to make famous, perhaps from dint of repetition, perhaps merely through its manifest untruth: 'If You Read It In *John Bull*—It Is So'. There were features on *John Bull* in Parliament, in the City, at the courts, at play. Some of the comments were in the best scandalmongering tradition. 'Who are the two Front Bench men who are in the habit of coming down to the House in an advanced stage of alcoholic stimulation?' is a typical example. There was the first of many Open Letters, this one to King Edward VII ('With your Majesty on the throne, a Parliament is almost a redundancy. . . . We have always believed that at heart your Majesty is a Republican'). There were the book and theatre columns written by Frank Harris. There was a City page, featuring particularly answers to investors, and a column of racing tips.

For some time this was the general pattern of the paper. Open Letters were written freely to Bottomley's legal enemies, including Mr. Justice Lawrance and Mr. Justice Grantham. There was an Open Letter to Lord Northcliffe, reproving his low standards of journalistic ethics, remembering old times when 'You came to us—pale-faced, sleek, pensive—to continue, under our guidance, the Press career on which your heart was set', and reminding him that the young Harmsworth had been hoaxed by boys from Eton into the belief that they played football with an Eton Pudding. This letter ended sternly: 'Lose no time, we admonish you, in clearing your stable of this filth. Let it not be said that to all the new-found passports to the Peerage has now to be added the prostitution of the Press.' In the same issue 'Anti-Humbug' attacked 'indecent advertisements' in another paper; the advertisements were obligingly printed in full. An appeal to national chauvinism was sounded in such articles as those on 'The Foul French' and 'The Gentle German'. ('Note on Cleanliness. There is no cleanliness in Germany.') After the second issue a circulation of half a million copies was claimed. Ingenious methods were used to advertise the paper. The most amusing of them was Bottomley's insistence that his selling plater, John Bull, should run in the Derby. The horse had no chance of winning, but Bottomley gave instructions that he should be run all out for the first few furlongs. The jockey, Hare, obeyed orders, and next day Bottomley issued his already-prepared posters which said: 'John Bull Leads the Field'. But in spite of such little tricks the circulation claims were at this time almost certainly exaggerated: for in 1910 a dinner was held to celebrate the achievement of the half-million circulation announced in 1906. Among the more distinguished guests at this dinner were F. E. Smith and E. G. Hemmerde, K.C., among laywers, and a variety of M.P.s. The menu included: 'Bortsch Masseuse Bisque Bramwell Booth', 'White Bait of Kill-Joy', 'Stiggins Quailes', 'Horace Savoury', 'Bull's Eyes' and 'Dessert of Evil Doers'.

The staff of the paper in its early years was full of colourful characters. The most notable among them of course was Harris, who acted as chief 'sub' and leader writer, as well as covering theatre and books. Theodore Dahle came over from the *Sun*. He was capable of turning out at short notice a pseudo-Kipling poem, a short story or an article, and as 'Anti-Humbug' he was responsible for many of the paper's 'exposures'. Also from the *Sun* was the correspondence editor Ernest Wray, a one-time shorthand teacher who could turn his hand to any journalistic job. Wray had a dog-like faithfulness to Bottomley, who placed more trust in him than in any other member of the staff. Most of the material for 'The World, the Flesh, and the Devil' column was written by the gigantic twenty-three-stone, hard-breathing assistant editor George Wedlake. The notes were written by Wedlake from material supplied by Bottomley, who finally approved them, softening or sharpening remarks according to his tactic of the moment. The racing column was handled by handsome, bearded William Lotinga, once famous as 'Larry Lynx' of the *People*, and later to be engaged in a bitter feud with Bottomley. The faithful A. P. Sinnett contributed many articles on occultism. Service affairs were handled by the 'Special Commissioner', Robert Edmondson, a one-time sergeant-major who had been cashiered for leaving his post in the South African War. Perhaps to convince himself of his own courage Edmondson still went about with a revolver in his belt. Later he was replaced as Services editor by a Captain Robert Reilly, a roaring six-footer with waxed moustaches in the Kitchener style who was often first in and last out at the local Long Acre public houses, the *White Horse* and the *Enterprise*. Add a number of 'special investigators' recruited from private detective agencies and retired policemen, a flutter of secretaries and a rush of office boys, remember that the *Enterprise* across the road took on during opening hours the aspect of another office where Tommy Cox sat with one or another crony, bubbling with dubious ideas, telling dirty jokes, dispensing patronage, handing out tickets for theatrical enterprises in which the Governor was interested; and you have some idea of the editorial workings of *John Bull* —as distinct from its financial and general administration, which was controlled by Elias.

The paper's editorial offices were arranged to allow Bottomley the utmost freedom of movement in case of trouble. He had a special entrance behind a door with a brass plate reading 'Mr. Bottomley'. This led to a small 'bogey' room with nobody in it, separated from Bottomley's office by another locked door. This office was a handsome room,

all oak partitions and green leather. A large lifesize bust of
Bradlaugh painted cream stood on the oak mantelpiece, a
framed copy of the first *John Bull* poster decorated one wall
and a picture of The Dicker on another. Rows of black
deed boxes, most of them empty, but lettered in gold with
the titles of Bottomley cases, lined the walls. Bottomley
himself appeared in a large photograph, statesmanlike,
benevolently stern, holding a roll of papers in his left hand.
There was a great boardroom table in the room as well as
Bottomley's own desk; eight oak chairs, green-leather-
seated, were grouped round it, massively respectable. In
times of stress, however, Bottomley would abandon this
respectability. Next door was his private secretary W. H.
Holland, impeccably frock-coated, almost overwhelmingly
gentlemanly. Next door to Holland was Wedlake, next
door to Wedlake was the Special Commissioner. Through
these and other doors the tubby little man would speed. A
corridor led him to a back stairway and thence to an emergency exit in Anne Street, some fifty yards away: from
which emerged, unruffled and unhurried, Mr. Horatio
Bottomley, M.P. on his way to the House of Commons to
defend the people's rights; or Mr. Bottomley the patron
of Romano's; or Horatio the punter's friend.

What were these moments of stress? There were visits
from irate cast-off mistresses, determined to get into the
sanctum, quite prepared to make a nuisance of themselves
and to hammer on the locked doors. There were crooks
and blackmailers, who thought mistakenly that Horatio
Bottomley might be a soft touch. There were duns, persistent, innumerable: for Bottomley's objection to paying
bills was almost pathological, and in 1906, the year when
John Bull was founded, forty bankruptcy petitions were filed
against him. There were process-servers looking for him
every week, in connexion with one or another little matter.
There was an asylum inmate who arrived with a razor,

threatening to cut the throat of the medical superintendent of the establishment from which he had escaped. There were people anxious to tell Mr. Bottomley in person about some particular national scandal, so that he might put it right. There were people who claimed that they had been unjustly treated by *John Bull*, and who swore to 'get' Bottomley. From all these troubles the little man skipped away when necessary, on his short legs, through the doors and the corridor, down the stairs, out of the emergency exit.

In the office Bottomley was liked, admired, even worshipped, by almost everybody from the most junior of clerks to the hardest-drinking reporters. He was always busy, always in a hurry: but never in so much of a hurry that he forgot those personal gestures in dealing with his staff which cost so little to make but mean so much to their recipients. At first sight of one junior clerk he asked a few rapid questions and then pointed out to Elias the boy's heavy boots. 'Get somebody to buy him a pair of *good* shoes for the office, Elias. The petty cash can stand it,' he said, and added benevolently to the clerk: 'You, my good little fellow, can change them when you come and leave.' His benevolence was unplanned, irresponsible, and for that very reason impressive to those who saw him daily. He would stop beggars in the street, ask them questions, and if the answers pleased him he would give them money and find them jobs. One man he helped had been acquitted on a murder charge, and several had convictions for petty larceny. One day on arrival at the office he passed a man hobbling up on two sticks, and discovered that he was the victim of a lift accident and that the firm involved denied liability. The man had walked from Dulwich to ask *John Bull* to take up his case. 'Walked!' Bottomley cried, pulling up the man's trouser legs to verify the genuineness of his injuries. 'And with those sticks. You'll not walk home again!' He opened his wallet and extracted two pounds, had the man driven home in his own car, took up the case personally with the firm concerned, and obtained compensation.

The staff were almost equally impressed, in a different way, by his efforts to avoid Elias's grip upon the financial side of the paper. He would come in, stress his urgent need of money, and plunge a fat hand among the sovereigns in the cash box. Sometimes the cashier managed to restrain him, at least until the money had been counted; but Bottomley almost always got what he wanted in the end.

From the first, Bottomley showed an inclination to use his usual financial methods in support of the paper. Within a few months readers were invited to take part in the *John Bull* 'Co-operative Partnership' scheme, through an issue of £25,000 in £10 debentures. Mr. Dalton Eason, the well-known accountant, testified that the paper's profits would provide 5 per cent per annum for debenture holders. Readers were invited also to transact their stock and share business through the *John Bull* Investment Trust, 'and thus keep out of the hands of undesirable "outside brokers" and "bucket-shop keepers".' 'Anti-Humbug' was very strong about the scandalous behaviour of bucket-shop keepers. More personal invitations were extended also to selected candidates to invest in the Investment Trust itself. When one day the minute book of the Trust came to be examined, it was found to consist of 146 blank pages: a fact very reasonably explained by Bottomley on the grounds that he was the Trust's sole director and had not thought it worth while to enter details of the meetings he held with himself.

Observant readers noticed also a curious feature of the paper. Advice on City and sporting matters was given to correspondents, on receipt of a shilling in stamps or postal orders. The replies often used strong language, for *John Bull* was a fearless paper. One might read: 'Have nothing to do with Mr. Abrahams of Jerusalem Street. He is a notorious bucket-shop keeper.' Or another: 'We are making inquiries to discover whether the Samuel Johnson to whom you refer is Samuel Johnson the welshing bookmaker against whom we have already warned our readers. We will let you know the result of our investigation.' The investigation would, presumably, be made, but its result seemed to depend very largely on whether or not Mr. Abrahams or Samuel Johnson paid a visit to Bottomley's office. If he came he would certainly be admitted—there would be no need for trotting down the corridor on this occasion. Then, in a week or two, a handsome apology would be made in *John Bull*. This Samuel Johnson was not, after all, the welshing bookmaker, but a most estimable character; Mr. Abrahams' business had been reorganized and he could now be recommended with confidence.

This was trivial stuff: but large firms were not immune from attack. The financial situation of Waring and Gillow was examined in a series of articles designed to show that the firm was almost in extremity. An article one week was headed 'The Coming Crash'; a fortnight later the paper listed thirty-five writs issued against the firm in the past three months. In the page of puns and bad jokes called 'Bull's Eyes' it was suggested that Gillow was not Waring well. Suddenly the attacks stopped, and a brief paragraph appeared: 'We are glad to hear, upon good authority, that the financial pressure under which Waring and Gillow have been labouring for a long time past has recently been relieved.'

In the background of this particular reconciliation was the ubiquitous Osborne O'Hagan, who was a personal friend of Samuel Waring. O'Hagan was told by Waring that if the attacks continued the ruin of the company was certain; Waring and Gillow had recently spent a great deal of money on their new premises in Oxford Street and were very hard pushed for money. O'Hagan agreed to see Bottomley, and called at his Pall Mall flat. 'Bottomley knew there was something in the wind, as it was not my custom to call at people's offices, except on bankers and people of the very highest position in the City.' Bottomley received him cordially, and showed him an even stronger attack which was to appear in the next issue. O'Hagan reproached him, and Bottomley was moved. He telephoned the printers and told them to delete the article on Warings. 'Does that suit you?' he asked. O'Hagan expressed his astonishment. 'Have I ever refused any request you have ever made me?' Bottomley asked. 'I always try to do what you advise me is right.'

This was O'Hagan's account of Bottomley's change of heart in relation to Waring and Gillow. Other firms, however, found no Osborne O'Hagan to intervene; instead they appointed Bottomley as special investigator to handle complaints, at a figure generally amicably settled at £500 a year. Thus, after an attack on the conditions alleged by *John Bull* to exist in some Lyons' shops, payments were made to him by the Company for some unspecified services; and, much later, he was engaged by Harrods as 'unofficial investigator'. Here the method adopted was that Bottomley approached the firm with complaints sent to him by discontented workers, and suggested that he should deal with such matters privately on their behalf. In the case of Harrods it should be added that only one payment was shown to have been made, and thereafter, it seems, the matter mysteriously dropped: but there were other firms who paid their yearly sum without complaint, either directly or by way of extensive advertising.* More

* There is no suggestion that the attacks made by *John Bull* against these famous firms had any factual basis. The important point is that an attack in the paper had such a great nuisance value that Bottomley was able to make unscrupulous use of it.

than once Elias and W. J. B. Odhams tried to induce Bottomley to abandon these attacks on important firms. There is no evidence that they had any inkling of the purpose which the attacks served: but many of the other periodicals printed by the firm objected strongly to the association of Odhams and such a muck-raking periodical as *John Bull*. The printing, however, was immensely profitable to Odhams, as Elias frequently pointed out to his fellow-directors; they simply could not afford to give it up. They passed resolutions at board meetings viewing with concern the increasing tendency of *John Bull* to attack well-known commercial firms, and left it at that.

Such, in its early years, was *John Bull*: defender of the poor and the oppressed, opponent of humbug, financial guide, moral adviser. Its editor was famous as a publicist and as a public character: but most of all, perhaps, he was esteemed in his personal affairs and on the race-course as a typical English sportsman.

Chapter VIII

THE SECOND TRIUMPH

'There is a thing named Mr. Bottomley
Who's an absolute VIPER, is what I say.'
                              Letter in *John Bull*.

IT WAS IN connexion with the Joint Stock Trust that
Bottomley first came into personal contact with the
solicitor Edward Bell, a tall gaunt eccentric figure with
a love of lost causes exemplified by his enthusiastic Jacobi-
tism, and with a fanatical dislike for all financial tricksters.
Bell was acting for several shareholders in a company
named Selected Gold Mines, and it was his object to obtain
a compulsory winding-up of the Joint Stock Trust through
the Official Receiver, as distinct from a voluntary winding-
up in the hands of a receiver friendly to Bottomley. When
the law courts opened one day Bell's clerk applied for and
obtained a debenture holder's writ; the clerk from
Bottomley's solicitors, with a similar application on behalf
of a debenture holder friendly to Bottomley, was a minute
behind him. He was too late. Bottomley saw Bell and tried
to bribe him. This was a tactical error, for Bell was wholly
incorruptible. Henceforth he was an implacable enemy, for
years little more troublesome than a gadfly, brushed off by
Bottomley as partner in a firm 'whom I shall not libel
when I describe them as not standing at absolutely the
head of their profession', but turning at last from gadfly
into deadly hornet. The immediate result of Bell's prior
application was that the Official Receiver dealt with

87

Selected Gold Mines, and was led direct into an investigation of the Joint Stock Trust.

The confusion created among the transfers has already been mentioned: but in spite of this confusion the investigators, Bell among them, noted that on various transfers appeared the names of five people who appeared to have been transferring away the whole of the shares. A further more or less surreptitious look at these transfers (surreptitious because the company's offices were crowded with Bottomley henchmen eager to helpfully hinder) revealed the surprising fact that each of these five people had been transferring away shares bearing the same serial numbers; numbers, also, that had already been allotted to the original subscribers. In other words, duplication of these shares had apparently been taking place, on an enormous scale. On the day that the compulsory winding-up order for the company was made, Bottomley was heard to say: 'We must not let them have those ledgers at any cost.' On that same day one of the clerks at the Joint Stock Trust offices was sent out to lunch earlier than usual, and when he returned he saw another clerk packing up parcels which looked very much like books. On that day also the Official Receiver called, as directed by the judge, to collect the company's books and papers, and discovered that the five share ledgers containing the details of the transfers under letters B, C, H, M, and S, were missing. This was a setback, but not a knockout blow. The chief examiner in the Official Receiver's winding-up department spent a great deal of time in reconstructing the share issue of the company from the remaining ledgers and the counterfoil share certificates, and after more than a year's work he came to the conclusion that the Joint Stock Trust had issued nearly ten million shares in excess of its stated capital, and that these shares were held by hundreds of people all over the country.

The charge was fraud, as it had been in the Hansard case. Mr. Horace Avory, K.C. (later Mr. Justice Avory) and Mr. Richard Muir (who later became Chief Counsel to the Treasury) conducted the case for the Crown. They were a formidable pair: and apparently they felt sufficient confidence in the strength of their case to prefer the general charge of fraud to the particular one of duplication of the share issue. Opposed to them were Bottomley, who defended himself, George Francis Fewings, to whose help in connexion with his first bankruptcy Bottomley had long ago testified, that obliging accountant Dalton Eason and a clerk named Stevenson. F. E. Smith and E. G. Hemmerde were among the defending counsel. The case lasted twenty-eighty days over a period of three and a half months, and caused considerable distress of person to the aldermen who tried it. Sir George Smallman took the case from its opening in December 1908, to the 20th of February 1909. Then he was suddenly taken ill, adjourned for one day—and never returned. Four days later the case was resumed with Sir Horatio Davies presiding. Within a week he also was taken ill, and the last days of the case were taken by Sir James Ritchie who had a necessarily imperfect knowledge of the proceedings. Bottomley was singularly fortunate in the aldermen's illnesses.

At Bottomley's examination a year before he had indicated the line of defence he would adopt in relation to the missing ledgers. With the coolest audacity he suggested that they had been taken away by Bell. He had seen Bell removing books from the court on the day of the winding-up order, he said, had congratulated him and said that he hoped the books and papers would do him good. How could he have thought that the books would be removed for the purposes of destruction? Bottomley had scored repeatedly off Avory at his examination. When Avory attempted to fix responsibility on him by reading a

passage in which he had told a meeting of shareholders
that it was desirable to have one leading character on the
board with financial experience, and then to give him a
free hand, Bottomley replied happily: 'Quite a little
classic. I rather like it. It reads splendidly. I did not know
I could speak so well.'

Avory was smarting from many such pin-pricks, and he
opened powerfully and harshly, complaining of the continual obstructions suffered by the prosecution, and pointing out that the disappearance of the books could benefit
nobody but Bottomley. Then he came to the question of
the duplicated shares, and here the evidence seemed damn-
ing enough. Bottomley had apparently sold no less than a
million shares to a Dorsetshire landowner named Carter,
in respect of the Woking, Aldershot and Basingstoke
Canal; another 300,000 had gone to an old gentleman
named Platt; many thousands had been sold to other
people. All of these shares, Avory promised to show, were
unauthorized duplicates, on which no duty had been paid
at Somerset House. Those defrauded by Bottomley would
tell their stories. Through his victims would come retri-
bution.

That was not quite the way it went. The principal witness to the deliberate confusion created in the Joint Stock
Trust offices was a dismissed clerk named Levie, who said
that Fewings had suggested the mixing up of the books
and share transfers. When the investigation became more
obviously dangerous Fewings had tied up a bundle of
transfers, put them in a locker and said: 'If they see these
it is all up.' Later still Levie had been called in by Fewings
and told to tear up some of the transfers. Bottomley's cross-
examination of Levie was masterly in its blend of jocu-
larity and seriousness. He suggested that Levie's object had
been blackmail. This was indignantly denied. Levie insisted that he had been dismissed because he was too honest

to do the dirty work asked of him. Have you been asked to do nothing against your conscience during all the years you have been in my employ? Bottomley blandly asked. Is is not curious that you should begin to be troubled now? The witness found it difficult to reply, and Bottomley pressed home his advantage. Reluctantly Levie admitted that he often had too much to drink, that he had been suspended more than once for being fighting drunk in the office, that he had implored to be taken back. With a flourish Bottomley produced several letters written to him by Levie after his dismissal, in which the clerk had expressed deep gratitude for money sent him. When Bottomley sent no more money the tone of the letters became menacing. Then Bottomley stopped writing altogether. 'And getting no answer he went to the Official Receiver about my terrible crimes,' Bottomley said humorously. The claque in court laughed dutifully. There was not much left of Levie's evidence by the time Bottomley and F. E. Smith had done with him.

There followed days and days of evidence from people who said they had been defrauded by Bottomley. Edward Bell had taken the unusual step of circularizing many shareholders to discover the position of their holdings, and the witnesses were extraordinarily varied; engineers, architects, leather merchants, doctors, printers, farmers and clergymen were included among them. During the course of their evidence Avory was teased and badgered almost past the limits of his endurance by Bottomley, and to a lesser degree by Smith and Hemmerde. Bottomley had made great play, in *John Bull* and elsewhere, with the political motives which he alleged to be behind the prosecution; he was fined £300 for contempt of court in publishing an 'Open Telegram' to Avory in *John Bull:* 'Congratulations on first witness in Rex *v.* Bottomley' and a cartoon showing Justice, scales awry, besmeared with mud.

91

He had said also in *John Bull* that the Official Receiver would not dare to enter the witness-box. Now, in response to a question of Hemmerde's whether the Official Receiver would be called Avory incautiously answered 'Yes.' Bottomley intervened to say that he was satisfied and Avory immediately corrected himself, saying that his representative would be called. There was derisive laughter, in which Bottomley joined. The subsequent exchange shows how badly frayed were Avory's nerves.

> AVORY: I am not going to be snapped up in this ridiculous way. When I said the Official Receiver I meant his representative.
>
> BOTTOMLEY: Then I understand the Official Receiver will not be called at all?
>
> AVORY: Mr. Bottomley will be good enough not to understand anything.
>
> BOTTOMLEY: I was anxious to know whether I should see the Official Receiver in the box.
>
> AVORY: Mr. Bottomley will find that out when the time comes.

When Avory asked ironically whether a company could commit a fraud the question was immediately objected to, and disallowed. When he said that he was anxious not to put irregular questions Bottomley said that he was much obliged for the forbearance and assistance of the learned counsel. On another occasion Bottomley, speaking with some emotion, complained of a band of detectives who were following him about in cabs and motor-cars wherever he went. Sir George Smallman expressed his shocked surprise and Avory, unable to contain himself, said: 'So far as I know there is not a word of truth in this statement.' Unfortunately on the following day Avory had to admit the truth of Bottomley's statement. He had been watched, apparently because somebody had forged a telegram to an important witness and put Avory's name on it. There may

have been good grounds for believing that Bottomley was
associated with the forgery: but Avory had to eat humble
pie. Perhaps Avory's worst moment was when Sir Horatio
Davies replaced Sir George Smallman and said that he
would come to a decision on evidence brought before him.
Bottomley immediately said that he assumed the evidence
already given was thought unnecessary, redundant or unsatisfactory. Avory exploded furiously, 'Of course you
must not assume anything of the kind. Nobody but a
lunatic would.' Bottomley commented calmly, 'Mere vulgar abuse,' and to the accompaniment of cheers from
Bottomley supporters Avory was ordered to withdraw the
remark.

Among this continual bickering, infuriatingly good-
humoured on Bottomley's side, increasingly irritated on
Avory's, the witnesses gave their evidence. An engineer
complained that he had paid for his shares but had received
no certificate. He had called at the office and seen a clerk,
whom he pointed out. 'He happens to be my solicitor,' Bottomley commented, and confused the witness by a series of
questions designed to show that the shares had in fact been
issued to his wife. Other witnesses complained that they
had not received share certificates, or that they had received
shares in other companies. They had received no answer to
letters, they had tried to sell their shares and discovered
that there was no market for them on the Stock Exchange,
they had expected a quick cash profit and had received
nothing. Bottomley dealt with them all cheerfully, with the
air of a man clearing up some regrettable mistake. A paper
merchant who had expected to get Joint Stock Trust shares
had received Selected Gold Mines instead. He had written
to say he did not want any more unsaleable stuff, and had
been given some Salvage Syndicate shares. On a further
complaint these had been exchanged for shares in the John
Bull Investment Trust. An honest man justified, Bottomley

triumphantly pointed out that there was a market in these last shares, and that they could be sold.

Some witnesses were more intransigent. A printer from Carmarthenshire would give way to none of Bottomley's blandishments. He said that he expected a cash profit and had continually asked for it. He asserted that the dealings of the Joint Stock Trust stank in the nostrils of all honourable men. Bottomley saw his chance when the man said he had consulted solicitors:

BOTTOMLEY: Who; circularizing solicitors?
WITNESS: Is it necessary to answer?
SIR GEORGE SMALLMAN: Yes.
WITNESS: Carter and Bell.
BOTTOMLEY: Did they ask for a subscription?
AVORY: I submit this has gone quite far enough.
BOTTOMLEY: I agree, I agree—quite far enough.

Most of the witnesses were clay in Bottomley's podgy hands. They so very obviously liked him, so plainly wished against all evidence—against their own presence in the witness-box even—to believe in his good intentions. Almost all had written things like: 'I put myself with confidence into your hands, despite the many disappointments I have had in the past.' An architect called for the prosecution said in cross-examination: 'I have always thought a great deal of you, Mr. Bottomley.' Another prosecution witness who held 27,000 shares said that he believed the charges against Bottomley to be 'absolutely unfounded'. Even the savage printer, it turned out, had written a letter assuring Bottomley that he believed in his good intentions and would take up some more shares. Somehow the question of share duplication faded into the background; interest was concentrated on the struggle between Bottomley and Avory, and the almost uniformly favourable view of the defendant's intentions discovered in each cross-examination.

Slowly the case slipped away from the prosecution. A charge regarding the destruction of the books was withdrawn for lack of evidence; too late they tried to stem the flow by putting into the box an accountant to prove the duplication of shares. In his five and a half hour speech for the defence Bottomley called attention to the fact that the Official Receiver's representative, Mr. Fox, had not, after all, given evidence. He had been taken ill, Bottomley said, but why did the Official Receiver not give evidence in person? Why, since the prosecution alleged duplication, had they not called two people to say that they had the same numbered shares? (The reason was the extraordinary confusion in the numbering, and the fact that many shares were not numbered at all.) It does seem, indeed, that near the end of the case the Crown abandoned hope of winning it, or they would hardly have relied on the evidence of a mere clerk from the Official Receiver's office, instead of the responsible figure who might have appeared. Bottomley professed himself outraged by the behaviour of the representative of the Solicitor's Department of the Treasury— 'He goes down to the provincial hotels, and, on paper headed "The Director of Public Prosecutions", writes to law-abiding, industrious people in the town that it is necessary they should see him in regard to proposed proceedings against me.' There was no conspiracy on his part: the conspiracy, rather, had been directed against him. The peroration was worthy of the man:

> I say, in conclusion, Radical and Democrat as I call myself, I am one of those who honestly has always revered the traditions, the prestige, and the power of this Corporation, and I do not hesitate today, hunted, hounded and harassed on all sides as I am, to come to you as not the least respected and one of the senior members of the Aldermanic Bench to give me sanctuary.

Sir James Ritchie (who had heard only the last three days' evidence) retired for a short time: when he returned he dismissed the case, saying that he had come to the conclusion that no jury ought to convict. There were cries of 'He's a jolly good fellow,' and Bottomley was carried from the court in triumph. That night he gave a large dinner party to celebrate the acquittal. A fortnight afterwards he addressed a meeting at South Hackney which received him with great enthusiasm. The Mayor of Hackney took the chair and banners at either end of the hall said 'Vindicated' and 'Victory' respectively. A little later on there was displayed on the sideboard at The Dicker a handsome silver cup given to Bottomley, he said, by his loyal friends; on it were inscribed the closing words of his Guildhall peroration.

There was one further comment on this triumph, achieved against extraordinary odds. Avory had left the Guildhall in anticipation of the verdict, but his junior Muir said: 'Well, it will be a long time before anybody dares to prosecute Bottomley again.'

So far as a serious Crown prosecution of him was concerned Muir was right: yet the bungled Guildhall prosecution had revealed to those with suspicious eyes such flagrant irregularities, such an immense duplication of shares, that some further action was inevitable. Urged on by the indefatigable Bell a retired woollen merchant named James Platt brought an action to recover the £20,000 he had paid for some 300,000 Joint Stock Trust shares. Like so many thoroughly respectable men of his kind Platt was fascinated by Bottomley as a rabbit by a rat. He had held shares in several Bottomley companies, and often expressed himself indignantly about the way in which they were run: but exposed to the hypnotist's presence, lured on by his voice, made sportive by his champagne, Platt could hardly reach quickly enough for his cheque book. He lent Bottomley money with Joint Stock Trust shares as

96

security, he visited the luxurious Pall Mall flat in anger and came away £4,000 lighter in pocket and the dazed possessor of a £100 debenture bond on which Bottomley had altered the figures £100 to £15,000. The case resolved itself into a simple question: were the shares sold to Platt, which were unnumbered, duplicates of the issued and numbered shares or not? Bottomley did his best to lead the cross-examination of him down various sidetracks, but he was less successful than he had been at the Guildhall. The judge ruled that the shares were worthless, and that the stockbrokers who had delivered them to Platt must refund the money.

There is a temptation to tell the whole story of Bottomley's life in terms of law cases; yet the ironies of his career can best be appreciated by considering the simultaneous activities of this many-sided man. While the case of Platt versus the stockbroker Rowe was being heard—a case in which the judge expressed severe disapproval of Bottomley's financial conduct—and shortly after a retired miller named James Murray had obtained a verdict against Bottomley and the John Bull Investment Trust Agency for the recovery of nearly £2,000 invested by Murray through Bottomley's 'intentional misrepresentation' of the facts, the inaugural meeting of the John Bull League was held at the Albert Hall. The league was opposed to cant and self-righteousness and, it is interesting to learn, favoured 'the introduction of common-sense business methods into the government of the country'. It was said that 64,000 applications for tickets had been received, and certainly the meeting was packed out. A hundred Members of Parliament were present, including F. E. Smith and Hemmerde. Did they join in singing the league song, credit for which should be given to Tommy Cox?

If you would to Parliament
Business men of grit be sent,
Join the John Bull League.
Men and women who despise
Party tactics, party lies,
Foolish, fake election cries,
Join the League.

Members of the John Bull League paid a shilling for their membership badges. Any further donation was optional, but it was expected that the option would be exercised. The league never became an important influence in English political life, perhaps because no benefits whatever were provided for the members; but it lingered on for years as a useful adjunct to Bottomley's political career. At Lloyd George's 'People's Budget' election of 1910, the league provided a good rallying point for Bottomley's supporters. Ably led by Cox and Perkins and a follower of Bradlaugh's named Ramsey, his electoral machine worked smoothly. When Austen Chamberlain came down to address a meeting in support of the Unionist candidate he received a patient hearing; but when the candidate, a barrister named Conway Wertheimer, rose to speak, fifty men with their boots well weighted with iron at tip and heel clattered one by one towards the exit. By the time they had all left the meeting Wertheimer had lost heart for his speech. At this election also a string of Bottomley's race-horses, with jockeys up, appeared in the streets. Notices on their loincloths said 'Vote for my owner'. Another much-publicized incident involved the threat of violence to Bottomley from a Unionist tough; the courageous candidate stood up to the man, and thrashed him with a horsewhip. So at least it was said, although the circumstances and timing of the incident make it very possible that this heroic role was arranged for Bottomley by Tommy Cox. The result was never in doubt. At a time when the Liberal majority in the country was wiped out Bottomley held South Hackney by nearly 3,000 votes. A vicious piece in *John Bull* attacked Wertheimer as a Jew and as a foreigner. Bottomley apologized for this article when the election was won, and to show his comradely feelings gave Wertheimer a brief in one of his law cases shortly afterwards. In the second general election of the year, held in December, victory was won less easily. The Liberal party in the constituency split, one section supporting Bottomley and the other choosing as candidate a young schoolmaster named Roberts, who conducted a campaign so vigorous that Bottomley became alarmed. He gave instructions that Roberts should be given an uncomfortable time, and something like pitched battles took place at the schoolmaster's meetings; battles not by any means unequal, for Roberts was supported by a number of athletic colleagues. Bottomley then changed his tactics, and kept in the background personally in an attempt to remain above the battle, which raged between Roberts and Perkins. The intervention of a Conservative candidate ensured his victory, but his majority was down by more than a thousand votes. The Liberal party, who must have been very tired of the often-proclaimed independence of the member for South Hackney, had declined to interfere between the candidates, and after the election Bottomley gave up the Liberal whip saying that in future, whilst in no way allying himself with any other party, he would occupy a position of 'dignified detachment'.

It was during the course of these elections that a young man named Henry James Houston offered his services in the fight to hold Hackney. Houston worked in the house at Church Lane, Homerton, bought by Bottomley as his political headquarters. Here the great man kept a handsome apartment on the top floor for his own use; and here, one day after the declaration of the poll, Houston received an invitation to become organizing secretary of the John

Bull League, at a salary of £2 10s. od. a week. He did not stay there long. 'I want you on my personal staff,' Bottomley said (according to Houston). 'You must come and be one of Bottomley's bodyguard.'

So began the connexion between Bottomley and his political secretary and chief organizer, the man who was called, with very little justification, 'The brains behind Bottomley.' Tall, thin, tubercular, eagle-featured, with deepset eyes and carefully-brushed black hair, thin-fingered, Houston adopted an air of cultural and moral superiority which was found extremely trying by those fellow-members of Bottomley's bodyguard who were aware that his father had been a railway worker. This pseudo-aristocrat had other habits also which did not commend him to men who felt that comradeship should prevail among those enrolled in the service of a man of genius. One member of the bodyguard was given by Bottomley a pair of moon-stone cuff-links for cleaning. He left them in the office for a few minutes, and when he returned they had vanished. Several months later Houston, who had been in the office at the time, was seen wearing a pair of links quite remarkably similar to Bottomley's. Another lost a copy of a book and found it later in Houston's Forest Gate home. An astrakhan coat and a set of pornographic photographs vanished similarly and were traced to Houston; and he was held responsible, perhaps unjustly, for other things that disappeared. If Houston had not been an excellent organizer and therefore very useful to Bottomley it is likely that one or other of the boys would have protested about his conduct. After all, it is rather unpleasant for comrades to realize that they have what is practically a thief in their midst.

Houston's experiences as organizer of the John Bull League were typical of the rapid shifts of activity among Bottomley's most personal supporters. Work in obtaining

cash contributions was greatly speeded up when one day
Cox came in with a list which he had rented from a Jew
in Brighton, containing names of thousands of people likely
to send money to support such a patriotic enterprise.
Several desks were suddenly installed in a dirty 'office'
over a rat-ridden fruit warehouse in Soho, and under
Houston's supervision a number of junior clerks from
John Bull were paid a shilling an hour to work at night
addressing circulars containing league progapanda.

This continued for a week or two. Money was subscribed
in satisfying quantities. Fresh lists were obtained. But with
the approach of King Edward VII's Coronation Tommy
Cox had a brilliantly topical idea. This was nothing less
than the erection of a John Bull Coronation Grandstand,
to be opened on Coronation Day by the great man himself.
It was agreed that this was a splendid idea, and Cox,
Houston, and Bottomley's personal secretary Holland, who
was at this time also an official of the John Bull League,
tried to find a site. Unfortunately, Cox's idea had come to
him very late; and it was like almost all of his ideas, in
that the execution was not equal to the conception. An
announcement in *John Bull* said that a 'magnificent site'
had been secured facing the church of St. Mary-le-Strand,
and that seats were 'being allotted to the lucky persons
entitled to them'. The lucky persons were those who had
subscribed to one of the many schemes for their financial
benefit by taking up some of the 200,000 half-crown
Readers' Shares offered with a promised interest of 6 per
cent. Not all of these shareholders appreciated their luck in
being able to buy seats, and advertisements appeared saying that a few seats were vacant, 'and we should be glad to
hear from any reader who would like a good seat at the
relatively nominal price of two guineas'. The stand had to
be erected very quickly, and there was a little trouble over
this; in fact there was a great deal of trouble, because the

contractor threatened to stop work altogether unless he received some money. Bottomley's reputation was such that many people who worked for him asked for settlement before completion. In this case the contractor was placated with an open cheque, and the stand was finished within a few hours of the time when the Coronation queues arrived. The patrons of the John Bull stand, who had paid their fees in advance, arrived and took their seats. They discovered that they had an excellent view, not of the procession but of the church. Those on the extreme wings of the stand had a reasonably good view; all the others had to crane their necks to catch even a glimpse of the procession as it disappeared behind the church. Nor was this all. As the royal coach went by, the back of the stand collapsed. There were few injuries, and those not serious, but Bottomley was indignant. The collapse of the stand, he said, was caused by the inferior work of ill-paid artisans. He intended to institute immediately proceedings against the contractors. There were some who complained that the site itself was a swindle, and they received a ready promise that their subscriptions would be refunded. The little affair passed off with the minimum of unpleasantness. There was no mention of it in *John Bull*.

The affair of the Coronation stand followed fairly closely on another ill-fated idea of Cox's involving some Indian wrestlers who were paying a visit to England. Through the columns of *John Bull* the best of the wrestlers, Gama, known as 'the Lion of the Punjab', issued a challenge to any wrestler in the world and in particular to a group of Japanese who were then giving an exhibition of their skill. The Japanese ignored Gama, but his challenge was accepted by the self-proclaimed world wrestling champion, a Galician named Zybsco. The match was for £250 a side and a gold belt provided by the paper, and enthusiasm was worked up by several articles about the 'the match of the

Century'. The match proved a fiasco for Zybsco played safe, spending nearly two and a half hours either on hands and knees or flat on his stomach. The crowd complained, Zybsco perspired, Gama could get no grip on him and the match was adjourned for a week. Zybsco, however, did not appear for this renewal of the contest. He had gone home to Galicia.

Such fiascos as these were inevitable in the conduct of a sensational periodical. *John Bull* had also its triumphs, both legal and journalistic. Among the former was the successful defence by Bottomley, assisted by F. E. Smith, Hemmerde and Wertheimer, against a libel action brought by a man named Ronald, whose association with the Law Guarantee Trust and Accident Society had been persistently attacked in *John Bull*. The case was conducted in a high-spirited manner by everybody. When Bottomley asked what qualification Ronald had for making a report on a steam laundry, Ronald said that he had been in one at Richmond, where he sent his shirts. When Ronald said that St. James's Court was down at Westminster 'where the flats are' Bottomley asked in surprise 'Are you referring to the House of Commons?' All this humour was much appreciated by Mr. Justice Darling, who was always ready to enliven the dullness of the courts with a little facetiousness.

Among Bottomley's journalistic successes were exposures of various frauds, the publication of the Crippen letter and the affair of the Akbar training ship. The paper performed a considerable service in exposing frauds and swindles of many kinds. Almost every issue contained an attack on begging-letter writers, perverted schoolmasters, badly-conducted mental homes, the neglect of patients in hospitals, or such savage judicial decisions as that by which a twelve-year-old boy who stole a piece of coal worth five-pence was sentenced to live for seven years on a training ship and to receive six strokes of the birch. The technique developed in the *Sun* was now seen perfected in a series of articles by a 'Special Commissioner' on massage establishments. Evidence had been obtained, readers were told, which 'is simply unprintable. No decent compositor would set it up. In point of fact its lewdness has never been equalled in any country or at any time.' Extracts from this evidence, suitably condensed for family reading, were printed in subsequent issues.

The Crippen letter played a large part in ruining Arthur Newton, at that time a well-known solicitor. It is said that Bottomley paid the costs of Crippen's defence, on the understanding that *John Bull* was to get the exclusive benefit of any special story that might be involved in the case. Whether or not this is true, it is certain that, three days after Crippen's execution, the paper published what purported to be a communication from him, 'sent to us through Mr. Newton'. The letter offered no revelations. There was a hint in it that Newton might reveal some secrets 'when all is over'; but Crippen himself would say nothing that might bring trouble to others. Ethel le Neve wrote a letter in the same week's issue of *John Bull*'s companion paper, *Mary Bull*. Crippen's letter itself was of less interest to the authorities than the way in which it had reached Bottomley, in view of the fact that Crippen had not been given access to pen or paper. Newton rashly wrote to the *Daily News* certifying that the letter was genuine. An explanation appeared in *John Bull* to the effect that Crippen had made a verbal communication to Newton, who had then come straight to the *John Bull* offices and dictated a summary of what Crippen had said. The shorthand notes supposed to have been taken from Newton's dictation were reproduced, and readers were asked to notice that no *letter from Crippen* had been mentioned, but a communication *sent to us through Mr. Newton*. Called before the Law Society to explain his conduct Newton said that he had told

Bottomley that no communication had been obtained from Crippen, and that Bottomley had dictated one on the spot. Later, when Newton's conduct was being considered in the King's Bench Division, his counsel said that of course Mr. Bottomley's staff did not possess as much knowledge of law as the Bench. 'Ah,' said Mr. Justice Darling, 'that will be news to them, I am sure.' Newton was suspended from practice for twelve months and ordered to pay the costs of the case. A few years later he was tried at the Old Bailey for fraud, and sentenced to three years' penal servitude.

The *Akbar* Reformatory scandal throws a curious light on Bottomley's character. The *Akbar* was a reformatory training ship lying in the Mersey, and the headmaster of the ship and his wife came to *John Bull* with an appalling story of what happened there. They said that it was common for boys to be gagged and then birched until the blood flowed, for trifling misdemeanours. Another punishment was immersion in ice-cold water for some length of time. A boy who complained of feeling ill was immersed in this way and died within a few hours. The treatment of the boys generally was harsh and often brutal.

The matter was raised in the House of Commons and the Home Secretary, Winston Churchill, agreed to the demand for an inquiry and put in charge of it the Under-Secretary of State for the Home Department, C. F. G. Masterman. It was more than four months before Masterman issued his report. During that time the two men accused of brutality were left in charge of the *Akbar*, and a boy sentenced to be birched tried to cut his throat. In the report Masterman called the charges 'random and reckless', but admitted the practical truth of them, saving only certain minor details. He defended the two men accused, but at the same time advised their removal. Bottomley's observation that Masterman 'had done his best in the way of whitewashing' seems a just one.

In his youth Masterman had invested much of the loose capital left him by his father, some £2,000, in one of Bottomley's companies, and had lost it all. He had gone, hotly indignant, to a shareholder's meeting and been so far conquered by Bottomley's eloquence that he had taken up more shares. No doubt Masterman made an effort to be fair in the report, but the whole tone of it shows his feeling that the information about the *Akbar* came from a tainted source. The effect on Bottomley was extraordinary. He took no part in the debate on the *Akbar* (when the motion came on he was watching his current mistress playing in a musical comedy) and he did not serve on the committee appointed: but his personal pursuit of Masterman was relentness. Perhaps, as a boy brought up at an orphanage school, he resented Masterman's ready assumption that the children would answer honestly when asked if they had any complaints. Perhaps he felt indignant that *John Bull* should not be given credit when it called attention to a genuine abuse of power. A personal antipathy for Masterman, an intellectual member of the Liberal party's left wing, also played a part in deciding his actions.

Whatever were the conscious or unconscious reasons for Bottomley's vendetta, its consequences were disastrous for Masterman. He was attacked as 'the Whitewasher' in imaginary interviews and open letters. In Parliament Bottomley moved unsuccessfully to reduce his salary from £1,500 to £400. When, as the result of an irregularity on his agent's part, Masterman was unseated at North West Ham, Bottomley wrote that 'whatever constituency he woos next will have an opportunity of pronouncing judgment on that *Akbar* Reformatory business. We will see to that.' The seat chosen for Masterman was the presumedly safe Liberal one of Bethnal Green: and there Bottomley fought a most vicious campaign against him. The former headmaster of the *Akbar* was sent down to the district to make speeches. Many members of the John Bull League readily accepted the invitation to 'Run down to Bethnal Green and give the "whitewasher" a hand—backwards.' Vans were overturned and free fights took place in the streets. Masterman was returned in his 'safe' constituency by 184 votes.

Bottomley had failed; but he did not accept this failure as final. He had Masterman followed, he received verbatim reports of every speech Masterman made, he commented on Masterman's activities week by week in *John Bull*. His chance came in February 1914, when Masterman was given a place in the Cabinet as Chancellor of the Duchy of Lancaster. At that time any member of the Government promoted to a higher post had to stand for re-election: and at this second Bethnal Green by-election Bottomley's organization excelled its previous efforts in bribery, scandal-spreading, and oratorical and physical violence. Bottomley himself entered the battle, hiring halls at a cost of £30 a night, having himself shaved and shampooed every day in different barbers' shops, drinking champagne in half the pubs of the district. Masterman was unseated by twenty-six votes.

Bottomley had been joined in the pursuit of Masterman by the Northcliffe Press and by Hilaire Belloc. When Masterman fought and lost Ipswich a few months later, the Bottomley organization again headed the opposition to him. After being seatless for a year Masterman was told by the Government Whip that he must resign from the Cabinet. The political career of this brilliantly intelligent politician, who had been told when he joined the Cabinet: 'The fact is, you are *l'homme indispensible*,' was over. He did not return to Parliament until the mild Liberal revival of 1924, and in that Parliament he had no effective place. Three years later he died, a sad and embittered man.

The Masterman campaign cost Bottomley a great deal of money over the years, particularly in the form known to members of his staff as 'S.A.' or social activity. No doubt he considered it money well spent.

Chapter IX

THE SHADIEST SIDE

'There is just one person in this world to whom I would like to pay tribute, and if I were a foreigner I might very well call him "Master". This is no other than my old friend, Horatio Bottomley.'—*Confessions* OF ERNEST TERAH HOOLEY.

AT THE TRIAL of Henry Hess in 1901 there had been a brief, spectacular intervention, presumably made on behalf of Bottomley. The counsel for Hess complained that Mr. E. T. Hooley had threatened Hess, saying: 'I have a good mind to thrash you now, but I will wait for you.' The judge sent a warning to the indignant, ebullient Hooley, and no thrashing took place.

In some ways Hooley was a more remarkable figure than Bottomley. The son of a Nottingham lace manufacturer, he early abandoned the tedium of life in a lace factory for the profitable pleasure of company flotation. During the nineties he brought out one cycle company after another. He bought the Dunlop Tyre Company for £3,000,000 and sold it with £2,000,000 profit. The Bovril, Schweppes and Singer companies all knew for a time his touch—hardly a Midas touch, as he maintained, but rather a leaden one covered with quickly tarnishing gold leaf—and he carried out also dozens of deals in houses, land and breweries. Bottomley aspired to become a political force, Hooley a social one. Bottomley was a self-proclaimed Radical, Hooley the loudest sort of Tory. He set the fashion of appointing 'guinea-pig' titled directors. According to Hooley he 'got hold of an earl' and offered him £10,000 for a duke and £5,000 apiece for a couple of ordinary peers. They were duly supplied, to the benefit of Hooley, although perhaps not of his companies. In his prime Hooley owned dozens of farms, as well as Risley Hall in Nottinghamshire and the Papworth Hall Estate in Cambridgeshire. The Papworth property had a circumference of sixteen miles and was furnished in style by Hooley's 'old friend' (by his own account) Sir John Blundell Maple, at a cost of £40,000. The cellars were supplied by 'my friend Sir Thomas Kingscote, the keeper of the Queen's cellar' at a cost of £10,000 for wines and £2,000 for cigars. Dashingly attired in a light grey check suit, scarlet waistcoat and light bowler hat Hooley rode around to the cattle markets ('in those days I drove some spanking horse-flesh') buying as many as two hundred beasts in a day. By a little use of injudicious influence Hooley was appointed High Sheriff of Cambridgeshire and Huntingdonshire, to the consternation of the county families. He was sponsored for the Carlton Club by Sir William Marriott, an influential Tory, and the Earl of Albemarle. He dined and supped with the Prince of Wales, and nursed hopes of entering Parliament and becoming Minister of Agriculture.

This glory did not last. Perhaps Hooley did not even expect it to last. He was a more reckless man than Bottomley, and a more generous one. When Osborne O'Hagan was called in (as he was called in so often) to arbitrate in a case brought against Hooley by Emerson Bainbridge, partner in a firm of mining engineers, O'Hagan was horrified not by the iniquity but by what he contemptuously called the 'amateur nature' of Hooley's flotations. During the course of this inquiry Hooley in the most casual way tried to bribe O'Hagan with a yacht. It was the royal yacht *Britannia*, which he had bought from the Prince of Wales for £10,000. No cash must pass between them, Hooley realized, but he suggested that O'Hagan might have some unwanted shares which he could exchange for the yacht. When O'Hagan said that they had better close the interview, Hooley said breezily, 'No offence meant.' When the question of O'Hagan's fee was mentioned, Hooley said that it should be five hundred pounds a sitting; Bainbridge suggested thirty pounds, and this was the figure accepted by O'Hagan, who awarded £10,000 and the disputed deeds of a Scottish estate to Bainbridge. In 1898 Hooley filed his petition. He had made careful provision for it in advance, and in a financial sense he survived it splendidly. He had made elaborate arrangements which preserved Papworth Hall and Risley Hall from his debtors, and in other ways had salted money away untouchably. The bankruptcy was Hooley's financial salvation, but it was the end of his social dreams. Although at Papworth 'my stately butler was still able to open the door to visitors, and the furniture continued to bear its customary look of opulence', he had to resign from the Carlton, the Badminton and the Royal Yacht Clubs. When Bottomley first had dealings with Hooley, it is said in 1905, the squire of Risley was rich but no longer respectable.

The activities of the two men often intercrossed, and it might be thought that some rivalry would have developed between them: but among business men of all kinds it is understood that friendly co-operation, where it can be managed, is more profitable than rivalry. Clients who visited Hooley's elegant Bond Street chambers would often be sent to Bottomley's flat in Pall Mall; and sometimes one of these financial wizards would find his client's problem of such complexity that he would be inclined, like a specialist, to call for a second opinion. A typical visit was described, rather extravagantly perhaps, by the victim of it, from the moment of arrival at the Pall Mall flat in Hooley's private cab:

Upon the door being opened, he was ushered into a wigwam sort of tent, of red cloth, with a light outside. Inside was a brazier, and the victim was asked to warm himself and compose his feelings until the great man was enabled to appear. In the ruddy glow, Hooley spoke of the difficulties of the introduction, and tentatively feared that the great man was too busy to be seen, However, the curtain of the tent was opened by a plumaged servitor, and in the red light Bottomley was seen. He approached Hooley and told him how he had torn himself away from urgent business of national importance, but he would give him five minutes. . . . From the wigwam he was ushered into a drawing-room with blue and gold furniture. There was a large armchair in the middle of the room . . .

This armchair was often jovially called by Bottomley the extracting chair. It will be seen that nothing in these methods was new. There was even the very old gag of a telephone call supposedly made by Hooley to some immensely important City figure, who offered a favourable opinion about the shares to be foisted on the victim. The magic was in the men themselves, the floridly eloquent Hooley and the more robustly democratic and down-to-earth Bottomley.

They could turn anything to profit. One day a Dorsetshire landowner named Carter came to see Hooley and said that he had bought the thirty-three mile long Basingstoke Canal for £10,000. This canal was not precisely non-existent, but it carried no traffic and in fact contained no water. What could be done with it? Hooley took Carter to see Bottomley, who floated it as the London and South-Western Canal. It is said that he thought the title might be connected with the South-Western Railway. Both Hooley and Bottomley sold shares in the canal. Bottomley sold several thousands of them to two innocent brothers named Reginald and Vincent Eyre. When the Eyre brothers discovered that they had sold out their gilt-edged securities for worthless shares they sued Bottomley. To keep the matter quiet Bottomley consented to judgments against him for £44,000, on condition that the young men withdrew their allegations. He was always eager to retain some loophole through which he could subsequently wriggle in any law case. When he was asked, in relation to the Eyre case, why he had released the brothers from liability if the transactions were honourable, he replied:

> Because they were not liabilities of mine. I had nothing to do with the transactions. You had better ask Mr. Hooley. He settled the action and paid every penny necessary.

There is a limit to co-operation as it is practised by businessmen.

Hooley was involved in a case brought against Bottomley in 1910 by the executors of an insurance broker named George Parker. There had been various transactions between Bottomley and Parker, and at the broker's death his executors found that Bottomley owed Parker some £20,000, for which the broker had obtained a friendly judgment in the courts. In answer to the charge Bottomley produced two letters which, he claimed, absolved him of all liability. One was a letter from Parker to Hooley, dated the 7th of November 1908. It simply said: 'I confirm the arrangements contained in Mr. Bottomley's letter of this date as regards the settlement of accounts between him and me.' The other was a letter from Bottomley to Hooley, with the same date on it. According to this letter a form of settlement had been agreed by which Hooley was to pay Parker a percentage of all profits from any business in which Bottomley and Hooley might be mutually interested, 'Mr. Parker agreeing in consideration of this authority, to take no further steps of any kind against me.' Any claim, Bottomley maintained, should be made not against him but against

Hooley, and Hooley was at this time going through his second bankruptcy. Both letters were witnessed by Tommy Cox. There was no proof, of course, that the letter from Bottomley to Hooley was the one referred to in Parker's note; and equally there was no proof to the contrary.

Hooley was indignant that he had been involved in the case at all. 'It's too bad to drag me into it, considering I never had a damned farthing out of the business,' he wrote. Nevertheless he entered the box, gave evidence against Bottomley, and confirmed that he had sent Parker at the relevant time in 1906 a cow, some pigs, a ham and some cigars. A pig was Hooley's favourite peace-offering, and he offered to send one to the leader for the plaintiff, Mr. John Simon, K.C. In spite of Hooley's evidence Bottomley (who for once did not defend himself, but was represented by F. E. Smith) obtained a verdict. Mr. Justice Darling, who obviously enjoyed the case, told the jury that it was a peculiar affair involving peculiar people; and the jury found that the agreement in the Bottomley-Hooley letter was valid.

There is no doubt that nine-tenths of Bottomley's association with Hooley will stay forever submerged. Their names were not often publicly linked. When Bottomley lunched one day with Marie Corelli at Stratford, he said to her afterwards: 'Now I must go and meet my friend.' She reproached him for not bringing his friend to lunch, but Bottomley winked and said engagingly: 'It's Hooley. I thought the two of us together might be too much for you.' There are many anecdotes of the two laying exclusive claim to a prospective victim, accusing each other of shameful dishonesty, quarrelling and making up. In one letter, no doubt typical of many, Hooley handsomely relinquished all claims to one client, handing him over to Bottomley. Hooley told many stories, in all of which he played the part of the innocent confounded by the wicked

Bottomley: but, wisely, neither he nor Bottomley ever put pen to paper unnecessarily in relation to such matters, and nobody will ever know how many sheep were sheared of their warm financial fleeces at Risley and The Dicker, in Bond Street and Pall Mall. From what came to light through their law cases it is clear that the shearing was highly personal—unlike Bottomley's earlier operations, in which the emphasis was on public subscription—and that it was carried on quite ruthlessly, until the victim was penniless. Old men, or very young ones like the Eyre brothers, were the sheep most generally favoured; and the degree of their complaisance was astonishing. It must be said, nevertheless, that Bottomley's tactics in uniting himself with Hooley in carrying out these large-scale and highly personal operations, were ill-chosen, and likely to take him, where they took Hooley more than once, to prison. It is very much easier, in the way of ordinary business, to rob five hundred people of ten pounds each than it is to rob one person of five thousand pounds. Very few of the five hundred people are likely to take action over the trivial sum involved; those who do can usually be kept quiet by the return of their money; and it is easier to raise a smokescreen of complication and obscurity where five hundred people are involved than in the case of one single complainant. Bottomley began and ended his financial career in the comparatively safe, large-scale, public subscription way. He was led into these treacherous personal engagements perhaps partly by the example of Hooley, who for all the stories that he told of his own innocence was in many ways Bottomley's exemplar (his discomfiture of the 'stags' who sold Waitekauri mining shares, for instance, paralleled an exactly similar operation of Hooley's carried out several years earlier with the Humber Cycle Company): and partly by the fact that he found it extremely hard at this time to make a living. He said only half-jokingly that he needed a thousand pounds a week to live on, and the money he obtained through *John Bull* was not half enough. Men will do anything, as we know, for money; and Bottomley was driven by his need of it to courses that he was never able, afterwards, to regard as completely honest.

Acting involuntarily as his conscience during this period was the firm of Carter and Bell. The John Bull Investment Trust had been registered in Guernsey, thus placing it at one remove from proceedings in the English courts. An attempt was made to wind up the company in Guernsey, and to destroy the books, but as *John Bull* put it:

> Carter and Bell are at it again. . . . They are now distinguishing themselves in Guernsey, where they are endeavouring to upset the liquidation of a private company, whose affairs are of no public interest; but it has the attraction for them of a possible annoyance to Mr. Bottomley.

Bell's activities stopped these books from being destroyed in Guernsey. This was a mere pinprick. Much more serious was Bell's part a year later when he acted as solicitor for the executrix of a man named Robert Edward Master. The story is one which must have brought home powerfully to Bottomley the unwisdom of the personal, or Hooley, approach.

Master was an elderly retired Indian Civil Servant who in 1904 lost his memory as the result of an accident, and afterwards seems never to have fully recovered the use of his wits. Bottomley sold him shares in the John Bull Investment Trust, which held no property whatever, in one of his Guernsey-registered companies called Carter's Deep Leads, which had always worked at a loss, in the Southern Counties Stores (also registered in Guernsey, and admitted to be insolvent almost from the start), and in Hedon Park Estates and the John Bull Agency. The loss on these shares amounted to some £57,000. Further than this, Master backed bills for the John Bull Agency to the extent of £37,500. He also lost a lot of money to Hooley who, when an action was threatened against him, paid a considerable sum in compensation.

Master had lost money originally in the West Australian gold mining companies. Bottomley re-established contact with one of his standard letters:

> I have been going over the names of my old supporters and it struck me that I might now be able to do something for those people who have lost money in my companies. Would you mind letting me know approximately the amount you consider you are out of pocket and I will see what I can do towards recouping your loss.

The wording was ingenious, yet in retrospect it seems astonishing that anybody should have been deceived by it. Master congratulated himself perhaps that he was not deceived: but he was tempted, and he fell. 'Bottomley was most cordial and offered to repay my losses,' he recorded in his diary. After that there was a whirl of luncheon and dinner engagements with Bottomley and Hooley:

> Walked Mr. Bottomley's chambers in Pall Mall. Took me small hotel in Coventry Street where we had much champagne and unnecessarily gorgeous lunch. After discussing business went home.

A few months of such discussions saw Master poorer by nearly £100,000, but the possessor of the shares already mentioned. The luncheons and dinners ceased, the old man was left alone. He made no complaint of his treatment, then or afterwards, and it was not until after his death that the exchange of money for shares was discovered.

Bottomley realized the seriousness of the action threatened against him, and did his best to avert it. He had become involved in what was, even for a man of his legal appetite, too many law cases. He tried to strike a bargain with Dade, the solicitor acting for Master's executrix, Mrs. Curtis. 'Leave me out of these proceedings and I will help you against Hooley,' he said. 'I have had a bellyful of litigation and don't want any more.' He ended with an implied threat. If the plaintiff persisted in proceeding against him personally he would file his petition, and nobody would get anything.

That did not check the proceedings. A writ was issued. Shortly afterwards a burglary took place at the offices of Dade and Company, and Master's diaries were taken. Six months later the offices were burgled again. This time a tin box full of documents and a brown paper parcel containing Bottomley's letters to Master disappeared. These burglaries were labour wasted, because all the documents in the case had been copied.

Before the Master case came on Bottomley found himself compelled to bring a libel action against a paper called *Modern Man*, which had said that much of the money remitted to *John Bull* to help the 'Human Documents' cases published every week was simply appropriated by the editor. The article mentioned the case of Warings, and said that the firm had taken half-page advertisements in *John Bull* after the attacks on them ceased and had also 'had the honour of carpeting the office floors'. The case was hurriedly withdrawn and the costs of *Modern Man* were paid in full. There was no reference to the withdrawal of the case in *John Bull*.

In the Master case itself Bottomley adopted the desperate strategy of calling no witnesses and not entering the box himself. Had he gone into the box and then lost the case he must have made admissions which would have led to a further prosecution: but by staying out of it he made a verdict against him almost certain. The plaintiff's counsel, Mr. Ritter, seems to have been moved by a moral

118

zeal almost equal to that of Edward Bell. 'I hope that after this case there will be an inquiry which will put Mr. Bottomley in the dock and render him liable to a long term of penal servitude,' he said. When Bottomley asked if Ritter had any idea of the length of the term his supporters dutifully laughed, but it is doubtful whether the Lord Chief Justice, who was trying the case, laughed with them. In his speech in his own defence the defendant adopted a rather haughty tone. He had not gone into the box, he said, because had he done so it would have greatly lengthened the case. Besides, he was not prepared to go into the box and submit himself to counsel, not always of the highest class, who under the protection of their gowns could make such suggestions as they pleased. Ritter, in his final speech, had referred to Bottomley as 'the cleverest thief in the Empire' and he retorted by saying that those who had brought the charge were a 'blackmailing attorney and most discreditable member of the Bar.'

The jury were out for an hour. They returned a verdict against Bottomley, and awarded damages of £50,000.

He did not underestimate the seriousness of the verdict against him, in relation both to his political and journalistic careers. Many men would have considered the position hopeless, but he would not give up. A large, empanelled notice in *John Bull* struck a note of sober concern, blended with optimism. The verdict was a very heavy blow, he was overwhelmed with anxiety, but still, 'as far as anything in the law can be certain, it is certain that before long a superior court will set matters right.' As he had done before in extremity he turned to writing about himself, analysing his motives and character in consecutive articles and acquitting himself of any intention but that to serve his king, his country, and his fellow men and women. Then came the decision of the superior court. It was against him, although

119

one of the judges thought there was a case for a new trial. At the last moment he withdrew his claim for judgment in an unsuccessful attempt to avoid comment on the facts of the case. Lord Justice Buckley commented on them nevertheless. 'I was not prepared to allow you to enjoy that advantage,' he said. 'I deliberately went into the facts because I thought it right to do so.' Bottomley said that that was what he complained of and Buckley observed acidly: 'So I understand. It was astute.'

Must a man with none but good intentions be branded finally a swindler? Could nothing, then, be saved of moral tone? Remarkably, it could. A few days after the failure of the appeal a letter from Dade appeared in *The Times*. The letter said that the plaintiff 'having had her attention drawn to a certain document, the contents of which were unknown to her advisers when she commenced the action' agreed that her claim was not based upon any misrepresentation of fact by Bottomley. By what means Dade was induced to write such a letter is unknown: but, such as it was, Bottomley used it. He gave a full page to the letter in *John Bull*, referred to the withdrawal of the imputations upon his personal honour (about which, in public, he always came out very strong) and commented loftily: 'The case is over; and although it has seriously dislocated my affairs and interrupted my work, I am busy repairing the mischief, in order that I may go back to the House of Commons and take up again the role of Independent Critic.' Would he be allowed to take up that role again?

At a great gala day held by the John Bull League at the Crystal Palace he spoke for an hour with hardly a note to nearly twenty thousand enthusiastic supporters. He told them that he was the victim of party, puritanism and priestcraft. He would make a statement in the House, and then if necessary would appeal to his own constituency. The league would go on, and plans had been made to fight twelve constituencies at the next election. Within a few weeks Walter Moore, a journalist on the staff of the paper, fought a by-election at East Buxton as a league candidate, and polled quite respectably. Bottomley made his statement in the House, and said that he hoped the Dade letter would clear his reputation. He was heard in silence, and afterwards was shunned.

Really, the game was up. He acknowledged this when he withdrew from candidature as Lord Rector of Aberdeen University, on the day after he had been nominated. He acknowledged it in the uncharacteristic letter he wrote to a shareholder when the John Bull Investment Trust was wound up: 'I am far too much engrossed in my own worries to be able to look into any of these outside matters, and it is useless your troubling me further.' He acknowledged it, finally, by seeking once more the protection of the Receiver against all the claims that were being made on him. To do this meant the interruption of his parliamentary career, but he was tired, he said, and ill. He wanted nothing now but a little peace.

Chapter X

BOTTOMLEY'S HARD TIMES

A. L. M. (Manchester) wants to know if the Editor has ever been incarcerated in one of H. M. Prisons?

The answer is—not yet, but you never can tell.

EDITOR'S POSTBAG, *John Bull* 1913.

HE WAS NOT allowed to live peacefully, not even though his medical adviser testified that he was suffering from ptomaine poisoning or under severe emotional strain, or the victim of an 'acute nervous collapse with intense headache and sickness'. Process servers sought him in vain at the *John Bull* offices and in one or another hotel. At the Pall Mall flat his valet Wade met them with a serious face and told them that the Governor was really in a bad way. He showed them a thin, hollow, pliable lengthy tube which, he said, had to be inserted in the 'Old Man's' genital organ twice daily, night and morning. Were they still doubtful? Did they think they heard voices raised in laughter, a popping cork? A starchy nurse came out, snapped at Wade, told him that Mr. Bottomley was suffering from intense nervous prostration and must have absolute quiet. Cowed, the visitors went away.

Still, he was not left alone to order his affairs with the simplicity that he would have wished. He made a suggestion, a handsome one surely, that he would vest in a trustee the whole of his property and income, to an amount of not less than £7,500 a year. The trustee was to be Sir

122

William Peat, who might be called perhaps Bottomley's favourite trustee, and the appointment was proposed by Henry Dade—who, rather strangely, had been Mrs. Curtis's solicitor in the Master case. The Committee of Inspection appointed included Julius Salter Elias, the business director of *John Bull*. This appointment was carried against the strongly-expressed opposition of Edward Bell —and of the Prudential Assurance Company.

The Prudential's intrusion into the case was occasioned by another instance of Bottomley's remarkable rashness. There had appeared in *John Bull* a series of savage attacks on the Prudential Company and its methods of business. They were accused of mis-statements, and of inducing poor people to take out policies on which they were wholly unable to maintain the terms. It was said that the company tried hard to effect the lapsing of policies, which were 'wheedled out of the hands of poor people who have paid premiums for years upon them by means of all kinds of plausible misrepresentations'. Case after case of alleged trickery was printed in detail. It was said that the agents, who deceived the small policy-holder, were themselves victimized by the company. A list was published containing the names of more than a hundred agents who had committed or attempted suicide, with the method used—'cut throat', 'drowning', 'hanging'. Another list gave the company's published profits and some details of the directors' fortunes, which were contrasted with the agents' poverty. A cartoon showed policeman John Bull picking up a trail of papers marked 'illegal policy' which led to the Prudential offices in Holborn. The company was invited to issue a libel writ. They did not do so, but sent out a reassuring circular to all of their superintendents and agents.

Perhaps Bottomley expected an approach from the Prudential, such as he had received from other firms, asking him to drop the attacks; perhaps his feelings were of the

part-false, part-genuine kind that seem to have moved
him in the case of Masterman and the *Akbar* scandal. He
added foolishness to hardihood by himself issuing a writ for
libel against the Prudential. It did not take him long to see
that the time (judgment had just been delivered against
him in the Master case) was not propitious for this kind of
action. He decided not to go on with the case, but the Prudential, stung at last to action, set it down for hearing
themselves. When he abandoned the case they presented
him with a bill of costs totalling £1,559. This comparatively
small unpaid sum allowed the Prudential to be ranked as
creditors of his estate, a fact which had unhappy consequences for him. He was particularly anxious to have his
scheme of arrangement accepted, because through it he
might be able to retain his seat in Parliament and would
certainly avoid a searching bankruptcy examination. To
the London Bankruptcy Court, however, he was taken in
February 1912.

Before this, however, the Prudential brought a case
against him for contempt of court, alleging that he had
been 'attempting by threats to prevent the due administration of justice in the present bankruptcy proceedings'.
A representative of Bottomley's solicitors had approached
the Prudential solicitor and said that they had got the old
man into a tight fix now. Had not the time come to try to
arrange for peace? But apparently no terms acceptable to
both sides could be arranged, and another emissary of
Bottomley's named Wenham threatened two directors of the
company that unless they agreed to the scheme for settlement the attacks on the Prudential would restart. In fact
they began again in the week that the case for contempt
came on.

In a long and eloquent speech before a packed court
Bottomley defended himself and accused the Prudential
solicitor of perjury. Such perjury was, he said, 'The last

card of a desperate company which was smarting under the lash of charges for which he was responsible, and which had been made and persisted in for the last twelve months.' It had been suggested that he was running away. Mr. J. M. Astbury, K.C. had been retained by the Prudential. Remembering his triumph over Sir John Rigby he referred to Astbury scornfully as a 'distinguished equity lawyer who had now come upon the scene to try his hand at cross-examination' and said that 'the learned counsel would not by the first member of the Bar who had not enhanced his reputation or practice by acting on insufficient instructions.' Astbury revealed that he had been approached by a barrister friend of Bottomley's, who had suggested that as Astbury had acted for Bottomley some years before, it was not quite ethical to act against him now. The barrister also suggested that Astbury should tell the Prudential that they should pursue Bottomley no further, because he had almost finished with them.

The Prudential had accused Bottomley of systematic fraud and blackmail. A good deal of entertainment was offered when their solicitor, Mr. A. E. Pratt, was in the box.

BOTTOMLEY: Where did the evidence as to blackmail come from?

PRATT: I showed it to Counsel in print. Here it is (showing book).

BOTTOMLEY: What! Are those books all printed about me?

PRATT: Yes.

BOTTOMLEY: Printed at the expense of the shareholders of the Prudential?

PRATT: I am afraid so.

BOTTOMLEY: Is it my life?

PRATT: Some of the worst parts of it.

BOTTOMLEY: Read me the worst part of it. (Laughter.) You say that you have evidence of blackmail against me.

Point to me something in that book on the facts of which
you said that.

PRATT: There is a book here which I will call Compulsory
Advertisements so as not to hurt your feelings. . . .

Later questions were asked about a man named Birch,
which show Bottomley's quickness of wit in noting the
mistakes of a legal witness:

PRATT: I believe he is your election agent. Have you an
election agent named Birch?

BOTTOMLEY: One of the rules of evidence, Mr. Pratt, is that
you must not ask *me* questions. (Laughter.) Well, a man
named Birch came to see you.

PRATT: No, he did not call on me. He approached a man
named Robinson, and Robinson told me.

BOTTOMLEY: Oh, Mr. Pratt, Mr. Pratt. (Loud laughter.)

It was all most delightful, most amusing. Nobody seemed
to be enjoying it more than Bottomley. Eventually, in the
King's Bench Divisional Court, he and Wenham were
fined £100 apiece, and two of the three judges trying the
case—Darling and Bucknill—expressed doubts that the
allegations of blackmail and fraud against him had been
proved. Mr. Justice Darling, who had added much to the
liveliness of the affair by his asides and interjections, said:

I am not going to send the parties to prison. Mr. Bottomley
has a duty to his creditors which he will not be able to perform if he is incarcerated in Brixton Gaol. Also, it would be
a mistake to fine him a large sum of money which ought to
go to his creditors.

After the case came his public examination: and
Bottomley must have realized fully his error in attacking
the Prudential, when Astbury cross-examined him for four
days. In general Astbury was not noted for keeping his
temper, but in this case he seems to have paid attention to
some advice he was given by Osborne O'Hagan shortly

before the case: 'The way to meet Bottomley is to hold yourself in, smile when he insults you, laugh more heartily than the rest when he scores a point against you.' The technique can be seen clearly in operation when the Official Receiver read the judgments in the Master case and Astbury politely suggested that Bottomley might find it useful to have a copy of the judgment.

BOTTOMLEY: No; I know the wretched thing by heart.

ASTBURY: You can have a second copy of mine.

BOTTOMLEY: No, thanks.

REGISTRAR: Mr. Bottomley does not appear to want any assistance.

BOTTOMLEY: It is Mr. Astbury's assistance that I do not want, sir.

ASTBURY: Quite right. Don't you take my advice about anything.

At times Bottomley went to almost extravagant lengths in an attempt to irritate his examiner:

ASTBURY: You keep race-horses, Mr. Bottomley?

BOTTOMLEY: No.

ASTBURY: You do not keep race-horses?

BOTTOMLEY: Certainly not.

ASTBURY: Then you did keep race-horses?

BOTTOMLEY: No, never. . . .

ASTBURY: You have a place in Sussex called 'The Dicker'?

BOTTOMLEY: Yes.

ASTBURY: You have stables there—large stables?

BOTTOMLEY: Yes.

ASTBURY: You breed horses there—race-horses?

BOTTOMLEY: Yes.

ASTBURY: Then why did you tell me that you never kept race-horses?

BOTTOMLEY: I gave you a correct answer. I never kept race-horses. They keep me.

There was loud laughter, but the loudest laughter of all came from Astbury. Before the encounter with Astbury,

Bottomley had admitted to the Official Receiver that he
kept six or eight gardeners at The Dicker, and also six in-
door servants and two chauffeurs. And yes, his London flat
cost six hundred pounds a year. The Registrar said that he
hoped he was not pinching himself when he lived in
London. Bottomley replied amiably:

> I hope I was not pinching anything. . . . I am very modest.
> For tea I have bread and butter and egg as a rule. I have no
> breakfast, and today I have not had much lunch. I do not
> smoke, and I rarely drink between meals. Now, I think, I
> have told you all about myself.

He was in excellent form also during his examination
by the easily-baited Bell. 'You look at me in such a tragic
way you always take my memory away,' he said. 'You
scowl and frown at me and bite your lips.' Bell apologized,
and by way of rejoinder asked whether Bottomley had
paid his friend Hooley a visit when Hooley was in prison.
'I will come and see you one day,' Bottomley responded.

In answering Astbury's questions, however, he could
not keep things on this plane of pleasant facetiousness. He
turned and evaded, he parried and made jokes, he
threatened continually that if he withdrew his scheme the
creditors would get nothing, he pleaded illness. The
Registrar asked him, one day when he complained of
stomach pains, whether he would be well enough to
attend on the day following. 'I will come, sir, if I am
alive,' he said. On the next day he was alive, but not present. Instead there came a doctor to say that he was not in
a fit condition to attend the court. It would be a fortnight
before he could appear. He came back in a week, and the
relentless examination was resumed. The task of finding
factual material discreditable to him was well within the
Prudential's resources.

It must be acknowledged that there was by now really a

great deal to discover. There was the matter of Bottomley's old friend, the furrier Saul Cooper. Astbury asserted that Cooper had visited a firm named Arthur Williams and Company and promised to stop attacks made on the firm in *John Bull* in consideration of a payment. He had actually obtained cheques from the firm. Bottomley was shocked. 'Mr. Cooper is a gentleman of high standing in the City. . . . It will come as a shock to the City in which Mr. Cooper is very eminent, very highly respected in the fur trade, to have it suggested that he goes about blackmailing people. It is a monstrous thing.' He was more than shocked, he was disgusted. 'Every thief in London could put up questions like this to me, if he could get counsel dirty enough to do it.'

Astbury remained unperturbed. He passed on to the winding-up order of the John Bull Investment Trust, made in Guernsey on the petition of a man named Bennett. Who was Bennett? Was he one of five brothers, all convicts? Was his real name Samuel Bangham?

'I have not the slightest idea, Mr. Astbury, any more than the five gentlemen instructing you might be described in a few years' time.'

Astbury refused to be diverted, and worked his way through a series of transactions involving Cox, the Master case, and another Bennett. The questioning in relation to this second Bennett is of some interest in view of later events.

ASTBURY: Is this Bennett a brother of J. H. Bennett?

BOTTOMLEY: I do not know whether he is or not. I believe he he is a brother of J. H. Bennett.

ASTBURY: Do you know who J. H. Bennett was?

BOTTOMLEY: I do not know who J. H. Bennett was.

ASTBURY: Did you introduce J. H. Bennett to various people who brought actions for fraud against you as a financier in Paris?

BOTTOMLEY: Never in my life.

ASTBURY: Did you obtain the acceptance of a number of Mr. Master's bills by this man Bennett?

BOTTOMLEY: I did not.

ASTBURY: Did J. H. Bennett in fact accept a number of Mr. Master's bills?

BOTTOMLEY: J. H. Bennett did in fact accept some bills in favour of Master. I happen to know that.

ASTBURY: Was he a man who could pay upon his acceptances?

BOTTOMLEY: If you ask me for my opinion, I should say yes.

ASTBURY: Was he ever sued on his acceptance by anybody?

BOTTOMLEY: You are up in the clouds. You will make my re-examination a week long. This Mr. Bennett of whom you are speaking now, who is not the Bennett you began talking about, did accept some of Master's bills, and he subsequently threatened criminal proceedings against Master for conspiracy in obtaining these bills, and he released him from all obligations upon them.

ASTBURY: Was he another of the brothers Bangham?

BOTTOMLEY: I do not know. I know nothing at all of his name.

ASTBURY: Prior to these episodes had J. H. Bennett been sentenced to 15 years' penal servitude?

BOTTOMLEY: Is it not wicked when I say I know nothing about it?

ASTBURY: Did not J. H. Bennett at one time occupy the same building as yourself?

BOTTOMLEY: A Mr. J. H. Bennett once had a flat in the same block of buildings that I had. That is how I met him.

Jokes, laughter, appeals to the Registrar proved ineffective. Insults were useless. 'I heard you ask a gentleman behind you which was the debit side,' Bottomley said jeeringly as a ledger was passed back in the court. Astbury made no reply, but moved on to discuss the Eyre brothers and others who considered themselves Bottomley's victims. Bottomley complained again, and said that one distinguished counsel had refused the brief, saying that the endorsement should read: 'Brief to throw mud at Mr. Bottomley during his public examination.' Astbury, who had already accused Bottomley of answering untruly, pressed hard for the counsel's name, but could not get it. 'There is some limit even to perjury,' he commented. Bottomley threatened to 'run down to the House and introduce a Bill to curtail the privilege of counsel', saying indignantly that 'It is time that some members of the Bar were made responsible for their outrages upon fair play and decency. Under a Business Government a reckless barrister would have his licence endorsed—just like a chauffeur.'

At the end of the examination Bottomley was, in the sense of public credit, a ruined man. He withdrew the scheme, since there was no longer any chance of its acceptance. His last speech in the House of Commons was made on May the 3rd, on the Clubs Bill. Like a true democrat he argued that there should be no difference between the liberty granted in workmen's clubs and in those of the richer classes. A few days later he applied for the Chiltern Hundreds. At a meeting in the Queen's Hall he said that the House of Commons was played out. He was not sure but that it was an illegal assembly, now that members had voted themselves an annual salary. He heard a call, distant at present but growing more distinct, 'Wanted—a Man!' Members of the *John Bull* staff were turned on to this meeting in full force, and struck a note uncommonly high in dealing with it. Theodore Dahle said that Bottomley had gripped the upper and lower middle class and praised particularly his phrases 'here biting in like vitriol, and there stinging like nettles' and Walter Moore was impressed by his rich humour and mellifluous tones. 'Libel, slander, persecution, lies,' said the paper's tame Socialist Norman Tiptaft, 'what matter it how they get rid of him so that he be quieted.' He was a true and gallant Chevalier. Most members of the House of Commons felt relief at the Chevalier's departure, though F. E. Smith paid him a high tribute:

> His House of Commons style was almost ideal, self-possessed, quiet, irresistibly witty, and distinguished equally by common sense and tolerance. . . . His absence has impoverished the public fund of gaiety, of cleverness, of common sense.

He was ruined, apparently, as a public man; and his emotional affairs also were in some disorder. In the midst of the Prudential affair, on the evening after he had been fined £100 for contempt of court, he was attacked as he left Romano's by a man named Aubrey Lowe. The affair was conducted, it seems, in a somewhat leisurely way. Considerately taking along a cab driver as witness of his actions, Lowe said to Bottomley: 'Now I've got you. Look out, because I'm going to hit you.' Afterwards, Lowe said, 'I gave him one, two, three, and knocked him flat on the pavement. After he got up I hit him again.' Bottomley refused to prefer charges.

Aubrey Lowe was the dashing, extravagant, somewhat reckless husband of a musical comedy actress who used the name of Peggy Fitzmaurice or Peggy Primrose: and it was in the slightly ludicrous role of ill-treated husband that he made the assault which was referred to in some papers as a 'horsewhipping' and in others as a purely technical assault in which Bottomley's hat was knocked off. The assault was ineffective, for Bottomley's friendship with Peggy Primrose did not cease, and at his death she said truly that she had been his more or less constant companion for over twenty years. More or less: for anyone who aspired to a position as Bottomley's companion had to understand and forgive a great deal. There was Mrs. Bottomley, for instance, to whom Bottomley's devotion, though not unswerving, was real. Eliza Bottomley had now changed her name to Alyse, as she had changed the colour of her hair to a most vivid red. She spent most of her time in a villa at Nice, with occasional visits to The Dicker. What she thought of her husband's way of life is not recorded.

Peggy Primrose must also at times have been annoyed by the number and variety of Botty's (as he was familiarly known to her) girl friends. There were girls in a dozen towns, waitresses and shop assistants, who were expected to be on call if needed when he paid the town a visit. There were girls installed from time to time in various London flats, there were members of his staff who were delighted to be the great man's companion for an evening. One might say cynically that he believed it impossible to have too many friends: or, more generously, that an eagerness to be loved made him genuinely kind. A girl whose home he sometimes visited remembers that his arrival would always be preceded by masses of flowers. Had he sent them himself, or was that merely a part of his efficient organization? He always affected surprise at seeing them, a surprise not meant to be taken seriously. ' Did I send all those? It makes the place smell like a damned conservatory,' he would say. *Damn* was the strongest swear word he used. Young women trying to write, girls hoping to find work in the theatre, found him—at least for a time—an enthusiastic and immensely helpful supporter. He would readily make appointments to talk with them all, to give them lunch or dinner. At times, indeed, he would arrange to meet three or four of them at the same time but in different places. Then there would be some telegrams, or telephone calls made by Houston or Cox, and a little sputter of anger on the part of the unlucky ladies. Of anger soon forgotten: for who could really be angry with a man who sent such delightful telegrams, flowers, chocolates, even (more rarely) jewellery?

133

A man, moreover, with a business government on his mind?

Among all these amiable and perhaps rather tiresomely admiring ladies, Peggy Primrose remained a permanent attachment. She was a dainty, vivacious blonde, with a talent for singing and dancing which perhaps appeared enlarged by her friendship with Bottomley. Certainly she was a chorus girl when Bottomley first began to send her notes at the Gaiety or at a rehearsal-room near the Adelphi Theatre: playing, perhaps, in *Peggy* or *The Sunshine Girl* or another forgotten musical of that time. It may have been through Bottomley that she obtained a three weeks' engagement as 'Mimic and Dancer' at the 'Old Mo', the Middlesex Music Hall in Drury Lane. Here she parodied Gertie Millar in *The Quaker Girl* and Alfred Lester singing 'I've Gotta Mother.' She played a straight part in a play at the Savoy, written by Bottomley's good friend Hemmerde. Bottomley backed this unhappy production. 'All London is flocking to *A Cardinal's Romance*,' said *John Bull* optimistically, and mentioned the 'bewitching archness' of Peggy Fitzmaurice. *The Times* also emphasized her pretty playing, but remarked that *A Cardinal's Romance* was in no sense a good play. It lasted for only fifteen performances, and must have cost Bottomley a great deal of money. Later he backed her most elaborate London appearance as the star of *The Dear Little Lady*, a musical comedy on which he was said to have lost £40,000 in the few weeks of its run, in spite of the 'House Full' notices obtained for a few nights by the simple expedient of giving away almost all the tickets.

Bottomley, like Hooley, managed to live very comfortably during this bankruptcy. Some race-horses were handed over to his trainer Jimmy Hare as part payment of his debts, others were made over to his friends Saul

Cooper (that 'gentleman of high standing in the City') and the moneylender Thomas Tanqueray Todd. His furniture was all nominally owned by relatives, and his son-in-law, the American millionaire Jefferson Cohn, owned The Dicker. His debts totalled nearly £250,000, but he did not allow the fact to perturb him. His way of living did not alter. There was no less champagne, there were no fewer girls, his betting was as rash as ever. 'Unfortunate I may have been,' he said, 'but never dishonest'; and to show that he was still a man of the people, unbroken, he took the members of the Clapton Orient Football Club to a pantomime and was photographed, beaming, in their midst. At Christmas the poor of South Hackney once more blessed his name. Many figures from the district were present at a banquet in his honour at the Great Eastern Hotel, when he was presented with a magnificent gold cup, subscribed for by an immense number of residents in the borough of all classes, creeds and political complexions. Readers of *John Bull* were thanked most movingly for their support:

> If we fall it shall be in the last ditch, and we shall want no better epitaph than that, like our Roman namesake, we fought as he fought, 'in the brave days of old'.

With all this there were necessarily a few tribulations. The John Bull League became moribund. He regretted that he was unable (unable because uninvited) to be present at a luncheon given for Mr. Asquith—'one of the men whom it is an honour to honour'. He could no longer run down to the House and introduce a Bill. A few cranks and killjoys shunned him. Yet what appears remarkable in retrospect is the large number of comparatively distinguished people who still found it possible to accept Horatio Bottomley's hospitality, at The Dicker, at Romano's, at the races. He had been found guilty in the Master case of what the judge called the most heartless fraud. He had been found guilty also of fraudulent breach of trust in relation to the shareholders of the Joint Stock Trust. His pretensions to honesty had been most mercilessly examined by Astbury. That many lawyers, politicians and business magnates, all of them no doubt honourable men, were content to remain on easy terms with such a man throws a great deal of light on—on what, exactly? On the charm of Horatio Bottomley, undoubtedly; on the wonderful elasticity of English social laws; on the healing power of hypocrisy, or on the generous impulses of humanity. Most of all, perhaps, on the fact that an accomplished swindler can survive many exposures, and has not really suffered disgrace until he is sent to prison.

So Bottomley retained many friends. But now there were no clients like Master and the Eyre brothers. Money was short. He had to find a new way of making it.

Chapter XI

SWEEPSTAKES AND LOTTERIES

'Be just and you will be known to history as "Bottomley's Boswell".'—*Horatio Bottomley to H. J. Houston.*

THE NEW MONEY-MAKING plans began when, in May 1912, readers of *John Bull* were invited to 'Hit the Bull's Eye.' The page of 'Bull's Eyes' ('We hear that Gillow is not Waring well') was a popular feature of the paper, and readers made up their own bull's eyes on certain given subjects, accompanying each entry with a sixpenny postal order. 'We hope as soon as the competition is in working order to be able to award prizes amounting to £500 per week' said the preliminary announcement. The response was poor, the maximum prize given was £50, and the competition was quickly dropped.

It was replaced by a 'Bullets' competition. In the *John Bull* form of 'Bullets' a phrase was given, and the first and last words of the 'Bullet' or answer had to include two letters from this phrase. Two prizewinning specimens are 'In a Hole' for which the winning Bullet was 'A Bolt Often', and 'In The Swim' for which the Bullet was 'Miles Without Smiles'. Here again a sixpenny postal order had to be sent, and the entries were judged by the editor. Before very long prizes of £500 a week were being offered in this competition, and it was joined by football and cricket competitions in which prizes of £5 a week for life, or £2,500 cash, were offered to anybody who could guess the top score made by the English and Australian sides in a Test Match, or could correctly forecast the results of twenty football matches. Sometimes four or five pages at the end of the paper would be taken up by details of competitions, together with little personal stories about the winners, and reproductions of the cheques paid out to them.

Were these competitions perfectly straightforward? Did all the winners receive their money? A certain doubt about this arose after the investigations made by *Truth* at a time when £1,750 was being offered each week for the correct results of twenty football matches. This should have been, as any student of modern football forecasts will agree, a pretty safe offer; but many successful predictions were made, and in one week, no fewer than seventeen people picked all the right results. In another week four people shared the prize money. Their names and addresses were given, and *Truth* was curious enough to investigate them. Three of them, whose addresses were in Torquay, Leicester and Manchester had made brief stays in lodging houses or hotels in those places; the fourth kept a boarding-house at Brighton, and was too ill to see anyone. *Truth* suggested that Mr. Bottomley had been 'the victim of some hanky-panky' and commented further: 'Whatever the odds may be against one person picking out by chance the winners of twenty specified football matches, I do not believe in the practical possibility of their being picked out by men who all depart from London about the same time to spend a few days respectively in lodgings or hotels at Torquay, Leicester and Manchester.'

Ten days later the villains were also exposed in *John Bull*, with an imposing array of solicitors' letters written on their behalf and staunch *prosecute and be damned* replies from the editor. The paper's investigators, it seemed, had been hot on the rogues' trail all the time, and congratu-

lated themselves on frustrating a clever plot. The exact
nature of the plot remained mysterious. As *Truth* said
mildly, 'It would have been more satisfactory if particu-
lars of how the attempted fraud had been worked and the
real names of the parties engaged in the attempt had been
published.'

A few months later there was a hearing of a libel action
connected with this affair, brought by Bottomley against
John Gulland, the Secretary of the Anti-Gambling League.
After *John Bull's* exposure Gulland had published a leaflet
in which he said that those exposed were employees of the
paper, sent to different parts of the country for a few days.
The name of one of the winners, F. Holland, was that of
one of the paper's cartoonists. Elias, called by the plaintiff,
made no attempt to explain this coincidence, but denied
that the winners were employees of the paper. Bottomley
in his opening speech said that Gulland put most of the
subscriptions to the Anti-Gambling League into his own
pocket. He was very powerful, but he got only a farthing
damages. It was something less than a triumph.

At much the same time that these competitions were
successfully launched there was an announcement in
John Bull that a Special Commissioner was to be sent to
Lucerne to investigate the sweepstakes on horse races
which were held there. These sweepstakes were illegal in
this country, but there was nothing to stop anybody apply-
ing for tickets to one or another firm in Switzerland. When
the Special Commissioner returned he praised the conduct
of the draws run by one or two firms, such as H. Diamond
and Smallman and Terry, but made dark references to
other less reputable organizers, 'Dirty Derby Diddlers' as
they were called. Diamond and Smallman and Terry were
referred to frequently during the next few months in the
most approving terms, and in February 1913 the name of
Patrick O'Brien was joined to them. Under the auspices of

Mr. O'Brien the John Bull Derby Sweep was to be run. Was Patrick O'Brien a proper person to conduct such a sweep? That was a point on which the editor needed some assurance, and he insisted to Mr. O'Brien that £10,000 must be deposited with 'a bank of first-class standing'. At an interview Patrick O'Brien handed in a slip of paper with the names of no less than three banks on it, and said that his credit was good for £10,000 at any of these banks. Sure enough, a half-page photograph appeared of a cheque for £10,000, lodged by Patrick O'Brien with the London, City and Midland Bank. That was really a clincher, and the sweepstake went ahead with a first prize of £5,000, which was later increased to £15,000. A visit made to Patrick O'Brien's offices in Switzerland was enough to dispel any lingering doubts. 'These offices,' said the admiring visitor, 'have more the appearance of a banking institution than of a sporting bureau. Every member of the senior staff is specially selected from the point of view of character and education, and the system of dealing with the coupons is such as to render anything in the nature of fraud an impossibility.' Craganour was first past the winning post in that year's Derby, but the horse was disqualified and the race awarded to Aboyeur. The first horse was held by a London taxi-driver, the second by a brewers' labourer in Islington. To prevent any dissatisfaction and the litigation that would have followed it, Bottomley very handsomely paid out money (and, it is said, also shares) to both claimants. In this particular case Bottomley, in general an uncommonly litigious man, had good reasons to want to avoid litigation. One reason was that the runner of the sweepstake, Patrick O'Brien, was in fact his old acquaintance the ex-convict J. H. Bennett. The other reasons were even stronger.

Bottomley's interest in sweepstakes was first roused when he took over a paper called *Lotinga's Weekly*, which had been founded by the sporting writer and racing tipster Willie Lotinga, or 'Larry Lynx', and found that many of the letters that came in to the paper contained inquiries about the repute of various sweepstake firms. 'What an enormous amount of money must be sent abroad to more or less shady firms in connexion with sweepstake and football betting schemes,' Houston remarked to him one day, and Bottomley replied that it would be a wonderful idea to run a *John Bull* sweepstake. There followed the visit to Switzerland of the Special Commissioner, who was coldly received; and on the way home from his annual cure in Carlsbad Bottomley himself visited Geneva and Lucerne. In Lucerne he met for the first time a man who was to play a vitally important part in his life. This was Reuben Bigland, a burly Birmingham printer known on many race-courses as 'Telephone Jack'.

Bigland had made a journey to Lucerne specially to see Bottomley, and found him staying at the Hotel National, famous for its stock of 1906 Pommery Champagne. His account of their meeting has a nice touch of unintended comedy about it:

> I took my stand at the foot of the hotel staircase and waited for the moment when the great little man should be seen coming down.
>
> Immediately I caught sight of the unmistakable figure, I commenced to stroll up, and when we met I exclaimed: 'Mr. Bottomley, I believe?' The great moment had come. He replied in his melodious voice: 'That's me.'
>
> I then went on: 'My name is Bigland—Reuben Bigland, of Birmingham.'
>
> He smiled, and said: 'Birmingham! Birmingham! Yes, that is a city I know very well. It recalls some pleasant recollections. I was reared and educated at Sir Josiah Mason's School.' Then he asked incisively: 'But what can I do for Mr. Bigland?'
>
> I replied to the effect that I should like to place a money-getting proposition before him, and craved the honour of a

few minutes conversation. To this he offered no objection, and in a very affable manner invited me into his rooms— and very splendid rooms they were that this 'poor bankrupt' had installed himself in on the first floor of one of the best hotels in Switzerland.

There seems no doubt that Bigland's suggestion for running a series of sweepstakes was already in Bottomley's mind. In any case he brushed it aside and asked for introductions to some of the football bookmakers and promoters. Bigland gave them to him, and received in return introductions to some of Bottomley's friends. 'This is my friend, Mr. Bigland,' Bottomley said. 'He is a large printer in Birmingham, a man I have known for twenty-five years. I want you to give him some of your printing and do what you can for him.' Through Bigland's introductions Bottomley was able to obtain financial support from some of the promoters, and it was these whose businesses were certified absolutely straightforward.

Presumably the instructions given by Bottomley were also useful to Bigland, for on his next visit to Bottomley he took with him as a present some 'very fine oil paintings of fruit and flowers' by a Birmingham artist. Ushered into the presence he placed the pictures on the mantelpiece, and there took place the following conversation:

'Well, well,' exclaimed the little man in his most suave tone. 'How nice; how splendid. And what are they, *oleographs?*'

I caught the tone and replied as soon as the words were out of his mouth: 'Scratch them and see!'

He did not relish my reply and the intonation of my voice, for he at once put on the covering air of friendship.

'Now, Mr. Bigland, it's very nice of you to present me with these lovely pictures by your local artist, but if you can let me have a "monkey" it will do me more good than pictures. This is an expensive office, and I'm an expensive man.'

142

In my simple and assured manner I played to get my own
back on 'oleographs', so I said: 'A monkey, sir?'

He fell into the trap and said, 'Yes, and I'm your friend
for life.'

My disappointing reply was: 'A monkey-up-a-stick is all
you will get from me before you have earned it.' I never saw
a man so perturbed at my audacity. He bustled me out of the
office, and that was the finish of my second personal interview with England's Superman, as he loved then to call
himself.

This brash, ludicrous, highly eccentric jack-of-no-trades
was in the future to be Bottomley's enemy: and he made
another enemy, too, in Willie Lotinga, who was promised
a substantial cheque by one of the sweepstake promoters if
he would go out to Switzerland and witness a draw.
Lotinga went out, wrote notices approving the conduct of
the draw—and received no cheque. He published furious
attacks on the promoter, H. Diamond, in *Lotinga's
Weekly*, and these attacks contradicted the eulogies of
Diamond that appeared every week in *John Bull*. Bottomley
told Lotinga that the attacks must stop: and at last, after
accusations on both sides of bad faith, Lotinga bought
back his paper. Even this was not a simple transaction.
When he first bought the paper Bottomley, characteristic-
ally, made part of the payment in *John Bull* shares. On
buying it back, Lotinga tried to sell these shares to
Bottomley at £2 each, the value placed on them at
Bottomley's bankruptcy examination. Bottomley refused to
offer more than ten shillings a share, and Lotinga was
violently angry at the way in which he had been cheated.
In a year or two's time his anger was expressed in a form
uncomfortable for Bottomley. Beneath the announcements
in *John Bull* worked this subterranean warfare; but it was
not enough to prevent the sweepstake's success. Hundreds
of thousands of tickets were sold and Bottomley, eager to

143

squeeze the orange dry, arranged a 'remnant sale' of 250,000 more books of tickets at three for five shillings instead of the previous price of ten for £1.

A few weeks before the draw he was summoned at Bow Street on the charge of promoting a lottery. He conducted his own defence very successfully and the magistrate, Mr. Curtis Bennett, refused either to convict him or to dismiss the summons, saying that there had been an offence under an antiquated law, which would be dealt with appropriately if Bottomley paid £10 10s. od. costs. 'That means, it seems,' said Bottomley, 'that on payment of ten guineas costs I am able to head an article in *John Bull* next week "No Conviction"!'

Shortly after the issue of the 'remnants' Houston went to Geneva where he found Bottomley installed in a handsome suite of rooms, occupied also by two of his lady friends and by Saul Cooper. Not until then, by his own account, did Houston find out that Bottomley meant to take the whole of the receipts from the 'remnants', for which envelopes of a distinctive colour had thoughtfully been provided. There followed feverish days during which Bottomley engaged taxis by the day, and went every few hours to the post office to collect several sacks of 'remnants'. A staff of several people, headed by Houston, opened envelopes, placed tickets for inclusion in the tombola and piled up the money—cheques, bank notes, postal orders and gold. At times the openers stood knee deep in envelopes, and postmen off duty brought round mail sacks to collect the waste paper. Occasionally Bottomley would cast an eye on the money, and take away a great pile of postal orders, bank notes, silver and gold, saying that he had somebody who could deal with it. In Bottomley's bedroom his lady friends were to be found banding up notes and postal orders and putting them into large wicker baskets. Bottomley himself took these baskets back to England,

and it is said that he was never troubled at the customs.

The envelope-opening continued without check until an hour or two before the draw. Invitations were sent to all the leading newspapers to witness the draw, but none of them accepted. A member of the *John Bull* staff was present, and Bottomley announced afterwards that at the draw the English press was represented.

Was the draw a fair one? According to Houston, and other acquaintances of Bottomley's, it was conducted with scrupulous fairness; by another account three of the winners were old friends of Bottomley and Hooley, and two of them were ex-convicts. It does seem an unusually sporting gesture on the part of the brewers' labourer who held the winning ticket of Aboyeur to share the five thousand pounds first prize with the taxi-driver holder of the disqualified Craganour, but perhaps Bottomley, a famous sportsman himself, was able to induce sportsmanship in others. The point is not of vital importance, for the total prize money was £15,000 and Houston estimated that the cash received amounted to over £270,000. There was a heavy bill for printing and postage stamps, but the profit was handsome. So handsome that it was natural to run more sweepstakes. The money that came in for the 1914 Grand National Sweep, although considerable, did not compare with the amount contributed for the Derby Sweep, and on this occasion Bottomley meant to take no chances. Every probable runner was allotted to a presumably reliable friend among Bottomley's wide circle of acquaintances. Every *probable* runner; but, with what must be called culpable carelessness, those horses which were thought unlikely to run, or if they ran were thought utterly incapable of getting past the first couple of jumps, were ignored. The draw was a genuine one so far as it covered these apparently hopeless animals. One of these was a horse named Sunloch. The owner of

L   145

Sunloch was in prison and the horse was not expected to run. It was quoted at 1,000 to 1 three days before the race. On the day before the race, however, Sunloch changed hands, was backed down to 100 to 6, and won. The ticket was held by a young Welsh electrician named Abraham Tibbs, who came up to London with his solicitor, and firmly refused to accept a parcel of valuable shares in lieu of prize money. Rather meanly, the suspicious Tibbs refused even to give any money to the 'Human Documents' Fund. It seems very hard that a well-laid plan should be spoiled by the inglorious uncertainty of racing, and there is a peculiar rightness in Tibbs' fate, as it was put down by a contemporary. 'It is a melancholy fact that the money proved a curse to the young man. He bought a motor-car, adopted a life for which he was ill-suited, and in two years was broke and dead.'

The Grand National was followed by a sweepstake on the F.A. Cup, and this was to be handled in conjunction with the Swiss firm of Smallman and Terry, who had 250,000 customers on their books. Much sweepstake material sent in bulk through the post had been held by the authorities to be illegal and Houston, who organized the distribution arrangements, decided to obviate this possibility by making sure that no single pillar box or post office was swamped. At a central office a large staff was employed in addressing and 'stuffing' the circulars and then putting them in hampers which were forwarded by train to agents in towns all over Britain, from north to south, from Aberdeen to Plymouth. These men moved about from day to day, and had strict instructions as to the distribution of circulars in various post offices and pillar boxes. Houston, a modern research organizer born a little before his time, had a wall sheet in his office showing the location of every hamper and the position of every agent. Test letters were enclosed in every bundle to check that the hampers of letters were

146

actually posted. This organization worked perfectly until a detective in Plymouth noticed one of the men going round from pillar box to pillar box and asked what his game was. What followed indicates the curious way in which Bottomley treated his staff. Houston was charged with conspiring with some person unknown to promote a lottery. He refused Bottomley's offer to send down F. E. Smith to defend him, pleaded guilty, and was ordered to pay a fine of £100 and the costs of the prosecution. Shortly afterwards Houston got married and went on his honeymoon. Bottomley had regarded the whole affair lightly, but said as Houston left: 'You didn't blow the gaff on me. When you get to Geneva you will find a handsome present waiting for you.' At Geneva Houston found the present. It was £50, a sum which could hardly be called handsome, since the costs of the proceedings amounted to nearly £400. Houston was allowed by Bottomley to go through the bankruptcy court for this sum, and was rescued only by Elias paying the debt. The sweepstake was held and there is no proof that it was anything but genuine.

The same cannot be said about Bottomley's biggest sweepstake before the war, the John Bull Derby Sweepstake of 1914. Yet another photograph appeared, showing a cheque for £50,000 which had been deposited in the London City and Midland Bank 'for the sole use of the prizewinners'. The cheque was undoubtedly deposited: what remained unrecorded, in *John Bull* and elsewhere, was the fact that after seven days it was withdrawn. The sweepstake was again run in conjunction with Smallman and Terry, and thus Bottomley obtained the benefit of their mailing list. The amount of mail coming in to their Geneva offices was so great that the police established themselves in a building on the other side of the street to watch what was going on. Smallman and Terry became daily more disturbed by the watch kept on them; so also, apparently, did Bottomley. At last he suggested to them that in their own interests they should let him have all the coupons and the money. He would then hold the draw in a boat on the Lake of Geneva, away from the prying eyes of French, Swiss and English policemen. Smallman and Terry agreed to this suggestion, either in fright or in return for a cash consideration. A boat was chartered, the sweepstake coupons were put in it, and it was taken out to a point three miles from the shore. There Bottomley, together with some friends, made the draw. This time the method adopted was really foolproof. All the horses thought to have even a remote chance were allotted to reliable characters. In the cases of the very few extreme outsiders that went to genuine entrants Bottomley laid off in advance with bookmakers against their possible success.

The 1914 Derby was won by an outsider named Durban II and those readers of *John Bull* curious enough to look at a copy of the paper containing the draw read that the horse had been drawn by 'Mdme. Hlne. Gluckad, Tour Bastard, Toulouse, France.' A lengthy article followed a fortnight later, which told a strange and pathetic story. Madame Helene Gluckman (not Gluckad) was, it appeared, a blind old lady, a widow for many years, who kept a small general shop. She was publicized as 'The blind widow of Toulouse.' Photographs appeared, showing her on her wedding day and 'as she is today'. There was also the usual photograph of the cheque. Where was the old lady to be found? She had been worried by proposals of marriage and had come to England to pay a round of visits to friends and relatives. 'We understand that other members of the family were interested in the winning ticket, but the old lady's share is a substantial one and comes to her as a very welcome windfall.' In gratitude for her good fortune the blind widow of Toulouse, as she was generally called, had sent a cheque for £500 as a subscription to St. Dunstan's.

Sir Arthur Pearson, the Chairman of the St. Dunstan's Fund, thought it prudent to make some inquiries about the blind widow of Toulouse; *Truth* also made inquiries. They discovered that the lady, though certainly old and blind, was not a familiar figure in the town but a visitor who had stayed there for a short time just before and after the Derby. It was discovered also, by *Truth*, that Madame Gluckman was a sister-in-law of Mr. Saul Cooper. There was no reason, as Bottomley protested, why Saul Cooper's sister-in-law should not win first prize in the sweep, but some suspicious-minded people did make ironic comments. The precise destination of the £25,000 was not known for another seven years. Then it was discovered that Saul Cooper and his friends had told Madame Gluckman to endorse the cheque for £25,000 photographed in *John Bull*. She had been paid £250, and the rest of the money found its way back to a Bottomley banking account.

After this sweepstake Bottomley bought out the potentially embarrassing Patrick O'Brien for £5,000. He retained the good Irish name, transferred the offices from Geneva to Lucerne and installed as 'manager' a man about town named Sir Brodrick Hartwell. With the sweepstake under his sole control he organized a 'Great Omnibus Sweep' on the Royal Hunt Cup and Stewards' Cup at Ascot, and on the St. Leger. A ticket for the first sweepstake entitled those who bought it to tickets for the second and third. Hartwell, however, became suspicious of the method adopted in the first draw, and instead of coming to Lucerne to witness the second draw he said that he was delayed on business at Ostend. Bottomley then sent Tommy Cox and one of his servants to make what he called 'a preliminary draw' of 2,000 tickets from which he proposed to make a final draw at Ostend. This second draw simply consisted of a mass of figures with no names at all attached to them. The third draw was never held and no prize money was paid out.

The end of this tale may be told here. It advances the story to a point after the outbreak of war, when the indefatigable Carter and Bell served Bottomley with a motion on behalf of a number of subscribers, that the prize money should be paid into court. Bottomley opposed the motion in person and followed his frequent practice of formulating his case as it proceeded. According to Houston, while Mr. Comyns Carr, K.C., for the plaintiffs was actually addressing the court, Bottomley was swearing to three affidavits conceived and written that day, to the effect that the draw had been made, that the money was in Switzerland, and that the dislocation caused by the war made its transference to England impossible. The judge ruled that there was nothing to connect Bottomley with the proprietor of the business, and hence that there would be no payment of the money into court.

'That's that,' Bottomley said to Houston as they drove away from the court to Romano's.

All this may be called background activity. In the foreground was H.B., the editor of *John Bull*, a man of the people although no longer the People's Tribune.

In an attempt to resuscitate himself as a public figure, and to revive the John Bull League, which had been transformed into the Business Government League, he went 'on the stump' with Houston and addressed dozens of enthusiastic meetings. His technique was brilliantly professional. He began always: 'Ladies and Gentlemen, I'm Bottomley,' and referred to himself as 'The editor of a more or less obscure journal—I forget its name at the moment— through the columns of which I advocate each week the cause of the bottom dog and the man-in-the-street.' The advertising of the paper was adroitly done, although it is doubtful whether it justified the sum of £100 paid to him by John Bull Limited every time he spoke. For three days

a week he would adhere to a routine by which he left
London for Glasgow one morning, arrived there at about
six o'clock, talked to friends and acquaintances over sand-
wiches and champagne, made a two-hour speech, had supper with the local officers of the league, and took the night
train to the next stop, which might be Edinburgh,
Manchester, Hull, Birmingham, or even Plymouth. On
one occasion he travelled up and down to Glasgow every
day from London to fulfil a lecturing engagement, for
which he was being paid £1,000, and keep his London
appointments also. His progress was a riotous one. He gave
a railway porter a pound for handling his bags and according to Houston a journey from London to Manchester was
never made for less than £25. The money went on champagne, tips, and a great sheaf of telegrams to his ladies and
to the office. When the train made a long stop he would
visit the bookstall, introduce himself as 'Old Bottomley'
and make inquiries about *John Bull*'s sales and position on
the stand, and about the placing of the contents bill. He
would cash cheques on trains for his bills, and would always
make these out for 'a good round sum' so that he had some
spending money. He was much loved, and with reason, by
train attendants. One day Houston told him that an atten-
dant who had often changed cheques for him was in
prison.

'Ah, we shall miss him,' Bottomley said. 'You had better
send his wife some money.'

'But he is in prison for bigamy.'

'What a hero! Ah, well! send both his wives some money
then.'

John Bull was full of predictions, exhortations, revelations, a few of which should be mentioned here. In the
shifting field of political prediction Bottomley was almost
unswervingly inaccurate, and fulfilled Ambrose Bierce's

definition of the word positive: *To be mistaken at the top of one's voice*. One such typical statement was his assertion early in 1912 that the Chancellor of the Exchequer, Lloyd George, was to be Prime Minister. Asquith would go to the Lords and retire. Lloyd George was busy with the re-arrangement of the Cabinet, and he would find a small place for Ramsay MacDonald, the leader of the Labour group. It would be dull to follow through a series of such mistaken predictions. What seems remarkable in retro-spect is the way in which their inaccuracy was blandly ignored by both readers and writer. It was in the field of revelation that the paper was most successful, and a few sample headings should be preserved, for nowadays their like is hardly to be found:

SHOCKING SECRET CINEMATOGRAPH SHOWS.
FILTHY FILMS FROM THE CONTINENT.
THE RACKETTY RECTOR OF RICKINGHALL.
A WORTHING WORKMAN AND A PHOTO FIEND.
MAMMOTH MERCHANTS' MONSTROUS MEANNESS.
'PRINCE' PAUL RIEDELSKI—SERENE SWANKER.
ROSEFIELD'S ROSY RAMPS.
BLACK PASTOR'S UGLY SIN.

Some of the revelations were of more interest than the comparatively commonplace attacks on the activities of petty swindlers, and the wicked practices of rectors, hidden by such titles. The paper had become sufficiently influential for men with a genuine grievance to come to it; and men with secrets to sell came to it also, in the generally mis-taken belief that they would get a good price. It happened occasionally that these visits were of some importance in a criminal case, or at least that they could be made to appear so. Such were the affairs, forgotten now, of the Hooded M.P. and the Starchfield Murders.

'The Hooded M.P.' was the name given by an ingenious

sub-editor, or perhaps by Bottomley himself, to a Member of Parliament whose name they did not wish to mention. A young man named John Williams, disturbed in a burglary, murdered a police inspector and was sentenced to death. Williams was known as the 'Hooded Man' because he had been removed from court to prison with a scarf over his face. After the sentence *John Bull* said that Williams, and an associate of his named Power, had come to the office a few days before the burglary was committed and tried to sell to Bottomley documents about an M.P. They said that they were 'acting in the interests of certain young men' who had fallen victim to the M.P.'s 'depraved habits'. Bottomley sent the documents back to Power and suggested that he should approach the Public Prosecutor.

This was the background of the affair, which had really little to do with the murder committed by Williams, but was handled with such adroitness by the staff that it obtained immense publicity. Bottomley sent the M.P.'s name in a sealed envelope to the Speaker of the House of Commons, and professed himself ready to serve in any way the cause of justice and morality. The Speaker rather disappointingly returned the envelope unopened. After one or two more articles which promised to announce the name in a later issue there was a stern editorial in response to 'many requests from readers to "let the poor devil off"':

> We have decided to give the culprit a chance—but our terms are inalterable. He must at the earliest opportunity and in any case not later than the next General Election, leave the House—*and in the meantime he must lead a clean life*. Thus and thus only, may his identity remain unrevealed.

A little later it was announced that the M.P. would take an early opportunity of resigning his seat. The name inside the envelope remains unknown: it is not even certain that there was a name inside it at all.

The Starchfield case is a murder mystery which in its day filled many columns of *The Times*: an unsolved mystery, although it may be thought that the weight of evidence points overwhelmingly in one direction. In January 1914 the body of eight-year-old Willie Starchfield was found strangled under the seat of a train running from Chalk Farm to Broad Street. He was not seen to board the train and no explanation of how he got on to it was ever offered by the prosecution or defence. Willie Starchfield's mother and father lived apart. His father, John Starchfield, sold newspapers outside the Horseshoe Hotel in Tottenham Court Road, and rather more than a year before had played such a courageous part in the arrest of a man who had committed a murder in the hotel that he was awarded £50 by the judge, and given a grant from the Carnegie Hero Fund. It was this man who was now arrested for the murder of his son.

The principal witness against Starchfield was a timber porter named Moore, who destroyed Starchfield's alibi by saying that he had seen Starchfield with the little boy. Moore had not gone first to the police, but to the offices of *John Bull*, where he had seen one or two minor figures and had then made a statement to the 'Special Commissioner' Edmondson, in which he said that he saw Starchfield actually commit the murder. Why had Moore gone to the offices? Not for money, he said, but to ask Mr. Bottomley's advice whether he should go to the police or not. And had Edmondson advised Moore to go to the police, or had he intended to use his evidence for a 'scoop'? In the box Edmondson was indignant. He said he had had to coax the story out of Moore ('Why should you coax a story out of him?' asked the magistrate), and had then advised him to go to the police at once. Why then had Moore come back on the following day, if he had not been promised money? Edmondson could not say. Bow Street police station was nearby, and Moore had been seen crossing the road towards it. Or had he been going to the Enterprise for another drink? It was a nice point, and the magistrate made some severe comments.

Another witness changed his mind about the time he had seen Starchfield in bed in the lodging house, and the newspaper seller was committed for trial. Bottomley immediately took up the defence of this 'rough, honest fellow', and engaged Hemmerde on his behalf. He was very strong about the public duties fulfilled by the paper: 'We are compelled to employ a little army of Special Commissioners, Investigators, Legal Advisers and other experts. We have become an unofficial State Department.' On the night before Starchfield was committed, Moore attempted to commit suicide. He was found in a room in his Hampstead lodgings, with a gas-filled tube in his mouth. His evidence at the trial was much less certain than it had been in the magistrate's court, and he wilted under Hemmerde's cross-examination. Mrs. Starchfield also made a very bad impression in the box. When Hemmerde's examination of the Crown witnesses had finished the judge stopped the trial, and Starchfield was acquitted. Two months after the end of the trial Mrs. Starchfield also made an unsuccessful attempt to commit suicide. A short film was made to celebrate the acquittal, which emphasized strongly the part played by *John Bull*, 'The Public Defender', in the case.

The years between Bottomley's application for the Chiltern Hundreds and the war brought more than the usual crop of law cases. Most of them were libel actions against *John Bull*; and, anxious as always to have no possible source of cash untouched, he sought counsel's opinion as to whether he could act as advocate for the company as well as for himself when they were joined as defendants. He was not permitted to do this; had he been allowed to do it

he might have drawn an additional sum as counsel for
John Bull.

His conduct of many of the cases added to the legend
(in which the Master and Eyre cases were conveniently
forgotten) that he was invincible in the courts. To those
who knew his casualness, his ability in mastering compli-
cated cases at very short notice seemed almost miraculous.
An article headed 'Black Baptist's Brown Baby' brought
a libel action from a well-known Baptist minister named
William Hughes, head of the African Institute. The case
was heard at Ruthin Assizes, and at five o'clock on the
afternoon of the opening day Bottomley was still in London
and had not looked at the brief prepared for him. In the
waiting-room at Chester station, he looked quickly at the
brief, and at eight o'clock in the morning met solicitors,
counsel and clerks. His respect for solicitors was small.
He believed that they were interested only in their costs,
and his standard greeting to them was: 'How are you?
How much?' He was slightly contemptuous also of the Bar,
as became one who was now generally called the greatest
lay lawyer in Britain, but he granted that barristers had a
limited usefulness in cases of misfeasance. It was in the
same spirit that he eagerly pocketed the shilling conduct
money that came with each judgment summons served
on him, observing generally to the clerk who served the
summons 'Must observe the law. A shilling's a shilling
these hard times.' On this occasion his rapid survey of the
brief enabled him to cross-examine Hughes for five hours
and obtain a verdict. A few weeks before this case he had
defended himself almost as successfully against a libel
action brought by a bookmaker who had been called a
welsher in *John Bull's* correspondence columns. The bookmaker was given a farthing damages after a cross-examination in which Bottomley said that 'his assertion was
that as a bookmaker the witness was a welsher, and as a

money lender he was a bloodsucker,' Another libel action indicates his ready understanding of the necessity for compromise. A retired Army officer named Captain Field brought an action against *John Bull*, Bottomley and Odhams after the appearance of an article headed 'An Officer and a—Cur, Army Officer & Child Wife' which described how Field had married a 'child wife' when he was nineteen and the girl was two years younger and had subsequently neglected her. Bottomley cross-examined Field ruthlessly for several hours, but was unable to obtain any admission that bore on the central fact that at the time of their marriage Field had been seventeen years old and the 'child wife' twenty-two. At the end of his cross-examination Bottomley suddenly said that he had come to the conclusion that the article was one which perhaps ought not to have been written and F. E. Smith, who for once appeared on the other side, said that compensation had been made on a very generous scale.

To its readers, however, *John Bull* did not appear to be by any means merely a scandal sheet or a medium for inaccurate political predictions. It was *British*, that was the dominant note always; a fearless Public Defender of the Truth, a sporting periodical, its ideal reader a bluff beer-drinking racegoing British workman, strong in the arm although perhaps a little weak in the head, fond of the wife and kiddies but ready to go out on the spree with the boys. For this ideal reader Bottomley was an ideal editor, sharing fully his delight in the great poster that appeared in Oxford Street, 'The largest pictorial poster in the world, showing the characters in *John Bull's* Revue of Parliamentary and National life.' The ideal reader could appreciate too, the lofty moral tone in which this undischarged bankrupt addressed an open letter to Hector Morrison, who had succeeded him as M.P. for South Hackney, and had used his vote in a way which Bottomley did not approve:

Come, come, sir—this won't do. It was not for such things that I gave you the seat. South Hackney is very dear to my heart, and your parliamentary pranks are a cruel aggravation of the tragedy which tore me from it.

Most of all, perhaps, the ideal reader appreciated the sporting character of the ideal editor. It was a fine gesture when, on the death of Captain Scott, his small son Peter was adopted as 'John Bull's Boy' and a subscription list put in hand for a replica in gold or silver of Scott's ship the *Terra Nova*. The replica turned out to be silver, not gold, but the gesture was still a fine one.

The editor was eager to encourage sport, and at the same time to see that it was cleanly conducted. He put up a prize of £100 and a gold cup for the first swimmer to emulate Captain Webb's feat of swimming the channel. In the interest of honesty he made a powerful attack on Jack Johnson, the Negro heavyweight boxing champion; a receipt was printed in the paper which professed to show that Johnson had agreed to the 'fixing' of his fight with Frank Moran. Johnson, who was then making music-hall appearances, denied the accusation but it was repeated again and again in various forms. At last the boxer, flanked by two powerful friends, came to the offices and demanded to see the editor. The most intrepid members of the staff shrank from the grim-faced furious man who went into the editor's office. He was there for some time. When he came out (what caused the transformation we shall never know) editor and boxer, smiling, stood arm in arm.

The editor's most notable sporting gesture at this time was undoubtedly his attempt to win back for Great Britain the heavyweight championship of the world. Just before a fight between Georges Carpentier and an American heavyweight named Gunboat Smith took place at Olympia, the announcement was made in *John Bull* that a great new

British heavyweight had been discovered. His name was Young Ahearn, who had done some boxing in America where he had been nicknamed 'The Dancing Master'. Ahearn was rechristened 'John Bull's Boy' and a purse of £10,000 was put up (or at least announced) for him to meet the winner of the Carpentier-Gunboat Smith fight. Smith was disqualified on a foul, and the announcement was made that Carpentier would fight Ahearn. Bottomley invited C. B. Cochran to handle the fight, offering him a liberal percentage of the gross receipts, with a sum of £1,000 on account, and Cochran left Bottomley's King Street flat with a preliminary cheque for £150 as an earnest of good faith. When Bottomley told Cochran the terms he had offered the boxers, the latter expressed doubt whether there was a place in London big enough to make the match pay. 'You do not know the power of *John Bull*,' Bottomley replied. Articles about the fight appeared week after week in the paper, and opinions favourable to Ahearn were elicited from several critics. John Bull's boy was 'eager, alert and diabolically clever, boxing in the upright style, with a terrible punch'. Many seats were booked. Then the 1914 war broke out, and Carpentier was recalled to France. Not at all disconcerted, Bottomley arranged for him to be replaced by Gunboat Smith. This venture, however, was destined to be unlucky. Gunboat Smith suddenly, and without warning, took ship to America; an article in *John Bull* asked why he had run away. Not very long afterwards Young Ahearn also went to America. He won several fights there, but he never became world champion. Gunboat Smith's departure to America has never been explained, but it has been suggested that Bottomley found it wiser and more profitable not to hold the fight.

To balance this unfavourable view there must be put down the impression of C. B. Cochran:

I could keep no track of Bottomley's disbursements for the proposed fight. It seemed to me that he had only to be asked for money for him to 'shell out'. I could not reconcile such transactions with the man who was always advocating a 'business government'. His treatment of me was generosity itself. When the match was declared 'off', he offered to give me the balance of the £1,000 which he had promised; but I declined to take it. I did, however, accept a further £250, as I had done a good deal of work and given up a considerable amount of time.

The war has been mentioned, that struggle which lasted from 1914 to 1918 and once appeared a Great War. This war was to change altogether the scope of Bottomley's activities and to bring him within measurable reach of some real power. If credit may be given to one of the conversations recorded by Houston, this was a fact which he clearly understood.

'Houston, this war is my opportunity. Whatever I have been in the past, and whatever my faults, I am going to draw a line at August 4th, 1914, and start afresh. I shall play the game, cut all my old associates, and wipe out everything pre-1914.'
'Including the women, sir?'
'Including the women.'

Chapter XII

THE GREAT PATRIOT

And now they're off to the war
And they all need cartridges badly
And of course there are plenty of nice kind people
Who'll find them the cartridges gladly.
'No ammunition no war!
Leave that to us, my sons!
You go to the front and fight,
We'll make you munitions and guns.'
BERT BRECHT, *trans. Christopher Isherwood.*

THE ACTUAL OUTBREAK of what was to prove, for him,
a most fortunate upheaval, was embarrassing for
Bottomley both personally and politically. For some
months before the war he had found racing in Belgium
easier, because of his bankruptcy, than racing in England.
He would tell his trainer, Jimmy Hare, that they would
have a holiday and take the horses, with their stable boys,
over to Ostend. On one occasion Hare, who had been
poorly accommodated at Alfriston, returned to find that
a sizeable house had been built for him, and that on part
of the estate nearby a hundred men were at work building
a private race-course. Bottomley's idea was to hold small
meetings here for himself and his friends; but the idea
was never put into practice for the course was never
finished. In August 1914 he had made one of these trips
to Ostend with most of his stable and was installed there
at a hotel, together with several guests. His trainer and

jockey, with their families, were staying in two flats at Mariakerke. All racing in Belgium was stopped at the beginning of the war, and the Belgian Government refused to give him transport to take the horses back to England. He issued a statement saying that he had offered his entire stable of twenty thoroughbred horses to the Belgian Government for cavalry purposes. This offer was politely refused, and after much difficulty the horses were sent back to England in a barge. Their owner followed by passenger boat.

He returned to meet a ticklish situation. *John Bull* had always expressed itself as strongly opposed to Servia, and when the Archduke Franz Ferdinand was murdered at Sarajevo the paper asserted that the murder had been planned and carried out by the Servian Secret Service, which was said to have established a bureau in London. A facsimile of a document planning the assassination was reproduced, which purported to be written on the paper of the Servian Legation. How had this document been procured? 'Never mind *how*, but we have come into possession of it—rescued from the flames before its bloody story was forever lost. *And here it is.*' An article referred to Servia as 'a hot-bed of cold-blooded conspiracy and sub-terfuge' and ended 'Servia must be wiped out.' On August 8th, four days after the outbreak of war, the cover was still occupied with the Ahearn fight ('Have you Secured *Your* Seat?'), but a powerful article appeared headed 'To Hell with Servia.' The article referred to Austria's just demands, claimed that the letter reproduced in *John Bull* had led to the Austrian ultimatum, and expressed the wish that Servia should be removed from the map of Europe.

It was clear that this approach must be changed; and Bottomley, never a man to overestimate the length of public memory, executed a simple reversal of his position.

On August the 15th a new John Bull appeared on the cover, rather portly but undoubtedly militant, wearing a rifle belt, carrying a drawn sword and with a sailor's cap labelled 'H.M.S. Victory' on his head. The caption asked 'Do you recognize him now?' A double-page article with the editor's name below it struck a patriotic note which sounded in many hearts. The article was called 'The Dawn of Britain's Greatest Glory' and was the work of a free-lance journalist named Charles Pilley who at the outbreak of war had felt himself compelled to write 'A Spirited Call to the Nation to Throw Itself Heart and Soul Into the Impending Struggle.' Pilley sent the article to Bottomley and had the pleasure of seeing it printed, though not under his own name. After this Pilley composed many of Bottomley's wartime articles, for which the master would suggest the broad outlines and add the finishing touches. A few weeks after his first article Pilley received a note asking for a lengthy article within the next two or three days 'dealing in a human and indignant way with the horrible breach by the Germans of every code of humanity in warfare, and generally supporting an article I think of writing under the comprehensive title of 'On Which Side is God?' A week later another note asked Pilley for 'something of the kind every Saturday morning, adapted to the latest situation' and promised that he would be 'duly credited'. The credit did not consist in the attachment of Pilley's name to the articles, but of liberal payment for the material used, and of Pilley's attachment to the stable. Like others who worked for the great man, Pilley was altogether devoted to him and after Bottomley's death praised his generosity, tolerance and kindliness. 'During the ten years or more of our close intimacy he was never guilty in my presence of one unkindly or uncharitable word or deed.'

One of Bottomley's greatest assets was his quick perception of a public mood. His political predictions were often wrong, but his personal feelings about the susceptibility of his public to gambling in West Australian Mining shares, entrance into lotteries and other matters, were almost always accurate. So now he sensed, anticipated and used the wave of chauvinism and hatred for the Germans that swept through Britain. Through *John Bull* and in his speeches he interpreted this public mood so well that within six months of the outbreak of war a serious journalist could write without seeming ridiculous that 'next to Kitchener the most influential man today is Mr. Horatio Bottomley'. An effort is necessary to understand the mental climate in which Bottomley achieved such importance. During the war of 1939–45, when bombs severely damaged many English towns and cities, there was nothing like the sustained hatred of the German people felt by men and women of all classes in 1914. The exploitation of this hatred through *John Bull* was what might be called the negative side of Bottomley's campaign: the positive side appeared in his speeches.

Within a fortnight of the outbreak of war Bottomley, forgetful of the words that had so recently been written about Servia, was proclaiming that Germany 'must be wiped off the map of Europe', and her colonies and navy divided between France and Britain. The Kaiser received attention in such articles as 'The Potty Potentate of Potsdam' and 'No Mercy for the Berlin Butcher.' An article by 'a well-known physician' was headed 'The Kaiser Certified Insane,' and reproduced an order for his reception in a lunatic asylum. To Bottomley's public at home, however, Germans living in England were more heart-warming subjects for vilification, and they were eagerly smelt out. A man named Gottschalk who had lived in England for nearly thirty years was pilloried under the heading: 'Foreign Foe in a British Tramway Office.' Henry

Webb, who sat on the Treasury Bench, was attacked in a double-page article for employing a German butler and his wife, probably spies: a former cook had seen the butler cleaning a revolver in the pantry. There were some people with queer-sounding names in public departments: Major-General von Donop, Captain M. F. Sueter, A. A. Worzel, Sir Claud Schuster, Sir Eyre Crowe. Could they be trusted? Weekly lists were published of Germans who were treacherously changing their names from Knopp to Knox, from Baumann to Beaumont. And the British were so foolishly *nice* to these Germhuns, as *John Bull* felicitously called them. Indignant because the wife of an interned German, a woman with four children, was to be given 12s. 6d. a week public assistance, Bottomley wrote:

> On the whole we must be one of the nicest countries in the world for the Germhuns to live in. Somehow he can always rely on our tender feelings towards the Deutscher in distress. Even in time of war, when he is an alien enemy in our midst, if he is naked we clothe him, if he is hungry we feed him, and if he is athirst we give him drink bless his dear heart. . . . This shows what a splendid investment it is for Germhuns to come to Britain and marry British girls, it is money for nothing.

Several large firms felt it necessary to take space in the paper to confirm, or assert their British nature. Thus Lyons advertised that theirs was an 'All-British Company with All-British Directors, has 14,000 All-British Shareholders and 160,000 All-British Shopkeepers selling Lyons' Tea.' Bovril published a list of its own All-British Directors and emphasized meaningly that 'There has been no need to make any change in the constitution or directorate of the Company SINCE THE OUTBREAK OF THE WAR.' This was followed by an extraordinary attack made in an advertisement issued by the firm of De La Rue, manufacturers of Onoto Pens, upon Waterman's. In this

165

advertisement De La Rue warned readers that 'Every Waterman pen sold in this country means profit to the King's enemies' because Waterman pens were sold through the Austrian firm of L. & C. Hardtmuth. Waterman's took a full page in the following week to deny the accusation. Waterman pens, they said, were made by an American firm, Hardtmuth was only the agent for them and the contract with Hardtmuth had been cancelled for the duration of the war. A reply from De La Rue headed 'Is the Truth Unfair?' asserted that Waterman's letter was a justification of their original statement.*

As the Germans advanced into France the war hysteria in England grew. Looking forward a little, Bottomley announced: 'Under the Business Government, every editor who either knowingly or recklessly publishes false news will be shot.' He called for a vendetta against any Germans in Britain, whether naturalized or not. 'As I have said elsewhere you cannot naturalize an unnatural beast—a human abortion—a hellish fiend. But you *can* exterminate it.' He advocated hanging all German sailors or letting them drown. He said that the Zulus and Basutos should be armed and allowed to 'run amok in the enemy's ranks'. He suggested the use of poison gas (this was before the Germans had used it), and said that no prisoners should be taken. He had always believed that the war would be a short one, and these measures would certainly end it in a few weeks.

Since the government was too lily-livered to adopt such strong measures, what milder ones might be useful? First and foremost (it was a demand he repeated week after week) the banner of the Kaiser must not remain on the walls of St. George's Chapel, Windsor, as a Knight of the

* Such ancient history is mentioned only to show the way in which the anti-German feeling fanned by Bottomley affected even companies of the highest repute and integrity.

166

Noble Order of the Garter. This disgrace must be remedied. Then all German property should be confiscated, and all Germans without exception locked up. Those cunning enough to have obtained naturalization must be made to wear a distinctive badge. (How *those* words echo down time's corridor.) They must be indoors by dark. Their children must not be allowed to attend any school, public or private.

And after the war was over there would still be a certain code of conduct to be observed:

> If by chance you should discover one day in a restaurant that you are being served by a German waiter, you will throw the soup in his foul face; if you find yourself sitting at the side of a German clerk, you will spill the inkpot over his vile head.

Early in 1915 the immensely popular 'Tommy and Jack' column was started in the paper. Servicemen were encouraged to send in their complaints, which were then investigated; and those at home could send out 'Tommy and Jack Comfort Parcels' containing Bovril, Bryant & May matches, Wright's Coal Tar soap, Black Cat cigarettes, etcetera, at the bargain price of five shillings. All of these goods were provided by firms who advertised in the paper, and since their generosity was mentioned in the notice, it is at least possible that the parcels cost Bottomley nothing at all. The Tommy and Jack column was organized and run by Captain Reilly, but those who gave accounts of their grievances felt that they were in touch with Bottomley himself. It was, and remains, a serious offence for a serviceman to send such complaints to the Press: but they were openly encouraged to do so by *John Bull*, with the promise that no action would be taken against them while their protector, Horatio Bottomley, breathed. When the column was started the Government considered bringing proceedings against him for inciting servicemen to break King's Regulations, but they quickly realized the usefulness of such a column as a safety valve. So far from prosecuting Bottomley it is said that Lord Kitchener and Lord Derby, who were then Secretary for War and Director-General of Recruiting respectively, discussed these grievances at a weekly breakfast, sometimes with Bottomley himself, but more often with Reilly. Strength is lent to this assertion by the paper's immunity from prosecution on this score; certainly servicemen and women believed that they were perfectly safe in writing to *John Bull*, and the fact that some grievances were rectified added to their faith in him.

Worse almost than the Germans in Bottomley's eyes was that section of the Labour party, headed by Keir Hardie and Ramsay MacDonald, in opposition to the war. By another felicitous misspelling Keir Hardie was referred to as Kur Hardie, and the demand was made that these 'two traitors within our gates' should be court-martialled for high treason.

> As regards the elder criminal, we are not sure that a madhouse is not his proper place, for there have been evidences for years past of incipient insanity, fostered and encouraged by that overweening conceit which is one of its recognized symptoms.

Ramsay was a louse of a different colour, a 'soured and disappointed political adventurer' who had 'entered into criminal conspiracy with his fellow charlatan, Hardie'. A full-page cartoon showed policeman John Bull arresting the two criminals, one of them carrying a paper addressed to 'Dear Brother Sausage'. A few months later Ramsay MacDonald made a speech in which he referred to Bottomley as a man of 'doubtful parentage, who had lived all his life on the threshold of jail'. By way of retort Bottomley published a facsimile of MacDonald's birth certificate, which showed that the Labour leader was himself an illegitimate child.

Is it not brave to be a patriot? Especially a patriot commissioned, as was Bottomley in the midst of his personal struggle against Germans and traitors, to write a series of articles on the war entitled 'If I Were a Woman'?.

When, early in 1915, the Northcliffe Press decided to found a Sunday illustrated paper to be called the *Sunday Pictorial*, they asked Bottomley to write for it. The approach was made to Bottomley through C. B. Cochran, who says that he acted as an intermediary and that he persuaded a Northcliffe journalist named Randal Charlton, to give him a cheque for £1,000. It was agreed that £100 an article would be a fair price, but Cochran asked for the cheque because Bottomley was the kind of man 'who always needed £1,000, but never £100.' Cochran saw Bottomley and got him to agree to write ten articles at £100 each.

When Cochran returned to his office he received a telephone call. It was Bottomley, who asked: 'Do you speak French?'

'A little.'

'Then, avez-vous touche?'

Cochran told him that he had a cheque for £1,000 in his pocket, and Bottomley immediately signed an agreement to write ten articles. Their success was such as to make him the most famous journalist in Britain. When the series was finished he asked for more money. At first this was refused, but after Bottomley had been out of the paper for a few weeks Randal Charlton again approached Cochran and he returned to the paper at £150 a week and generally with his name above the page of pictures on the front. He continued to write a weekly article until 1921.

The success of these articles was no doubt based partly on the fact that the advertising given him was of an unprecedented scope and nature. At this time posters were allowed quite freely to disfigure the countryside, and it was difficult to travel anywhere by omnibus, tramcar or train without seeing the name and face of Horatio Bottomley on hoardings and telegraph poles, in fields and at railway stations. No advertising, however, can sell something that is unwanted, and Bottomley's articles were successful because in them he struck exactly the right tones of down-to-earth religiosity, patriotism and Radicalism. He might not feel these emotions, he might not even write the articles; yet, like the pieces in *John Bull*, they have his peculiar mark upon them. Not that the articles in the *Sunday Pictorial* resembled the editorial pieces in *John Bull*: the tone here was that of the lay preacher, a forthright man convinced of his high mission, addressing from his weekly pulpit a vast audience brooding on the problems of the world from the depth of their Sunday afternoon armchairs. His very first article in 1915 struck the comforting note of false prophecy:

> I am one of the few individuals who are predicting that we are now witnessing the beginning of the end, and that the month of June, even if it does not mark the finish of the war, will find hostilities suspended pending discussion of the terms of peace.

Thereafter his pieces were, as the *Sunday Pictorial* frankly said, a national tonic. A few phrases, gathered almost at random from many similar ones, help to explain the nature of his appeal. 'The Kaiser and his hellish hordes are possessed by the Soul of Satan. . . . Remember this, God always wins in the end. . . . This week I want to have a chat with my pals—with Tommy and Jack. . . . Where *is* the Great Preacher who shall teach us the lesson of it all?' After the death of Kitchener whom he had always proclaimed a great military leader, he wrote: 'It is a long time since I prayed. But let us all do so today. . . . Kitchener is not dead. We have lent him to God.'

These articles were written by Bottomley only on the rarest occasions—when all others failed him, as it were. The ghosts included Charles Palmer, who had come in as assistant editor of *John Bull*, the sporting journalist A. G. Hales, Charles Pilley and Houston, and the procedure generally followed was described by Pilley. The chosen ghost wrote the whole article from a title and a page of notes provided for him. The article was then 'soled and heeled' by Bottomley at King Street, at The Dicker, or even on a railway platform. Houston mentions a typical piece of soling and heeling, done while Bottomley sat reading the 'ghost's' article in the garden at The Dicker. The opening sentence was Bottomley's:

> As I write I am sitting facing the lovely Sussex downs, my favourite collie by my side, licking my hand and looking up into my eyes, and my thoughts turn to the simple country parson of the village.

Then came the ghost's copy. Bottomley continued:

> The bells of the old village church are ringing, calling the people to prayer. The simple country parson passes by on his way to divine service, and my thoughts turn instinctively to. . . .

More ghosted copy. And he ended:

> God bless that simple country parson. Another striking article by Mr. Bottomley next week.

At The Dicker he became during the war much liked, and even respected, although he was never accepted by county society. Those who knew him there had an impression of spontaneous generosity and charm, and felt that in no circumstances could he possibly be unkind. A small instance of this occurred when the vicar's son was wounded in 1916. The War Office telegram was sent to Bottomley because his was the only telephone in the village. He sent the message across to the vicar, who was in church and immediately telephoned the War Office and worried them until he had obtained information about the exact nature of the wound. His wife and daughter were now also installed at The Dicker for the war's duration. The war's meaning and nature impinged very little upon the impregnable stupidity of Alyse Bottomley. She had a vague idea that the shells fired from guns were of the nature of cannonballs and said plaintively to the vicar's wounded son when he came home: 'The shell hit you. But couldn't you have got out of the way?'

Bottomley valued the £7,800 a year that he obtained from the *Sunday Pictorial* and he appreciated the journalistic power given him by the weekly article; but the actual production of the piece bored him after a time, and his indifference communicated itself to the ghosts. One or two articles were returned for rewriting, and the proprietor approached Peggy Primrose, and urged her to induce Bottomley to pay more attention to his weekly piece. There was an improvement, but Bottomley remained restive. It was characteristic of him that he always wanted something more than he received. He exerted himself rather more than usual at Christmas, because he received a handsome Christmas bonus, but the religious message he addressed to the *Sunday Pictorial* readers at some festivals was a mere rewriting of what he had written the previous year. The tone of these articles distressed some of his staff, who had seen the great man's irreverence, and moved Tommy Cox to mild protest: 'You know, governor,' he said, 'you trotted out the Old Man again yesterday, but it's not your true self writing, and it sounds false. You ought to knock it off.'

'Well, Tommy,' Bottomley replied amiably, 'you can't deny that good old God sells the paper.'

Chapter XIII

THE GREAT ORATOR

Off you go, dear boy, to the front!
For they threaten your native sod.
March, for your mothers and sisters,
For your King and for your God!
BERT BRECHT, *trans. Christopher Isherwood.*

THE POSITIVE SIDE of Bottomley's personal achievement during these war years was his extraordinary success as a public speaker. Here again an effort of comprehension has to be made: for his speeches, like most others, seem on paper remarkably dull and tedious. Wit, intelligence, clear logical thought, are not the means by which a speaker charms a large audience into acceptance and applause. He weaves round them, rather, an incantatory spell of words, words which depend for their effect on the speaker's personality: in Bottomley's case upon the twinkling grey-blue eyes, the warm humour, the consciously common touch, the apparent deep sincerity. Yet the words one puts down are poor substitutes for an explanation of their effect, for in Bottomley's case, more than in that of any other great speaker, the triumph was personal, magnetic. It is impossible for anybody who did not hear him to understand how this man fascinated shareholders, magistrates, judges and others. One can set down only the cold inadequate facts.

Six weeks after the war began Bottomley made his first recruiting speech at the London Opera House, which was under the control of his friend Seymour Hicks. The success of this meeting contrasted quite remarkably with the comparative failure of an official recruiting meeting held there a week or two earlier. Two hours before the meeting several thousand people were outside the theatre, and by eight o'clock the crowd had grown to twenty-five thousand, of whom five thousand only gained admittance. Traffic in Kingsway was entirely suspended, and not until the meeting was over would the crowds disperse.

This meeting was the first of many. Seymour Hicks wrote a short recruiting play called *England Expects* and put this on also at the London Opera House. Isobel Elsom and Phyllis Dare played in it and the latter sang for the first time 'We don't want to lose you but we think you ought to go,' a song so popular that it was several times repeated. Bottomley provided the financial backing for this show and his lieutenants, Cox and Houston, superintended the recruiting side of it. In the interval Seymour Hicks announced Bottomley, and he moved many hearts with what afterwards became known to his familiars as his 'Prince of Peace' speech, from its peroration:

> If the British Empire resolves to fight this battle cleanly, to look upon it as something more than an ordinary war, we shall one day realize that it has not been in vain, and we, the British Empire, as the chosen leaders of the world, shall travel along the road of human destiny and progress, at the end of which we shall see the patient figure of the Prince of Peace, pointing to the Star of Bethlehem that leads us on to God.

When the speech ended many young men trooped up to enlist at the huge table in front of the stalls, over which a Union Jack had been placed.

Triumph followed triumph. Houston arranged for him a 'Grand Patriotic Rally' at the Albert Hall. The band of the Irish Guards was there, and the chairman of the meeting was the Reverend Arthur Waldron, the vicar of

Brixton. Waldron, a popular speaker in London parks and meeting places and the author of a controversial play called *Should a Woman Tell?* was a great friend and follower of Bottomley's, and took the chair for him at many meetings. The organization was in the hands of C. B. Cochran, who told the police that large crowds must be expected. They made the same arrangements that had proved satisfactory for a meeting held a few weeks earlier, addressed by Lloyd George, Asquith and Winston Churchill. These precautions proved utterly inadequate to deal with the huge crowds that besieged the hall. The meeting was arranged to begin at half-past seven, but the confusion was so great that Bottomley himself could not get into the hall until two hours after that. Peggy Primrose, who had a ticket for a box, was also unable to get in and lost a French pique hat in the crush. Cochran kept the meeting going with speakers he found in the hall, and with the famous Charles Coborn singing 'Two Lovely Black Eyes'. At last Bottomley got·in and spoke to an enraptured crowd. Then Constance Collier recited his great poem 'Why is the Red Blood Flowing'. Two verses will perhaps be sufficient to give the flavour:

Why is the red blood flowing—why do the women weep?
Why have our dear lost brothers gone to their long last sleep?
Come, comrade, come—consider; let's look things in the face;
For this is more than a war, mate—it's a call to the human race.
Listen! don't you hear it—ringing through the land—
Prepare and be ye ready—my Audit is at hand!

How do your books, and mine, stand—are all the entries made?
Is anything unsettled—are all our first debts paid?
The Audit will be searching, and this will be the test—
What have we done for England—have we given of our best?
And when the Audit's finished, what are we going to do?
And you, behind the counter—and you—and you—and you.

Several verses stressed, perhaps a little inappropriately in view of Bottomley's past financial troubles, this theme of a final Audit. And what we were going to do, it appeared, was, not very surprisingly:

> *To prove this world we live in, of all the worlds the best;*
> *And justify our mission, to put in highest place,*
> *O'er all the Peoples of the Earth, the Anglo-Saxon race.*

The writing of the poem has been variously credited to Cox and to Randal Charlton, who had become a member of the stable, but there seems no reason why it should not have been written by Bottomley himself.

After this Albert Hall meeting Bottomley wrote to Asquith, the Prime Minister, enclosed some of the press cuttings about it, and offered his services as Chief Recruiting Officer. The reply he received was ambiguous. 'Thank you for your offer,' the Prime Minister wrote, 'but I shall not avail myself of it at the moment. You are doing better work where you are.' Bottomley interpreted this letter in a complimentary sense, and carried it always in his gold card case.

He was then engaged by Cochran to bolster up a waning revue called *Spot the Winner*, at the Empire. He made a quarter of an hour appearance at the end of the first act, and was paid £100 a performance. Prices were raised considerably, but the receipts during the time of his engagement increased to £1,100 a week. At the Empire Bottomley first used what was to become more or less a standard arrangement for his stage appearances. During the interval a platform was quickly built up on the stage from tables and planks, and forty 'extras' dressed as Red Cross nurses or in the hospital blue of the wounded paraded on them, with a heavily-painted Britannia poised rather precariously on the topmost form. One night the bottom form collapsed just before he reached his peroration, throwing Britannia

SPEAKING IN TRAFALGAR SQUARE, 1915

BOTTOMLEY, ACCOMPANIED BY HOUSTON, ON HIS VISIT TO FRANCE IN 1917

and her fortunately unhurt supporters in a shambles on to the stage.

A series of engagements followed. A few of them were genuine recruiting meetings, but most were barely-disguised music hall turns. His greatest success was at Hull; after a meeting there he received a letter from the Chief Recruiting Officer telling him that over a thousand recruits had enlisted. Among his paid engagements were a ten-minute speech he made in connexion with the production of D. W. Griffith's film of *Abraham Lincoln*, his visit to Tagg's Island to speak at a Fred Karno show, and a week's engagement at the Glasgow Pavilion. For the first two of these programmes he received £100 and for the week at Glasgow an overall fee of £1,000. At Glasgow he went on the stage preceded by a chord from the orchestra, and spoke for only ten minutes. The management had increased the seat prices considerably, with less happy effect than at the Empire. Bottomley had obtained £500 in advance, but he became anxious about the second half of his fee. He managed to obtain this before it was due, and with the money safe blandly told the audience that he was getting nothing for his services, since any money paid him would go straight to a fund which he controlled, to keep the dependents of those who had volunteered.

In making these appearances he was prepared to engage in hard bargaining, and always insisted on money down before making the speech. In one town he was offered £50, and insisted that Houston had fixed guineas.

'No, pounds,' said the proprietor.

'It must be guineas,' Bottomley insisted. 'The opposition show will give me fifty guineas.'

'But you don't want to go there, Mr. Bottomley. It's a low down place.'

'I can't help that. I am an oratorical courtesan. I sell myself to the man with the most money.'

N   177

There can be no doubt that, although the Government was unwilling to give Bottomley any kind of official recognition, they understood the immense intangible influence he possessed with the working-class and lower middle-class. When a serious strike of shipwrights was threatened on the Clyde in April 1915, he went down to talk to them with the blessing of the Chancellor of the Exchequer, Lloyd George and the First Lord of the Admiralty, Winston Churchill. He spoke to a mass meeting of five thousand workers, and a short extract from what he said shows how adroitly he appealed to them:

> I do not want you to be treated like children by the state, or tied to the apron-strings of the parsons or the priests. Why, half the work of bringing about a better understanding between masters and men—between Capital and Labour—has been done already by the war itself. You will find new Rules of Trades Unions and of Employers' Federations—on a more human basis; you will find brotherhood and humanity covering the whole relations in the financial, commercial and industrial field.

The workers listened to him, and at that time there was no strike on Clydeside. In the following month Churchill suggested that he should pay visits to war munitions works. For a short time he did so: but, when he learned that the banners in St. George's Chapel were at last really to be taken down, he was unable to resist making the threat in a speech at Edinburgh that if the banners were not removed he would go down to Windsor at the head of a band of patriots, and tear them down in person. He was able to hail their removal as a great triumph, but such tactics hardly endeared him to officialdom.

He seems really to have believed that one day he would be called on to form part of the Government. The John Bull Bank, theoretically owned and founded by his friend Tanqueray Todd, offered for sale through a full-page advertisement in the *Sunday Pictorial* 'on Mr. Bottomley's behalf' 50,000 ordinary shares at par, with the condition that Bottomley should have the right to repurchase them at five shillings premium. It was said that the object of the offer was to enable Mr. Bottomley to adjust his business affairs finally, and return to Parliament, since 'Representations had been made to him from important quarters as to placing his services at the disposal of the State': but whatever the size of the subscription it did not pay his debts or take him back to Parliament.

Just before Asquith's resignation at the end of 1916 the *Evening News* placards bore the words 'Bottomley Wanted', and an open letter in the paper suggested that the Government should send for Bottomley if they wanted some vigour brought into the conduct of the war. Soldiers on leave carried these placards through the streets, cheering Bottomley and demanding his inclusion in the Cabinet; and at the same time a letter in the *Daily Mail* suggested that he should be sent round the country with 'official' politicians to add a little zest to their speeches. At the time this placard appeared, however, he was ill; and ill, not in his King Street flat but in the rooms of a woman friend. His temperature was too high for him to be moved and he fretted, immured in these wretched rooms, while Houston and his valet Wade told all visitors at King Street that Mr. Bottomley was too ill to be seen. After four days he had recovered sufficiently to be returned in the night to King Street, bundled up in blankets and a fur coat, but the move caused a relapse, and he became delirious. He expressed himself 'ready and eager' to perform any service. 'When and where my country calls me there will I go.' Alas, Lloyd George had now formed his Coalition Ministry and the opportunity Bottomley envisioned—for it was really a vision with little relation to reality—had gone. He had to console himself with an account of his part in the governmental change which eased his own vanity, and no doubt pleased his *Sunday Pictorial* readers:

> I happened to meet Mr. Lloyd George, Mr. Bonar Law and Mr. Max Aitken, and I could not resist the temptation of acquainting them with my very decided view of the situation. The following day Mr. Lloyd George and Mr. Bonar Law intimated to Mr. Asquith that they had had enough of it, and called upon him at once to consent to the reorganization of the Government, on a business basis.

So it was a Business Government after all, although the greatest businessman of all was not in it.

On his recovery he began what were called his patriotic lecture tours, in towns and cities everywhere in the United Kingdom. These lectures were organized by Houston, on the profitable basis that the speaker obtained between 65 and 85 per cent of the gross admission fees, the proprietors paying all expenses. In addition to this he was paid £25 by *John Bull* if he addressed one meeting in a day, or £17 10s. od. per meeting if he addressed more than one a day. This charge was justified on the basis that Bottomley's lectures were incidentally a good advertisement for the paper. The first two meetings were held at the Winter Gardens in Bournemouth, in front of a large audience of a much higher social class than that which he generally addressed. He spoke with immense success, using a brief prepared for him by Houston in which he appeared in the congenial role of prosecuting counsel against the Kaiser and the German nation, who were charged with the wilful murder of civilization. It became his custom whenever two meetings were being held in one town, to give the first part of the indictment in his afternoon speech, and then to sum up in the evening. By this means he cannily ensured that a large part of his afternoon audience came back again.

In his lectures and addresses he generally avoided the more blatant vulgarities of the *John Bull* articles and even of his *Sunday Pictorial* pieces. The tone was altogether higher. The German nation was still attacked as a blight upon civilization, but they were not called Germhuns and there was nothing about throwing soup in the face of a German waiter. In essence, however, he used the same material. A master in the art of telling his audience what they wanted to hear, Bottomley spoke with assurance of an early end to the war. He had said in 1914 that it would be a short war. When the German armies were sweeping through France he proclaimed their exhaustion and imminent defeat, and as months and years went by he was not deterred from repeating this heart-warming, though time-corrected, message. Within a few weeks, he said always, the Huns would be on the run, through France and Belgium, over the Rhine. There they would get a necessary taste of their own medicine. 'Bear in mind, I speak of that which I know. Tomorrow it will be officially denied, but take it from me that if Bottomley says so it is so!'

The proprietor of the hotel he stayed in at Bournemouth was impressed by the success of these lectures, and he gave instructions that whenever Bottomley visited the hotel he should receive a special five per cent discount. The concession was trivial in comparison with the amount Bottomley spent even in tips, but it was the kind of gesture that delighted him and he never failed to stop at the hotel afterwards. The Bournemouth lectures brought in nearly £200, and two more meetings at Torquay the next day were even more profitable. The patriotic lecture tour had begun. For the next eighteen months he lectured on two or three days a week. Like his Business Government League lectures these involved frequent dashes to London, much champagne drunk on trains, many telegrams, many small disbursements. One of the pleasures of these tours for him was the sight of his own face from the carriage windows, repeated hundreds of times on posters and billboards. He was often accompanied on tour by one or another of his mistresses.

As the lectures developed a regular rhythm of their own, Bottomley learned to judge his audience and vary his speech accordingly. His judgment was purely a monetary one. By means of a simple code Houston told him the amount of money taken, and his performance was adapted to it. The variation was particularly noticeable according to Houston, who was his constant companion on these tours, in his peroration. He had a number of perorations, varying in loftiness according to the cash receipts. To an audience that had contributed £50 or less as his share of the proceedings he made an appeal to the public to rally round the Empire and to support the King as (a phrase he often used) 'The hereditary President of the British Empire.' This peroration ended: 'Remember the words of that grand old anthem which says: 'Confound their politics. God save the King.' An audience that had contributed between £50 and £75 got a quotation from 'Land of Hope and Glory' which ended with the hope that God would make us mightier yet. For £75 to £100 he moved upwards in the emotional scale with words about England's unsullied name and clean escutcheon. And anything over £100 received the full accolade, the Great Audit of the Universe, the Prince of Peace, the Star of Bethlehem leading us on to God. When he had learned, or divined, that the takings were worth more than £100 to him he would say: 'Right! I will trot out the Prince tonight.' And out the Prince was trotted to the edification and delight of the audience; like all theatrical artists he worked best under the inspiration of the box office. In moments of extreme elation he would provide a bonus for the audience. 'I'll give them something tonight,' he would say. 'I'll not only lead them to the Prince of Peace, but I will lift aside the curtain and take them right inside.'

It was rarely that the orator's activities were questioned. A note in the *Daily News* which gave the financial details of a lecture at Swindon ('Cash Taken £163 2s. 9d. Entertainment Tax £38 9s. 5d. Paid to Mr. Bottomley £87 12s. 0d. Balance for Soldiers' and Sailors' Fund £37 10s. 9d.') he treated with disdainful silence. He was more than a match for such hecklers as the one who shouted: 'Isn't it time you went and did your bit, Mr. Bottomley!'

'Would to God it were my privilege to shoulder a rifle and take my place beside the brave boys in the trenches,' he replied. 'But you have only to look at me to see that I am suffering from two complaints. My medical man calls them anno domini and embonpoint. The first means that I was born too soon and the second that my chest measurement has got into the wrong place.'

Not all of the engagements were mercenary. He still addressed recruiting meetings without payment, although the help he gave was apt to be embarrassing to officialdom. He spoke to a huge crowd at Clapton Orient football ground a few weeks before conscription came into effect, and said that Lord Derby and other ministers had told him that whereas men who joined the colours voluntarily now would do so only for the duration, those conscripted would have to sign on for five or seven years and would get poorer pensions and allowances. The statement was hurriedly denied, but had its effect on recruitment.

There were other occasions when he gave talks without being paid for them, and even at some expense to himself —or rather, to the *John Bull* advertising account. A young clerk working for the paper still gratefully remembers how Bottomley came down to address his army unit. So important was the visit felt to be that the new soldier was given several weeks' leave from his station at St. Albans to try to arrange it. To his own astonishment the arrangement presented no difficulty; the only stipulations made by Elias, who handled it, were that the words 'Under the auspices of *John Bull*' and 'In aid of Regimental Funds' should appear on all printed matter. At prices from half a guinea downwards all the tickets were sold, and arrangements were made for Bottomley to inspect a guard of honour. He arrived two hours late because of a car break-down, but carried out the inspection with the seriousness of a man who feels that a guard of honour is no more than his due. Tempers had been frayed by the delay, but Bottomley charmed the colonel and his subordinates by the good humour and good fellowship which masked his evident consciousness of himself as a man of destiny. The Regimental Funds benefited by more than £450, Bottomley got nothing out of it, and to top it all he trotted out the Prince of Peace.

These glimpses must be preserved in the balance against the moments of extreme disarming cynicism. Such moments as the one after a meeting at which he had recited 'Why is the Red Blood Flowing', with its appealing line: 'This is more than a war, mate—it's a call to the human race.' When he left the platform he learned that the receipts had come to the unexpectedly high figure of £200. 'This is more than a war, mate,' he chuckled happily to Houston.

Chapter XIV

DIFFICULTIES OF A PUBLIC MAN

Who wouldn't rather be polite than rough
If only things in general weren't so tough?
BERT BRECHT, *trans. Christopher Isherwood.*

HIS SUCCESS AS an orator and publicist during the war
changed very considerably Bottomley's view of himself and his likely future. He was at first bewildered
by the influence he exerted through speeches and articles;
and although he soon became accustomed to it the sight of
the crowds that assembled to greet him, and the pleasure
of seeing his own face a hundred times on a short train
journey were a never-ending delight. He became permanently intoxicated with great daily draughts of publicity;
they had an effect that made his indulgence in champagne
relatively innocuous. As the months went by, steadily increasing his popularity and fame, his conviction deepened
that the words he had spoken so often would, one day in the
near future, come true. Britain would call for a Man, a
Great Preacher, a Leader: and when the call came he
would be ready to answer it. He was surrounded by the
most dangerous sort of flatterers, those who believe their
flatteries to be sober truth. These men were not innocents,
but hard-headed journalists: Charles Pilley spoke for them
all when he said that at the zenith of his wartime popularity Bottomley could have had almost any Cabinet office
that he wanted. Such statements are exaggerations, but
they have a basis of truth. Bottomley's personal popularity

185

was greater during this time than that of any Minister of the Crown, and it seems likely that the possibility of silencing this persistent and influential critic by the offer of an important post was considered, and rejected, during the latter part of Lloyd George's wartime government. His touch with discontented workers was miraculous, and he was hurriedly sent to talk to miners and railwaymen when there was a possibility that they might strike. Finally it seems to have been decided that he was a man who should be used, but not officially acknowledged. There was all that dubious history in the background, the Hansard case, the Master case, the Guildhall prosecution, the intimate connexion with Hooley: most important of all was the fact that he was still an undischarged bankrupt. It was too much, a little too much for Bottomley's friends and acquaintances in high places to exert influence on his behalf. A small but typical incident occurred when Bottomley and Northcliffe met in 1917, for the first time in many years. They talked amicably together, and Northcliffe, who was at the time Director of Propaganda, and had just returned from an official mission to the United States, said that everybody in America was anxious to hear Bottomley speak. Always ready to answer his country's call, Bottomley suggested that Northcliffe should speak to the Prime Minister, so that he might be sent on an official mission. A few days later Northcliffe published in an interview the names of a number of Englishmen whom the Americans were eager to hear. Bottomley's was not among them.

Bottomley hoped in time to overcome the distrust with which he was regarded by the sheer force of popular feeling in his favour. It was obvious that the cause of the Business Government League would be much strengthened by some parliamentary representation, and he disturbed the wartime electoral truce by sponsoring candidates in several by-elections. In 1915 a Bottomleyite named Knight fought a by-election at Cleveland against Herbert Samuel. The issue which Bottomley chose to stress was, typically, the recent inauguration of a Liquor Control Board, and he addressed twenty meetings at which he pled feverishly against any interference with working-class drinking habits. Most of these meetings were addressed under the auspices of a newly formed 'League of the Man in the Street' which, as distinct from the Business Government League, seemed particularly devoted to the brewing interests. The founder and secretary of this league was A. Locke Cox. The effect of Bottomley's intervention was that Knight was called 'the right-to-get-drunk candidate', and was heavily defeated. A few months later Bottomley was nearly successful in his support of Pemberton Billing at Mile End; the theme this time was an insistence that air warfare should be carried on more vigorously. Zeppelin raids were causing a small loss of life but much anxiety, and Bottomley asserted that Pemberton Billing had 'invented an aircraft before which a Zeppelin would turn back and never come here again'. At this election Houston organized a non-stop meeting at a local cinema, in which a fresh audience was ushered in every hour. They were addressed by Bottomley, Pemberton Billing, the veteran Labour leader Ben Tillett, and Randal Charlton. The success of the meeting was marred by the fact that on the following morning several people went to the police station to complain that their pockets had been picked while they listened to the speeches. Pemberton Billing was beaten by 376 votes, and Bottomley's *Sunday Pictorial* article for that week was called 'The Moral of Mile End'. These votes, he said, meant more than a liking for Billing, Beer and Bottomley; they meant Business. In the other by-elections fought during the war Business Government candidates obtained a respectable number of votes, but in spite of Bottomley's energetic support they were not elected.

The attempt to establish the Business Government League as a political force had, then, to wait until its president could emerge from his bankruptcy and re-enter Parliament. In the meantime he understood the importance of preserving his war-given respectability by allowing no further noxious breath of scandal to tarnish his good name. He was unable, however, to resist offering readers of *John Bull* the chance to take part in a few more sweepstakes. One of these was Patrick O'Brien's John Bull (1915) Football Cup Sweep, another the John Bull Derby Sweep for 1915, and a third one the Great £50,000 Patriotic War Skill Competition. In this last competition the entrants were invited to forecast the month and year of the Peace Treaty, the country in which it would be signed, and the amount of the indemnity. The football and Derby sweeps could no longer be run from Switzerland, and entrants were invited to send their money to an accommodation address in Glasgow, from which they were sent back to London. The device was too simple to be effective and the Glasgow address was soon raided by the police. The Derby was not run in 1915, very little money was subscribed by optimists prepared to forecast details of the peace date and terms, and no prizes were awarded. Sweeps and lotteries, as Bottomley realized, were—at least in this straightforward form—pretty well played out. Nor did the *City John Bull*, a weekly supplement to the paper which gave lightly-veiled advertisements to some companies and ambiguous warning about others ('only the other day we detected a grave discrepancy in the accounts of one of the biggest companies in the City, and the directors are now in cable communication with their Colonial office on the matter') survive more than a few issues.

A small pendant may be added here to the story of his speech to the workers on Clydeside. Bottomley offered to send copies of this much-admired speech to every worker in the area at his own expense. Names and addresses were given to him by the Clyde employers and he forwarded to every worker an entrance form for the 1915 Derby sweepstake.

The usual crop of libel actions against Bottomley, *John Bull* and Odhams Press gave a certain amount of trouble. In some of these cases Bottomley was no longer joined as a defendant; by this device the plaintiff prevented his appearance as counsel, and it is noteworthy that in his absence almost all of these cases were lost by the paper. A man accused of 'cadging for the Cadet Corps' and putting some of the money into his own pocket was awarded £100 damages, an article headed 'Bloomer's Bloomer. Luton Lawyer's Lamentable Lapse' cost the paper £500, and a wholesale haberdasher falsely accused of selling press studs made in Germany on cards marked 'Made in Britain' ('Wood Street War Wangler's Wiles') received £600. Worst of all, Liebig's Extract of Meat, makers of Oxo, obtained £1,500 damages for a libel which, on the evidence of a label found in a German soldier's possession, accused the company of supplying goods to the enemy.

These, however, were minor matters compared with the problem presented by Willie Lotinga. It will be remembered that Lotinga thought that he had been badly treated in the matter of some *John Bull* shares, and he suffered another misfortune in the loss of his job as 'Larry Lynx' on the *People* which left him determined to have revenge on Bottomley for all his troubles. Both Lotinga and Reuben Bigland appear to have regarded Bottomley with that curious loving hatred felt by a small miscreant for a large one. They felt, as it were, that they themselves should have been Bottomleys, and they were particularly infuriated by his patriotic words and writings. When Lotinga met Reuben Bigland (as the latter says, and as one would like to believe, by the purest chance in a Holborn teashop) there ensued a collaboration which was extremely embarrassing to Bottomley. Bigland agreed to print on his Birmingham machines a pamphlet which Lotinga had written about Bottomley. Two paragraphs from this four-page foolscap document will show that Lotinga did not mince his words:

> Just to recall a few of Bottomley's swindling Companies, I name the Hansard Union, the Joint Stock Institute, the West Australian Finance Corporation, the Associated Financial Corporation, the Joint Stock Trust & Corporation Ltd., 'John Bull' Guernsey, the John Bull Investment Trust Agency, and the present *John Bull.* . . .
>
> Even at this moment he is running a sham 'Bank' whose 'business' embraces that of a welshing bookmaker in one name, and a racing paper and tipsters' telegrams in another, and a Company fraud in a third false name—an absolute hotbed of fraud is the 'John Bull' Bank, Old Jewry, E.C. And all the dishonest schemes are advertised and recommended by *John Bull* and each 'dummy' principal refers to the other and receives a high reference.

Like all bankrupts of the Bottomley school, Lotinga did not suffer from an acute shortage of money through his bankruptcy; he paid Bigland £200 for the risk he was taking in publishing such material, and Bigland addressed the first copy:

HORATIO BOTTOMLEY
26 King St.
St. James, S.W.1.

and waited for some action to be taken. For a time nothing happened. According to Houston, Bottomley laughed when he first read such odd constructions as: 'He is the reputed father of a number of illegitimate children and is also the owner of a "dud" bank.' Lotinga travelled to towns where Bottomley was giving lectures and distributed his pamphlet free outside the lecture halls. Bigland joined in with the production of a booklet. On the front cover was printed: 'What Horatio Bottomley Has Done For His Country and The Wounded Soldiers.' The booklet contained twenty-four blank pages.

When Lotinga's leaflet had been in circulation for three months Bottomley issued a paragraph in *John Bull* offering a reward of £50 for the name of the printer of it. Bigland immediately sent a wire: 'Reference your reward of £50. Send me the cash and I will give you the type. Bigland.' This offer was ignored. When Bigland's claim remained unpaid he issued a writ in the County Court for the money, and Bottomley paid it rather than have the case heard. Now that Lotinga had been established as the printer of the leaflet Bottomley applied for an injunction to stop him from circulating it. The judge, however, ruled that the matter complained of must be read in court and Bottomley, fearful of his new-found respectability and disturbed also by the thought that Lotinga's revelations about his keeping a number of women would be made public, withdrew his motion. Defeated at every turn he sought the mediation of Thomas Henry Dey, a well-known bookmaker who was friendly with both parties. A settlement was finally agreed upon the basis that Bottomley paid Lotinga the price he had originally asked for the *John Bull* shares; he gave also an apology in writing, signed by himself and Elias. Lotinga on his side, it is said, deposited his proofs and documents with a neutral party for destruction.

That was the end of the trouble; but it was not the end of ill-feeling on Lotinga's side. The two men met frequently at race meetings up till the time of Lotinga's death a few years later, but Lotinga would never speak to Bottomley or shake hands with him. When his will was read it was found to contain clauses warning his sons never to associate with that scoundrel Bottomley.

At the same time Bottomley came to a settlement with Bigland. The cause of this quarrel was almost certainly more than the mere matter of £50 which Bigland says he lent Bottomley, although with so strange a character as Bigland was to show himself the root of enmity may be very small. Bigland's account of their reconciliation is in any case worth quoting for something odd and comic in the phrasing:

> On the sixteenth of May, 1916, I received a telegram from Bottomley to meet him at the Queen's Hotel, Birmingham, at twelve o'clock.
>
> I was on the platform to meet the train from London due in at 11.40, by which he arrived.
>
> He opened the conversation by saying: 'Well, Reuben The Daring!'
>
> I instantly replied: 'Well, Bottomley the Brave!'
>
> Thus we mutually chipped each other and eventually made our way into the hotel. Bottomley came down to business straight away by asking me a question: 'Bigland, I am determined to come to a settlement with you. What do you want?'
>
> 'I lent you £50,' I responded, 'and I do not want one penny more or less than the amount due to me.'
>
> He turned round to his secretary (Houston) and said: 'Henry, this is a man who ought to be in our stable. Give him a cheque for fifty pounds. . . .'
>
> He then displayed that subtlety of which he is a past master. He said casually:
>
> 'Bigland, you have done me a serious injury by your articles, not only upon my public but also my private life. Do you realize that you have damaged me in the eyes of my lady friends?'
>
> I said: 'Mr. Bottomley, I am gallant enough to apologize to any lady whom I have injured.'

Bigland then wrote out an apology for the distress he had caused Bottomley, and handed it to him. Bigland was

ARRIVAL AT THE HOUSE OF COMMONS, FEBRUARY 1921

ARTHUR NEWTON   BOTTOMLEY   RAWSON   UNKNOWN
(associated with some   (valet)
Bottomley enterprises)

ARRIVAL AT BOW STREET, OCTOBER 1921

now happy to think that he was on terms of friendship—
and of course equality—with 'this amazing man'. Before
many months had passed he was able to prove his usefulness
as a member of the stable in connexion with an action
brought by a man named Barrett, who sought to obtain a
reward of £1,000 offered by *John Bull* to anybody who
could show that the 'Bullets' competitions were not fairly
conducted. Bottomley was not joined in the action so that
Sir Edward Marshall Hall, who appeared for the paper, had
to proceed without the help of his unlearned leader; but
the trial was postponed because of the absence of three
witnesses whom Barrett wished to subpoena. One of these
was a man named Duos, who worked in the *John Bull*
office, and who had made a declaration in support of
Barrett's. Where was Duos? By Bigland's story, told much
later, he received instructions from Bottomley that Duos
should be got out of London for a little time. He was
removed as far as Birmingham, where he was paid £200
which Bigland had received from Elias. Duos then signed
a statement withdrawing his accusations, and this statement was passed on by Bigland to Elias for safe keeping,
Bigland said further that Bottomley and Elias gave
Barrett a sum of £725 to drop the case.

Bigland's statements were emphatically denied on oath
by Elias. It was not denied, however, that the case was
settled by a cash payment of £725 to Barrett: whether out
of the goodness of Messrs. Bottomley's and Elias's hearts or
for another reason will never now be determined.

There are many difficulties in the life of a public man.
In the autumn of 1915 a supporter of the Labour party
and conscientious objector named C. H. Norman published
an article about Bottomley in the periodical *Forward* and
later reprinted this as a pamphlet called 'Horatio Bottomley
Exposed'. This pamphlet was mild in comparison with
Lotinga's accusations. It consisted chiefly of factual details

O

from several cases, including the Master case and the Crippen confession. There was, it is true, a fine flourish at the end:

> Nothing could be more conclusive proof of the rottenness of British journalistic and political life than the fact that such a man is 'consulted' by the rulers of this country, leads Press campaigns, and is hearkened to by thousands of well-meaning dupes, in his endeavours to drive from off the public stage any and every agency that stands for national sanity, working-class freedom and decency in public life.

Bottomley at first threatened to take legal proceedings against Mr. Norman, but, when these threats had no effect, decided to bide his time. Later he made an ingenious use of this pamphlet.

It is pleasant to be able to end this chapter upon a note that shows Bottomley at the top of his form. The secretary of the Anti-German League was charged at Westminster with misappropriation of funds. In his defence he pointed out that he had had to pay considerable sums away to lecturers and musicians, including a sum of £52 10s. 0d. to Mr. Horatio Bottomley. Fearful that mercenary considerations might be imputed to him Bottomley asked permission to make a statement and, rather surprisingly, was allowed to make one by the magistrate. He said humorously that he was not a member of the Variety Artistes' Federation—his figure prevented him from becoming what he understood was known as a knockabout turn; then, gravely, that the money had been paid not to him but to his War Sufferers' Fund and that, moreover, he had donated a sum of fifty guineas to the defence of the secretary of the league. So far from having been paid fifty guineas he was fifty guineas out of pocket. He expressed his pleasure at having been permitted to clear up a small incident that had caused him considerable annoyance.

To Houston, as they got into a taxi outside the court, he spoke rather differently. 'Well, I got my shout,' he said. 'That will put matters right in the Press. What a nice old gentleman on the bench! He let me say what I liked. I think I shall retain him to hear all my future cases.'

Chapter XV

WHO IS MR. BOTTOMLEY?

> Past histories, earthly lapses, blotted pages in the book
> of life—well, what of them? Let him that is without
> sin cast the first stone! And remember that, whatever
> his faults, each man has been given the opportunity of
> supreme attainment.
>
> GREAT THOUGHTS *of Horatio Bottomley*.

THESE TROUBLES WERE mere spots on the sun of his
success. It must be remembered in reading Bottomley's
story that the things put down in the last chapter were
known to comparatively few people. Norman's pamphlet
was a mosquito bite, Lotinga's a wasp sting. The Barrett
case received no more than a few lines of attention in most
papers, and people were used to reading of actions brought
against *John Bull*, by people who, as the paper's faithful
readers always discerned, were in any case no better than
they should be. As a counterblast to Lotinga he issued a
little pamphlet of his own which was distributed free at
all his meetings. It was headed 'Who is Mr. Bottomley?'
and answered this question with considerable emphasis:

> He is the finest orator in the Kingdom.
> He is the first 'lay lawyer' in the land;
> He is our best recruiter;
> He is a fine sportsman;
> He is a great financier.
> He is a fearless and independent politician.

As the war went on, more and more people began to accept Bottomley at his own valuation. He was a particular favourite with those clergymen who favoured savage punishment of the whole German nation; those who were impressed by the Radical note in these speeches; and those who regarded him as a true sportsman. In one or other of these categories came the Bishop of Stepney and later Bishop of London, the Reverend Arthur Winnington Ingram who often received Bottomley at Lambeth Palace and seems to have felt a genuine personal interest in him; the Reverend Basil Bourchier, Rector of St. Anne's, Soho, who often mentioned in his sermons the part Bottomley was playing in keeping up national morale; the Reverend Arthur Waldron; and many others.

Distinguished men were happy to sit upon the platform at his public meetings, now that he had become respectable. The Racing Emergency Committee, supported by most of the leading bookmakers and trainers, elected him as its chairman. The committee's object was to ensure the continuance of horse racing during the war, and they subscribed £3,500 to provide funds for Bottomley to organize meetings throughout the country on their behalf. He addressed a number of meetings and asked for a continuance of full-time racing, until he learned from a member of the Government that they had decided to limit wartime meetings to Newmarket. His plea was then immediately changed to a request that meetings should at least still be held at the home of horse racing and when the official decision was announced he claimed it as a triumph for his campaign. The whole of the £3,500 had, of course, been disbursed, and none of the subscribers to the fund ever looked very closely into the balance sheet he casually presented. They were sportsmen, like Bottomley, and they were grateful for what he had done. At a luncheon given in his honour he was presented by that well-known trainer, the Honourable George Lambton, with a round silver-gilt rosewater dish made in 1826 and weighing 179 ounces. It went down to The Dicker, with many similar trophies.

Tributes of one kind and another, together with luncheons in his honour, came frequently nowadays. He made an official presentation to his fellow-director, J. S. Elias, of Elias's portrait in oils, executed by his relative Rowland Holyoake. Bottomley paid warm tribute to Mr. Elias's ability and energy. Mr. Elias, not to be outdone, paid a tribute to Mr. Bottomley: if *John Bull* had been founded and edited by anybody else, he declared, it would either be floundering with the mediocrities or have long since gone to its grave. Bottomley spoke indignantly at a meeting of the Imperial Defence Union to consider the Tragedy of Mesopotamia. If, after the disclosures made, Lord Hardinge still dared to wear the Order of the Garter, Bottomley threatened to go in person and tear it from his knee. He expressed his willingness to lead a procession to Buckingham Palace with a request to see the King. In response to ardent cries that he should lead his audience to the Palace there and then, he replied, perhaps a little lamely: 'Unfortunately His Majesty is not at the moment in residence.'

A luncheon was also given for him by the Aldwych Club with Sir Harry Dalziel, a well-known Unionist M.P. and business man, in the chair. This was in October 1917. Bottomley spoke of his recent visit to the front and the optimistic spirit of the men. We should not worry about the Russian defection, that was of no importance. There was little doubt that we should be able to sit down to our Christmas dinner with peace on earth once again.

This visit to the front was at once an astute move to maintain his popularity, which was greatest of all among servicemen, and a further attempt to obtain some official recognition from the Government. Permission for him to pay a visit was readily given, but there was nothing

official about it: Bottomley went as the representative of
the *Sunday Pictorial* and *John Bull*. His disappointment
was assuaged by the fact that he was able to obtain
£1,000 from the *Sunday Pictorial* and a substantial sum
towards his expenses from *John Bull*. Houston, who was
his travelling companion, says that these amounted to a
little under £100. The visit was an immense success. He
was greeted most warmly by the troops, and delighted
General Robertson by his reply when told to lie on his
stomach because of shellfire: 'My dear General, if you
want to afford the enemy the finest target in the world
you will insist on me getting down on my stomach.'
Readers of the *Sunday Pictorial* benefited also by some
heart-warming articles:

> What would I like to see first? Can you doubt my answer?
> I wanted to see and talk with the boys in the Casualty
> Clearing Stations and the Hospitals. After that I wanted to
> talk to the men in the Rest Camps.

Then he was in the trenches, 'with the boys who are
actually fighting; with guns roaring all around and above
me'; he was looking at the graves on the Somme and
wondering 'whether, perchance, I might for one short
moment be permitted to look beyond the veil'. This was
not permitted; he had to be content with a minor miracle,
the preservation of the figure of the Madonna in Arras
Cathedral from shell and bomb damage. How that would
have shaken his old-time Rationalist friends, he reflected.
His own feelings were summed up in a characteristic
couple of sentences.

> I have been in Hell—and from its depths have seen the
> striking splendour of Heaven. In the scorched and blackened
> track of the Devil—I have met with God.

By using the word 'characteristic' I do not mean that
Bottomley actually wrote these articles, but that they ful-

filled perfectly the image of him that was imprinted on the minds of his readers. This account of his experiences at the front was written by Pilley, whose brief was no more than four pencil-written sheets. Pilley exercised his imagination and wrote five long articles, which received a self-congratulatory accolade from their nominal author. 'Although I had to write to you under great difficulties I am glad I was able to give you such an accurate picture of what I saw in France. Please carry on.' The same material served for a series of articles in *John Bull*, with such titles as 'Somewhere in Hell' and 'What Haig Told Me'. What Haig told Bottomley was nothing more than that things were going well, but the visitor was much impressed by the fact that at lunch Haig passed round the vegetables 'just like any footman or waiter'. Bottomley commented wonderingly, 'And he is the Commander of the British Army in France.'

Later he paid a visit to the Grand Fleet and was involved in a small night sea battle. For this trip the *Sunday Pictorial* provided £500 and *John Bull* made a further contribution. Another, almost equally successful series of articles on 'What Beatty Told Me' appeared in *John Bull*.

Early in 1918 he was invited, at last, to Downing Street to an interview with Lloyd George, Sir Edward Carson and Lord Rhondda. Their conversation seems to have been limited to a discussion of various points in relation to food distribution made in *John Bull*, but Bottomley made a great deal of play with it. To his suggestion that a Director of War Propaganda was needed, he said that Lloyd George replied: 'I thought you were filling that role.' A week or two later he mentioned casually that he had been offered a post in the Cabinet. The statement was no doubt wholly untrue, but the fact that it remained uncontradicted gave it verity for his followers. The story was widely spread also of his behaviour when one night a bomb fell in the basement of Odhams' building, killing thirty-four people and wounding many more. Among those killed was his friend, the Rev. E. H. Moore, Rector of St. Paul's, Covent Garden. It is said that Bottomley preached to the survivors in the ruins; and, rather more probably, that he stood weeping among the dead and wounded. In the face of this dramatic display the presence of Elias, who had come up on a special night engine from his Brighton home, was perhaps less noticed.

The months went by; his fame grew, and so did the fame of his paper. It was known as 'Tommy's Bible', and it is not likely that the hospital librarian exaggerated who wrote that new arrivals from the trenches were cheered up at once by the sight of the well-known cover. The way in which he was linked with the paper is shown by the many pantomime and musical comedy rhymes of the period referring to them both, of which the following verse is a fair sample:

> *A wire I'll send to a gentleman friend,*
> *I'll call him Horatio B.*
> *He's noted today for seeing fair play,*
> *In a country that claims to be free.*
> *If you feel in a plight, to his journal you write*
> *And get reparation in full.*
> *So you'll all say with me, Good luck to H.B.*
> *And continued success to John Bull.*

He appeared in every episode of a propaganda film called *Truth and Justice*; and, best of all, the accusations of dishonesty against him seemed finally squashed with the prosecution of a Birmingham printer named John Greaney, who had republished Norman's pamphlet. Was there something queer about the publication of this pamphlet, in an edition of no more than six copies? And about the fact, noticed by a few people, that Greaney was sustained in court by another well-known Birmingham character, Mr.

Reuben Bigland? If so, it did not appear at the time. Bottomley was very strong in his opening and Mr. Cecil Hayes, appearing for Greaney, did not plead justification but contented himself with arguing about the amount of damages that should be awarded. Mr. Justice Darling, who appeared fascinated by the fact, alleged by Bottomley, that in the Master case the foreman of the jury knew so little English that he called the Lord Chief Justice 'Mr. Darling', instructed the jury that they must necessarily find a verdict for Bottomley, and had merely to assess damages. They did so, in a sum of £500.

With these malign voices silenced (for if damages were to be granted for the printing of Norman's pamphlet, which consisted almost wholly of facts, obviously nobody was likely to take the chance of printing more controversial material) he went from strength to strenth. He was the star speaker at Albert Hall meetings, supported by Lord Beresford, Sir Edward Marshall Hall, Brigadier-General Page Croft and a variety of Members of Parliament. The enthusiasm of the audience for his policies (no peace with the Kaiser, unconditional surrender, march to Berlin) was only exceeded by their feeling for him personally and he asked himself in print, as he had asked himself so often before, 'Am I Wanted?' He put it squarely to his readers: 'What can I do? For purely personal reasons I am compelled for the present to work outside Parliament.' He tried to reconcile himself to that unhappy fact by issuing 'A Call to the King' to fulfil the Bottomley programme.

When the end of the war did come, and the election with it, Bottomley, true to his talent for inaccurate prophecy, was totally unprepared. Every year but this one he had said that the Christmas turkey might be eaten with peace on earth; many times he had announced an imminent general election. This year he refrained from forecasting peace, occupying himself rather with the discovery of a group of German sympathizers associated with the Ministry of Blockade. When the Armistice was signed, however, he realized that an election was likely and hurriedly made preparation to clear himself from bankruptcy. On the day before the electoral nominations closed he went to the court with the sum of £25,000 in banknotes and another £9,000 in war stock. Most of his debts had been bought at a heavy discount by three companies: The Northern Territory Syndicate, the Mining Commercial and General Trust, and South African Petroleum Exploration. Mr. A. Locke Cox was a director of the two latter companies, and Bottomley nominees controlled the first. In spite of these circumstances, no objection was made by the Official Receiver to the annulment of the bankruptcy. It has been suggested that a certain pressure was exerted on the part of authoritative figures who thought that because of Bottomley's wartime services it would be ungrateful to probe too deeply into the methods by which he obtained release from bankruptcy.

On December 4th then, Bottomley was duly nominated. There was only one nomination form and Perkins slept with it under his pillow on the night of December 3rd, in fear that it might be lost. Houston, who had accumulated bills over a long period, smothered the division with them, and the campaign began. He stood as an independent under the slogan 'Bottomley, Brains and Business'. He was opposed only by a Liberal named Henri. The Unionist candidate withdrew. Houston's organization functioned well although it apparently received little help from Bottomley. Certain of victory, and conscious of his position as a man of destiny, he abandoned his old ways of lunching at local public houses and mixing with the constituents, preferring instead the company of the theatre managers, proprietors of revue shows, actresses and book-

makers who had come down to help the campaign. He
was late for appointments, or missed them altogether, and
addressed comparatively few meetings in the constituency,
where much of the work was done by Charles Palmer. His
readiness in reply to hecklers had not deserted him, however. Asked whether he was in favour of mixed bathing
for the unemployed he said that if such facilities were
granted they would not be unemployed for long. Questioned by an enthusiastic Zionist on his views about Pales-
tine as a Jewish National Home he replied: 'I haven't
made a study of the question, but I certainly think it is
high time Brighton was relieved.'

The burden of the campaign, then, fell on Houston,
Cox, Perkins, and Palmer; Bottomley, although none of his
many leagues in fact ran candidates at the election, had
bigger fish to fry. At an Albert Hall meeting directed
against a 'Patched-Up Peace' one of his staff greeted his
arrival on the platform with the cry, dutifully taken up by
the audience, 'Three Cheers for Britain's next Prime
Minister.' He was very stern about the fact that the new
House of Commons would not be summoned until the
Peace Treaty had been signed. 'Unless Mr. Lloyd George
—who I am not certain is coming back—calls Parliament
together a few days after the 14th of December 1918,' he
said, 'I shall take a taxi-cab to Buckingham Palace and
have a few words with His Majesty.' A well-developed
tendency towards megalomania was shown also by the
publication of a 'Black List' of more than seventy candidates against whom readers were advised to vote. The list
included the names of Labour candidates like Lansbury,
Ramsay MacDonald, and Snowden, but most of the people
in it were simply personal or legal enemies. In the first
category came Masterman, Herbert Samuel, and Sir
Matthew Wilson (who had resisted a suggestion that he
should pay Bottomley for support given him during an

election campaign); in the second, Comyns Carr, who had
given him a gruelling time during the last bankruptcy
proceedings, and Sir John Simon. Bottomley ignored the
advice of political and legal friends against the publication
of the list. He believed that it would have no effect on his
popularity, and he was right. The figures announced for
South Hackney were:

Horatio Bottomley	11,145
Arthur Henri	2,830

Chapter XVI

VICTORY BONDS

O, they are such charming people
If you'll leave them well alone
While they're fighting to recover
What has never been their own.
BERT BRECHT, *trans. Christopher Isherwood.*

THE IDEA THAT all gamblers work unconsciously towards their own ruin is reinforced by a consideration of Bottomley's conduct during the last years of the war and afterwards. Through his lectures, his articles and his editorship of *John Bull* he received sums of money so large that it would have been easy for him to clear off his debts without substantially modifying his way of living. In fact, however, he increased his expenditure to keep pace with his income, spending money more and more wildly during each successful year. Now he never tipped in silver but always in pound or ten shilling notes; he was accompanied wherever he went by great groups of hangers-on whose expenses were charged to his account; in a dozen different ways he thumbed his nose at destiny and made it a point of honour never to be prepared for adversity. On the racecourse his betting had an utter wildness that alarmed bookmakers almost as much as it delighted them. 'The Old Man's got his Macmerry hat on,' they would say, referring to the fact that when his successful selling plater Macmerry was running Bottomley would always wear a bowler hat instead of his usual wideawake. With his Macmerry hat on

206

Bottomley would bet in thousands rather than hundreds, and his winnings or losses in a week might easily be £10,000. As a loser he was imperturbable, as a winner greedy. He would lament the short price at which the horse had won ('The price was rotten, I've not won more than ten thousand on the race'), and would conceal the amount of his winnings from his trainer Jimmy Hare to avoid giving him a present. For all these touches of cautious meanness he was in general a gull ready for picking by any wide boy. He would buy his horses in at ridiculously high figures after they had won selling plates; he would make bets that were utterly to his disadvantage; knowing nothing whatever of horses he would often reject the advice of his trainer and accept that of a shyster who had no object in view other than that of selling a useless animal at a high price. In dealing with bookmakers he was for the most part punctilious in settling their accounts. To do so he endured on the Mondays when accounts were rendered a process which he described as going through the Garden of Gethsemane, as he borrowed money at high rates of interest to settle his racing debts.

In spite of the large sums of money he obtained by what may be called comparatively honest means, Bottomley found it necessary to devise some new way of obtaining public support. He found it through an ingenious and audacious scheme involving government bonds. A kite had been flown for such a scheme in 1915, when readers of *John Bull* were invited to subscribe to the John Bull War Loan Club, with a view to buying War Loan Stock, the interest on which would be distributed among the subscribers in the form of a draw. 'If you would like a chance to get £2,000 of War Loan Stock for 2s. 6d., write to A. L. Cox, John Bull Club, Lucerne, Switzerland,' the advertisement suggested. The scheme was frustrated by the Postmaster-General who returned most of the letters and subscriptions sent, presumably on the ground that such a draw would be a lottery. Early in 1918, however, this idea was developed in another guise, as a 'Premium Bond Scheme.' Money sent to Bottomley was to be used for buying War Savings Certificates, and the interest on these certificates would be used to award prizes after a draw which was to be supervised by Bottomley himself. Those who subscribed could combine a warm glow of patriotic self-righteousness with the more febrile excitement of having a little flutter which might, just possibly, bring them in several thousand pounds. The temptation was hard to resist, especially when the scheme was backed by the name of John Bull Bottomley. The amount subscribed is not known; estimates vary between £100,000 and £250,000. The amount of prize money disbursed is also not known, because the result sheet published gave only the numbers of winning tickets, without names attached to them. The War Stock Combination merged into another scheme called the War Stock Consolation Draw which offered 'consolation shares' to those who had failed to win prizes in the War Stock Combination. The Consolation Draw brought in more money, and some of it was used to obtain Bottomley's discharge from bankruptcy.

These schemes, however, were mere preliminaries to the Victory Bond Club, which was based upon the government issue of a Victory Loan. It is difficult now to gauge the extent of the emotional fervour that swept the country in the last months of the war and in the first flush of peace. nothing similar was felt in the war that ended in 1945, just as in the second war there was no hatred of the Germans comparable to that felt by an earlier generation strong in Imperial righteousness. In those days it seemed to many people, and not merely wealthy people, a positive patriotic duty to subscribe to the Victory Loan. Bottomley showed them an easy way to do so. He was helped by the

answer to an adroit question which he put to the Chancellor soon after his return to Parliament. He asked if the
Government would remove the wartime beer and railway
restrictions if he guaranteed a subscription of £100,000,000
in Victory Bonds. The Chancellor, Austen Chamberlain,
replied: 'I expect my honourable friend to get me that
amount in any case.' The answer was smoothly evasive, but
Bottomley used it to imply that his Victory Bond Club had
official approval.

The Victory Bond Club was operated from Bottomley's
flat, 26 King Street, its secretary was Tommy Cox, and the
essential feature of it was that one-fifth share in a Victory
Bond was offered for £1 whereas the government bonds
cost £5 each and were therefore out of the financial reach
of many people. A cartoon in *John Bull* showed a man looking up at two signs, one advertising Victory Bonds at £5
and the other John Bull's Victory Bond Club, minimum
subscription £1. John Bull, standing by the man's side, advised him: 'If you can't afford that, Jack, have a quid or
two in this.' The scheme was similar to the War Stock
Combination, in that subscriptions were to be used to buy
Victory Bonds and that a prize draw was to be held for the
interest. In addition, however, Bottomley's circular pledged
the return of all subscriptions in full on demand, and he
promised further that the whole of the interest would be
devoted to the prize fund without any deductions for
postage, printing or clerical work.

It may be thought that these promises should in themselves have aroused suspicion; but such thoughts ignore
the feverish temper of the time, and the absolute trust
felt in Bottomley by millions of people throughout the
country. His belief in his own power over the mass of
working-class and middle-class people must have been confirmed by the extraordinary response to the scheme.
Thousands of registered letters came every day to King

P

Street, where a staff of a dozen people tried to deal with them. Outside, the police lined up the daily queues of ex-servicemen, pensioners, clerks and other people who waited with ready money to buy certificates from the man they trusted. It must have seemed to him like the fulfilment of a dream. Every so often he wandered in to open a few envelopes himself, exclaimed delightedly at their number and at the sums of money contained in them, and then retired to another room to split a bottle of champagne with a friend. When there was ready money in an envelope he often pocketed it, and he took charge also of £600 subscribed in golden sovereigns, giving his cheque in exchange. The method of dealing with subscriptions was utterly confused. Subscribers were supposed to receive tickets on which their names and addresses had been entered, while the issuer of the ticket retained the counterfoil. Such finicky details, however, were soon abandoned, and a revised certificate was printed, simply certifying that the bearer held one ticket in the Victory Bond Club and was entitled to one chance in the annual draw. The clerks handling the tickets, some of them Bottomley's stalwarts and others ex-servicemen engaged for the work, entered into the spirit of the thing. No attempt was made to issue certificates consecutively; a clerk who ran short simply picked up any book of certificates he could find and began to hand them out. The applications were dealt with quite haphazardly and the letters with their accompanying forms were simply left lying about in heaps. It was, in consequence, impossible to deal with any complaint, since too much trouble would have been involved in finding the original letter; and it was impossible to query any cheque returned marked 'Refer to Drawer' since the certificates had been sent out on receipt of the cheque. In addition, all subscribers to such schemes of long ago as the John Bull War Loan Club or the Patrick O'Brien

Derby Sweep of 1915 who said that they had not been dealt with fairly were sent Victory Bond Club Certificates. After all, they cost nothing more than the money involved in printing them. Holders of War Stock Combination certificates were allowed to transfer to Victory Bonds for an extra 4s. 6d. per share.

The confusion involved in the issue of certificates was in part, no doubt, a deliberate device; Bottomley had realized through many experiences in court that it is more difficult to disentangle affairs which have become confused through incompetence than to discover one falsehood in an otherwise orderly statement. Confusion, however, presents its own problems: in this case primarily that of dealing with the demand for the return of money which began within a few weeks of the first rush of subscriptions. No system had been used by which it would have been possible to tell genuine demands from false: and since there was plenty of money about some of it was used to placate dissatisfied people. The return of money, also, was not systematic. It is said that some people received their money back three times over, that others received their money back on application without sending in their certificates, and that many forged certificates were redeemed. The redeemed certificates were not noted on the back of the counterfoils as a check, but simply torn up. The clerks had also realized the profitable possibilities of confusion, and there can be no doubt that several of them pocketed a proportion of the ready money that came their way, in envelopes or over the counter. It must have seemed to Bottomley that the most important thing was to keep discontent from spreading, and thus damaging his position as a Member of Parliament and a public figure. The loss of a few thousand pounds through forged tickets was comparatively unimportant.

Nevertheless he finally became alarmed at the position.

He had actually bought Victory Bonds to the nominal
value of £500,000 at a figure of 85, so that in fact he
paid some £420,000 for them. The Stock Exchange value
of the bonds fell to 73, and when he had to sell some to
pay discontented subscribers he did so at a considerable
loss.

He also held a prize draw, or said that he did so. This
draw, by Bottomley's own story, was very strangely conducted. He and six of his clerks put discs into sacks, one
disc going in for every subscriber, and then the discs were
thrown on to the floor. The lights were turned out.
Bottomley, with a candle, went in to draw the highest
prizes and the clerks drew the lower ones. There was a total
of 1,639 prizes ranging from £10,000 to £10 but since no
names were published, but only the numbers of prizewinning tickets, it is impossible to discover whether these
prizes were actually awarded.

He bought a set of filing cabinets and called in Houston,
with whom he had been at odds over an outstanding debt
of several hundred pounds. Houston has described what
he saw:

> I went downstairs with him, and in the massive boardroom
> I found stacks of correspondence, the various piles bearing
> such labels as 'People who sent in cheques; no tickets re-
> ceived', 'Tickets sent and cheques not met'; 'People who sent
> postal orders; no tickets received'; 'People who stopped their
> cheques; query tickets sent'; 'Advices from PMG that postal
> orders have been paid into Victory Bond account'.
>
> These are only samples. There were dozens of them all
> round the walls of the room, with heaps of correspondence,
> four or five feet high, beneath.

Whether Houston would have been able to create order
out of chaos—whether indeed he was ever meant to do so
—cannot now be known, for in January 1920, after the
Victory Bond Club had been operating for some six

months, Bottomley called a meeting of subscribers at the Cannon Street Hotel. He told them, inaccurately, as we shall see in a moment, that the funds of the club consisted of £500,000 worth of government bonds, and also that he proposed to merge the Victory Bond Club into a new Thrift Prize Bond Club, with its headquarters in Paris. The merger took a little time, but within a few months it was accomplished. Its primary object was to take pressure off Bottomley in London, but it had other purposes too.

It is interesting to place beside this glimpse of the backside of the sun a view of the activities that went on in an attempt to increase the prestige and political power of *John Bull*'s editor. Bottomley recognized that the end of the war was a time of crisis for him. Release from bankruptcy and re-election to Parliament gave him an opportunity to form his own political party and to consolidate his position as the Prophet of the Common Man. He understood this, but he was incapable of pursuing for long such serious ends. Success and flattery had transformed his egoism into an all-embracing guide to his actions. He suffered only intermittent pangs of doubt about the unwisdom of such projects as the Victory Bond Club. In general he was now incapable of questioning his own decisions, incapable perhaps in any rational sense of making decisions. He was simply borne onwards and upwards by the momentum of past success; his actions were no longer coherent but contradictory, stimulated by egoism and greed.

Egoism prompted the most disastrous folly of his postwar career. In October 1919, a notice appeared in *John Bull* that 'We have personally just acquired the *Sunday Evening Telegram* and a controlling interest in the *National News*.' These two Sunday papers had a small circulation, but Bottomley seems to have bought them originally with the vague idea of making himself a newspaper

213

proprietor, in competition with Lord Rothermere and Lord Beaverbrook. It was typical of his absolute certainty of success at this time that when he bought the *Sunday Evening Telegram* from Sir Henry Dalziel he did not trouble to inspect the accounts, Dalziel, the toughest of Scotsmen, sold for £20,000 a paper which he had been about to close down as a hopeless business proposition. Bottomley used one of the Victory Bond allotment letters for £100,000 to buy the papers, so that at the time when he told the meeting at the Cannon Street Hotel that a sum of £500,000 had been invested in Victory Bonds, one fifth of the money had already been used. After buying the papers, however, Bottomley lacked time and interest to organize them. He appointed Charles Palmer, already overworked as assistant editor of *John Bull*, as editor first of the *National News* and afterwards of the *Sunday Evening Telegram*. He refused to spend much money on the staff or on production. The editorial offices consisted of three rooms in a house near the Bell Tavern, and several of the people who worked on the papers did so only as a part-time job. The papers limped on for some months, losing several hundred pounds an issue; their owner took less and less interest in them, and friends advised him to cut his losses and close them down. Half of their advice was taken. Bottomley closed down the *Sunday Evening Telegram*, and at the same time decided to change the name of the *National News* to *Sunday Illustrated*, and to produce it as a picture paper, a rival to Lord Rothermere's *Sunday Pictorial*. The paper's success would be ensured, Bottomley told doubters, by the fact that his own leading article was to appear in it, instead of in the *Sunday Pictorial*. The profit that Lord Rothermere was making out of him (for he was convinced that his articles were responsible for the *Sunday Pictorial's* large circulation) would then come back directly to the man who was earning it.

The effect of this step was to cut off the income of £7,800 a year which he received from the *Sunday Pictorial*, and to deprive him of perhaps his most useful journalistic platform. He was the most important and influential journalist in the country: but he was taught painfully that one weekly article cannot by itself sell a paper. He knew nothing himself of the special problems involved in picture paper journalism, and he refused to employ expensive technicians. A great deal of money was spent, but most of it was used to advertise Bottomley, as the *Sunday Pictorial* had advertised him a few years before: this time, however, the money was (if the expression may be used of any money ever in Bottomley's hands) his own. Some of it went in an advertising scheme which he devised. He proposed to divide £25,000 among those readers of the paper who, during a given week, most effectively advertised *Sunday Illustrated*. The means of advertisement chosen by members of the public were not calculated greatly to increase the sales of the paper. A woman daily paraded Piccadilly with twelve balloons each bearing a message about the paper; a man tried to cross Central London on hands and knees with a placard in his mouth and a message on his back. At the week's end a large number of claims came in, but Bottomley's response to a suggestion that he should issue a list of prizewinners was vague. Many of his friends had helped, he said; their claims must be considered; and he invited the intransigent F. J. Cook, a member of Odhams' staff who had been loaned to him to help with the distribution of these two newly-acquired papers, to breakfast at King Street. Neither Bottomley nor Cook touched the breakfast that was brought in; and when food had been replaced by a bottle of Cordon Rouge and Bottomley invited Cook to drink to the success of *Sunday Illustrated* the latter refused (rather churlishly, one feels) to drink so early in the morning.

Bottomley rang the bell, instructed his valet to throw the glasses into the fireplace, and indicated that the interview was at an end. Later on in the day he invited Cook to have tea with him. 'You were bad-tempered this morning,' he said sadly. Cook, a tough and thrusting figure, was impervious to Bottomley's charm. While the editor sulked down at The Dicker he checked the claims, and announced the names of the prizewinners and the winding-up of the competition. Bottomley recognized defeat and paid out the money, murmuring only: 'Weren't you rather hasty, Cook?' Perhaps money had ceased to have very much reality for him; the thought of those allotment letters must have been a great comfort.

More than the distributive energies of Cook was needed to make *Sunday Illustrated* a success. Badly laid out, ill-organized, inadequately staffed, the *Sunday Illustrated* was unable to achieve a large circulation. One or two features were borrowed from *John Bull*, such as 'On The Carpet' in which a 'delinquent, of high or low degree', was summoned before the editor for 'suitable admonition'. George Lansbury was rebuked for inspiring riots in Poplar, Balfour for not having married, the Secretary of State for India for mentioning the words Home Rule, and the Lord Chamberlain for the arrangements made in connexion with Princess Mary's wedding:

> I have sent for you to ask a few questions about the impending Royal wedding. . . . Where is the Princess going immediately after the ceremony?

He suggested that she should take part in a procession through the East End.

> Princess Mary is a sensible girl. Put it to her.

Such pieces as these were a little too blatant for the audience they were meant to touch. The *Sunday Illu-*

strated suffered chiefly, however, from the editor's own refusal to be greatly bothered with the paper. It is said that he was out of town until the Thursday before the publication of the first issue; and he soon ceased to interest himself other than in the most perfunctory way in its production.

John Bull suffered less from his inattention to its affairs, chiefly because it was staffed by competent journalists; but the paper inevitably lost some of its force as the war, which had helped so much to make it famous, faded into the background of men's minds. The 'Tommy and Jack' column was retained to air the grievances of ex-servicemen but the note of defiance present in the column during wartime was necessarily absent. Moreover, such a paper needs always an object of attack, and the exposure of Germans who had treacherously changed their names soon became obviously outdated. There was little savour even in such attacks as that on Frank Harris, of whom Bottomley said that 'this scoundrel must not be allowed to pollute the soil of Britain' and suggested that if he put foot in the country he should be tried as a traitor. Unsuccessful also was the purchase of the German submarine *Deutschland* which was bought as a victory souvenir. Bottomley's friend Pemberton Billing had bought the submarine as a speculation for £5,500, and he speculated rather successfully because he sold it to *John Bull* for £12,000. The submarine was sent on tour to various provincial towns and was then placed on exhibition in London; the chief guest at the London opening was the Under-Secretary of the Admiralty. Unfortunately a good deal of work had to be done before it was fit for exhibition; then several people were injured in an explosion aboard the ship; and the offer of victory trophies made from Deutschland metal, among them 'a striking bust of the editor', proved to have little appeal.

The place of the Germans as an object for execration was taken by pro-Bolsheviks in Britain. These, it seemed, had gained great influence in the trade union at the expense of such trustworthy Labour men as J. H. Thomas and Bottomley's friend Ben Tillett. Week after week savage attacks were made on such militant figures as Robert Smillie of the Miners' Union and Robert Williams of the Transport and General Workers' Union. At one time a grand debate was projected between Bottomley and Williams, but after a great deal of epistolary sparring this was abandoned. The attacks on Smillie, Williams, Robert Blatchford and George Lansbury remained as virulent as ever; by their sides MacDonald and Snowden, so much execrated during the war, appeared almost worthy characters. A neat blending of the old anti-German and the new anti-Bolshevik themes was effected in the suggestion that the *Daily Herald* was financed by pro-Germans.

Aside from this the paper returned to receipts tried and true, but little used during the war. Palmer produced one more unmasking of massage establishments, and hinted at the unspeakable things he could tell if only he were permitted to speak of them; the 'Amazing Letters of a Degenerate' no doubt shocked many readers. The 'splendid brutality' of General Dyer in shooting down the Indian crowd at Amritsar received praise, and a strong hand with insurgency and disaffection everywhere was warmly advocated.

Unwarned by the moderate success of his earlier sporting ventures Bottomley also renewed the search for some 'John Bull's Boys' to bring back boxing championships to England. The paper's boxing correspondent, A. G. Hales, was sent on a tour of the country to discover potential world champions who were to wear 'John Bull Belts' in the ring. 'A year hence Great Britain will hold more World Championships than the rest of the universe put together,'

Hales rather oddly and optimistically wrote soon after the beginning of his search; and he was soon acclaiming Young Jim Slater as a very promising middle-weight. The process of discovery, and of training the 'boys' at Herne Bay went on for some months in preparation for the day when they were to be matched with first-class professionals at the Albert Hall. Hales was particularly optimistic about Slater who was, he said, 'an artist—nearly a great artist'. The day came and John Bull's Boys fought some fairly talented professionals. Hales had discovered a useful flyweight and featherweight but the artistic Slater proved to have little but courage to recommend him. He was toyed with by a boxer well out of the first rank, and finished flat on the canvas with a very badly damaged eye. After this the idea of discovering a world boxing champion was abandoned.

His political activities showed a similar irresolution. In an attempt to capitalize on the middle-class postwar discontent with rising prices he founded yet another league, the League of the People which was described as 'A Union of the Masses as Citizens, Consumers and Taxpayers'; members of the John Bull League were told that they could exchange their membership certificates into the new organization. Here again, however, 'organization' is almost too strong a word, for the League of the People had no reality beyond its grand inaugural meeting. Bottomley could not be bothered with it—he much preferred to spend a week at Ostend as he did soon after the league's foundation, accompanied by a dozen men and women friends and a string of sixteen race-horses.

Bottomley's first arrival at the House of Commons after the general election, was stage-managed as competently as usual by Tommy Cox, and he entered to the cheers of a good collection of his South Hackney constituents. His speeches were lively, and the House filled up always when he was on his feet; but his attendance was spasmodic, and he did not trouble to push any of his ideas through very far. It is true that these ideas were the same old measures he had so often advocated—larger pensions, easier divorce, a national lottery—and he knew there was no chance of their adoption. He was, it might be said, biding his time; certainly he had no doubt that his time would come. Invited by Lord Rothermere to go down to Margate and speak at a by-election on behalf of his son Esmond Harmsworth, Bottomley (who had met Esmond Harmsworth for the first time that week) opened his speech by saying:

> In the course of another few weeks His Majesty will send for me and ask me to form my first Business Government, and I am going to ask for young Esmond to join my Cabinet. This is the day of young men, and I want young men around me. I have been watching young Harmsworth for a long time, and am here tonight to ask you to give him your votes and so save me the job of finding him a seat elsewhere.

'You all think that I have been paid to come here,' he said in the course of the same speech, 'but the fact is that I have received nothing but some very indifferent champagne.' Harmsworth duly elected, proved too independent to be a recruit to the Business Party: but when a seat became vacant at the Wrekin, the assistant editor of *John Bull*, Charles Palmer, agreed to stand as an independent candidate, or Bottomleyite. Palmer was Bottomley's closest journalistic associate at this time; they had occasional tiffs, most of them based on the difficulty Palmer found in getting money due to him, but his admiration for Bottomley's personality was unbounded. Palmer was a genuinely idealistic Kiplingesque Imperialist, and worshipped Bottomley as a superior man devoted to his own ideals. The great man on his side confessed that he looked on Palmer as his successor, and felt a fatherly love for him. 'I am the big John

Bull; he will make a good little John Bull', he said to
Houston. 'Both on the paper and in the House he will be
invaluable to me. You know my philosophy—three meals
a day, if required, as much as I want to drink, a sleeping
suit and a good bed and bath, and what does it matter if I
peg out with my boots on?' Palmer was opposed by official
Coalition and Labour candidates, but gained the seat after
a vigorously conducted campaign. Bottomley learned the
news through a telegram from Palmer: 'Greetings to
Great White Chief from Little John Bull. Your great personality has won a famous victory.'

The strength of the Independent group was thus doubled
but Palmer was not for long a Member of Parliament.
More and more work was thrust on him in connexion with
John Bull and the two Sunday papers; and in addition he
took a serious view of his parliamentary duties. The strain,
combined with the uncertainty involved in any monetary
dealings with Bottomley, was too much for Palmer. In the
winter after his election he caught a chill while touring
his constituency; the chill turned to pneumonia, and he
died. A few days before his death Bottomley telephoned
Houston. 'Palmer is as good as dead,' he said. 'What about
General Townshend for the Wrekin?' Houston may have
been shocked, as he says, but he gladly acted as election
organizer. General Townshend, who was famous as 'The
Hero of Kut,' stood as an avowed supporter of a 'Business
Government', and acknowledged Bottomley as his leader.
He was elected by an overwhelming majority.

Chapter XVII

UP AND UP AND UP

'Mr. Bottomley belonged perhaps more to the eighteenth than to the ninteeenth or the twentieth century. . . . He had all the qualities and all the defects of an adventurer or a buccaneer. He had seen many men and many cities. His virtues and his failings were on the grand scale. Many humble and obscure persons rightly or wrongly regarded him as their champion against the tyranny of Church or State. He spoke as a cynic but acted as a romantic.

E. S. P. HAYNES, *The Lawyer, A Conversation Piece*.

THE MENTAL INSTABILITY that increasingly characterized Bottomley's actions and the growth of his always considerable vanity were evident only to a few friends; in the eyes of most people who knew him or read about his activities he seemed after the war to move from one success to another. In particular these years marked the emergence of his Independent Parliamentary Group as a political force. For the activities of such a group, declaring itself independent of all the established parties, the time was a happy one. The Government coalition of Liberals and Unionists led by Lloyd George was obviously an uneasy one, and no opposition party of considerable strength had appeared at the 1918 election. Many Liberals were distressed by the split in their party, many Unionists found it hard to reconcile themselves to the thought of serving under Lloyd George. The policy of the Independent Parliamentary Group was skilfully designed to attract discontented elements in the two main parties, and Bottomley's frequently-declared devotion to improving the lot of the working-man weaned away votes which would otherwise have gone to a Labour candidate.

Thus the group's 'official declaration of policy' demanded that payment of all war indemnities and reparations be sternly enforced, that British supremacy be maintained 'unfettered by Leagues of Nations', that undesirable aliens be rigidly excluded from the country, and that public expenditure be cut down. It also called for the abolition of dumping to check unemployment, 'the keeping of faith with ex-servicemen', the establishment of the office of a Public Defender, the reform of the House of Lords, and the equality of all forms of religion in the eyes of the law. The declaration advocated also, most strongly, 'the introduction of Business principles into the Government of the Country—including the issue of Premium Bonds'.

The parliamentary forces of the group were swelled by Sir Thomas Polson, who was elected as an Independent Anti-Waste member for Dover, Major Christopher Lowther, and Rear Admiral Murray Sueter, who had been mentioned some years before in *John Bull* as of possibly Teutonic origin, but was now enthusiastically supported by Bottomley. Sueter swept into Parliament with a majority of more than 7,000 votes and brought the group's strength up to five. Later still they were joined by Sir Cecil Beck and supported by General Nicholson, who was elected for the Abbey division of Westminster after a curious campaign in which Bottomley suddenly came out in his support after telling Houston to act for the Independent Anti-Waste candidate, Nicholson's opponent Colonel Applin. The group had a central office near the House of Commons, and Lowther was appointed as their Whip. Bottomley worked hard and effectively on behalf of the candidates, although he had to be provided with a 'minder' to make sure that he did not miss a meeting here and there in the interest, as he put it, of canvassing a few publicans. One day during the Dover by-election he slipped the leash altogether and used the Rolls Royce car provided by Lord Rothermere as election transport to take him for a day's racing at Gatwick.

The group was not a large one, and there was no question of it existing as a separate party, but its success caused the Government considerable embarrassment. Bottomley's objective, as far as he can consciously be said to have possessed one, was to use the group to enforce his own recognition as a serious politician. The men who supported him were impeccably respectable: was not that a guarantee of his respectability too? This question of maintaining an appearance of respectability was one that worried him often, although intermittently: and he produced in *John Bull* yet another explanation of the verdict against him in the Master case, which he seems to have regarded as the blackest spot on his career. He related an incident, long past, in which the Lord Chief Justice, Lord Alverstone, had been involved in an accident as a result of which a publican's house had been damaged. Alverstone had refused to pay any compensation at all until the case had been taken up by Bottomley; then, at Bottomley's insistence, he paid a beggarly five pounds towards the publican's losses. Could it be doubted that Alverstone was prejudiced, and should not have taken the Master case? That case in which absurdity was added to prejudice by the foreman of the jury calling the Lord Chief Justice, Mr. Darling?

How did Bottomley obtain the support of men like General Townshend and Sir Thomas Polson? He either suggested their candidature or if they were already in the field offered his support as a speaker and the help of his organization. The reaction of Admiral Sueter was probably a typical one:

> Knowing little about politics I accepted his offer at once. Bottomley came down and made several speeches for me and had great audiences. His organisation was headed by an expert in these matters named Houston. They all worked very hard for me. Their organisation included a Padre who held many a fine outdoor meeting for me. . . . Old Bottomley was perfectly straight with me over money matters, when I had to remunerate his workers. Not a hitch anywhere when I had to settle up their expenses with him.

It was easy to succumb to Bottomley's charm. He could appear quite transparently honest, even a little simple; upon occasion his punctiliousness in financial matters seemed almost excessive; to these distinguished military and naval figures he appeared in the guise of a robust humanitarian, unorthodox at times, with devilishly radical views about matters like reform of the divorce laws and of prison conditions, but a real man of the people—distinct from those Williamses and Smillies and MacDonalds— whose beliefs were quite obviously sincerely held. There were uncomfortable rumours, of course, but then every public man is subject to vilification by rumour, and half-an-hour's conversation with the man himself would bring conviction that the rumour was unfounded.

Man-of-the-people Bottomley accepted the invitation sent him by the President of the Oxford Union, Beverley Nichols, to come down and speak in a debate: but social climber Bottomley is perhaps also evident in the decision to answer the invitation in the third person. Mr. Bottomley considered himself honoured by the invitation, Mr. Bottomley would like to know the subject of the debate. He would prefer to speak in favour of the Independent Parliamentary Group. Failing that he would like to attack the League of Nations, which he considered a useless and pernicious institution.

It was arranged that he should speak in favour of the group. Mr. Nichols has recorded vividly his first impression of the man:

> A grotesque figure, one would have said at first sight. Short and uncommonly broad, he looked almost gigantic in his thick fur coat. Lack-lustre eyes, heavily pouched, glared from a square and sallow face. He seemed to have a certain resentment against the world at large. It was not till he began to talk that the colour mottled his cheeks and the heavy lines on his face were lightened.

He was childishly pleased to learn that there was some excitement at his coming, and that he followed men like Asquith, Lloyd George and Winston Churchill. At dinner he delighted a little group of undergraduates with an account of how he avoided paying income tax, but in the debating hall he seemed to Mr. Nichols suddenly nervous. He opened his speech with an unhappy historical reference, then looked round and said calmly: 'Gentlemen, I have not had your advantages. What poor education I have received has been gained in the University of Life.' This does not seem an approach calculated to impress a critical, sophisticated audience, but there is Mr. Nichols' evidence that it had precisely the effect he intended. The listeners warmed to him and he sailed on thereafter from one eloquent flight to another, up and up and up, dazzling his listeners by the force and flow of his oratory, dropping occasionally into lightning repartee, enlarging on the contemptuous reference to him by another speaker as a voice crying in the wilderness. 'All my life I have been a voice crying in the wilderness. All my life I have battled alone, fought alone, struggled for causes that other men have deserted as hopeless. . . .'

He won his motion by hundreds of votes, and at a party afterwards showed them a trick in opening champagne. He placed the bottle in the door jamb, half opened it, shut it again, gave the bottle a pull—and the cork was out. On the following morning Mr. Nichols asked what he would like for breakfast. He stuck out the tip of his tongue, winked, and asked for kippers and brandy. He drank the brandy, left the kippers, and went back to London. A man of the people indeed! What did it matter that some of the students referred to him as Hotairio?

Yet successes in Parliament and at the Oxford Union did not still the rumours. They were not quietened even by the merging of the Victory Bond Club with the Thrift Prize Bond Club, and its transfer to Paris. The reason given for this was that, because of prosecutions on the ground that the various Bond schemes were lotteries, it was easier to operate them from abroad. The scheme was operated by the typical Bottomley technique that if a man held £10 worth of certificates in the Victory Bond Club he was invited to send another £5 and exchange these certificates for a £15 French Credit National Bond. Many thousands of subscribers made such an exchange, and the whole procedure helped further to confuse the position regarding the bonds. Some people called at King Street and left their certificates and additional money to buy the French bonds. Others called to complain, to ask for their money back, to ask for details of the prize draw that was to be held in France. More confusion was caused by the fact that every day new lists of people were being circularized with details of the scheme and were asked to send their subscriptions to Paris in Treasury notes. Bottomley went to Paris once or twice a week, and every time brought back with him a suitcase full of Treasury notes. It seems to be true that his baggage was passed through without examination by Customs officers; or at least that is the simplest explanation of the fact that he took large sums of goods and money backwards and forwards with impunity. His office in Paris was simply an accommodation address from which letters were collected every day. It is said that the son of Bottomley's barber was the collector and that he took them to the house of one of Bottomley's mistresses in France to await collection. No attempt was made to buy French bonds with the money.

This riotous progress was checked when the banker in Paris refused any longer to let his premises be used as an accommodation address. A genuine office was opened and bonds were really bought; since the £15 Credit National Bonds could be bought at £9 in the market, Bottomley made a profit of £6 on each bond purchased. Generously he offered all subscribers who had bought one bond the chance of buying another at the reduced price of £12; thus his own profit on the second bond was reduced to a mere £3. Money was plentiful, even making allowances for the suitcases full of notes taken back to England. Many complainants at this time received their money back in full, and without delay.

The rumours persisted in spite of these repayments. They were based in large part on the articles or notes about 'Mr. Bottomley's Bond Clubs' which appeared in *Truth* almost every week for two years. Week by week *Truth* printed facts which led inevitably to the conclusion that the Bond Clubs were being fraudulently conducted, although the word *fraud* was never used. They printed in full the letter sent out to subscribers, signed by A. L. Cox, and pointed out that people were being asked to pay £15 for Credit National Bonds which could be bought for £9; they warned subscribers that they were 'handing over their money to the unfettered personal control of the promoter of a so-called club, having neither a committee nor any rules, nor indeed any sort of legal construction or

existence'. They printed letters from people who wanted
their money back, and referred to other letters which were
'the reverse of complimentary to the distinguished President'. They quoted from an ironical letter written by an ex-
serviceman, apologizing for troubling Bottomley when he
was taking up cases involving the inadequate sentences
passed on German war criminals for cruelty to British
troops, but saying that he had himself been treated a little
cruelly. This subscriber recovered his money through a
solicitor and *Truth* was soon advising others whose letters
remained unanswered to approach their solicitors immediately. When Bottomley unwisely tried to answer some of
the accusations the paper commented:

> Who can fail to be moved to the heart by this cry from the
> heart of a public benefactor? Did he not, purely in the way of
> patriotism and philanthropy, go to the trouble and expense
> of receiving subscriptions for over £500,000 to his Victory
> Bond Club. . . . Yet the subscribers are dissatisfied. Some
> rudely characterise as trash the reasons that are given for
> pricing at £15 bonds which at the time the offer was first
> made could be bought for about £9. . . . Imagine what a sore
> trial this ungrateful and inconsiderate treatment must be to
> such a high-souled man as Mr. Bottomley.

This was too much. Bottomley issued a writ for libel.
This writ, however, did not have the usual effect of stopping
the articles. They continued, week after week, in a ruthless
examination of various aspects of Bottomley's schemes.
Some duplication of numbers in the lists of prizes distributed in the Victory Bond scheme was noted, an attack
was made on his projected Derby sweep, the hints of fraud
became stronger each week. Twenty-five letters a day came
in to the paper from subscribers to the schemes, and these
subscribers were given the name of a solicitor who would
handle their claims. A whole series of writs descended on
the paper, but the editors of *Truth* seem rightly to have

guessed that these writs were a mere bluff and that Bottomley did not wish to have the merits of the Bond Clubs debated in court. When the writs proved ineffective Bottomley took the desperate measure of sending to the principal firms in the newspaper trade a suggestion that they should cease to handle a periodical which made libellous accusations against his good name. The trade ignored this suggestion. *Truth* continued to be circulated, and the attacks continued.

In October 1921 Bottomley made his customary move to escape from financially difficult situations. He consented to a solicitor's application that a Receiver should be appointed for the Bond Clubs; the Receivers mentioned in the application were Sir Harry Peat of W. B. Peat & Co. (auditors of *John Bull* and trustees of Bottomley's account in bankruptcy) and Mr. Percy Garratt (who had acted for Bottomley in a contract arranged with Odhams in 1920 by which they took control of the paper, while he obtained a share of the profits, and for the sum of £88,000 agreed to edit *John Bull* for the duration of his life). Messrs. Peat and Garratt were appointed Interim Receivers, and Bottomley must have felt that he had fallen among friends. He briskly sent out a letter from Paris admitting that things had become a little confused, and offering to help all subscribers to formulate their claims. *Truth* commented acidly on 'Mr. Bottomley's kind offer':

> We have no hesitation in saying that Mr. Bottomley, or any representative of Mr. Bottomley, is the last person from whom subscribers in the Club should seek help.

It was too late even for the appointment of Receivers. A subscriber to the clubs sued Bottomley in person and obtained a verdict for £468. The political meetings he addressed now were subject to noisy interruptions; even in his own Hackney constituency there was derisive laughter during one of his speeches. At the end of 1921 the directors of Odhams, who not so long ago had thought it desirable that he should edit *John Bull* for life, decided regretfully to dispense with his services. He was paid £25,000, and severed his editorial connexion with the paper. One can well believe that this step was most reluctantly taken, for the names of Bottomley and *John Bull* were inseparable, but by this time a shadow more menacing than that cast by the *Truth* articles had fallen over Bottomley's career: the shadow of Reuben Bigland.

Chapter XVIII

THE WAY DOWN

Of fair estate and good repute,
He fell against the Law,
And, though his hands were free from guilt,
Was drawn within its maw.
        HORATIO BOTTOMLEY, *Songs of the Cell.*

REUBEN BIGLAND'S VENDETTA against Bottomley was prompted by the latter's refusal to back a scheme for converting water into petrol. This, at least is the explanation of their quarrel given both by Bigland and Bottomley. Shortly after the end of the war Bigland was told of this remarkable invention; he investigated it, found that the process seemed perfectly genuine, and arranged for a demonstration at Newmarket on Cesarewitch day. In a quiet racing stable he 'gathered together such a company of financial notabilities as has rarely been seen' in order to show that a pail of fresh water could be converted into motor fuel. The inventor of the process stripped almost naked to show that no kind of conjuring trick was involved. He took from a small black bag three bottles containing the preparation and sprinkled them on the water. When lighted they burned with a flame five feet in height. The liquid was then poured into the empty tank of a motor-car, and Bigland stepped into the car and drove off. This was, as he frankly confessed afterwards, an error of judgment; for after he had gone 'the company dispersed to the races and I never had an opportunity to gather them together again.' Nor, apparently, were the financial notabilities sufficiently interested to look further into the matter: so Bigland approached Horatio Bottomley. They split a bottle of champagne while Bottomley listened to what Bigland had to say. Then he nodded pleasantly and told Bigland to come and see him early on the following morning.

Bigland took him at his word and called at seven o'clock the next day. He found Bottomley sitting up in bed writing. He read attentively a cutting from the *Daily Express* describing the test at Newmarket, and then said: 'Reuben, this is a swindle!'

'But, Horatio,' Bigland said, 'the man is not born of woman who could swindle you and myself, jointly and severally.'

Again Bottomley refused to back the scheme and Bigland, as he admits, became rather excited. He had been hoping to obtain some £60,000 backing from Bottomley for the invention, and he was angry at being refused. 'You call this friendship, Horatio?' he asked. 'You have taken a million pounds of the people's money and when I retire from this room I shall make it my business, as one of the club members, to see that they have fair play. From this moment I shall be your enemy.' Bottomley laughed at him and suggested, ironically it is to be presumed, that he might obtain help from Elias. Bigland actually went to see Elias, and saw also one or two speculative financiers, but they refused to help him, and the petrol scheme collapsed: not, as Bigland insisted, because water could not be converted into petrol but because the cost was prohibitive. After this incident, however, he 'formed a fixed determination' that 'Mr. Bottomley must be ruthlessly exposed.'

Bottomley's account of this interview, given later, was that Bigland had in effect tried to blackmail him for £60,000 on the pretence of obtaining backing for this ridiculous scheme. In this he was supported by the evidence, for what it was worth, of the couple who ran the flat, who said that they had heard Bigland threatening Bottomley, demanding £60,000 and saying, 'I will bring you down to the gutter.' It has been suggested, less romantically, that Bigland claimed £1,000 for various services rendered, and that it was Bottomley's refusal to pay this sum that prompted the vendetta. The relations between the two men were never as simple as those maintained between Bottomley and his faithful camp followers. Bottomley recognized Bigland's usefulness, particularly in the Greaney case (which will be discussed a little later), but was contemptuous of him as a foolish bragging figure, 'Reuben the Daring'. Bigland was fascinated by Bottomley, often lent him money, and much resented the slights he received.

After Bigland had sold to Hooley a process for keeping fish fresh without ice ('I had previously taken a box of fish to 10 Downing Street to get the Prime Minister interested, as the food shortage was then very acute', he records) he turned almost his whole energies to exposing Bottomley. He wrote to Austen Chamberlain, told him that the Premium Bond Scheme was a swindle, and was advised to see a solicitor. He sent letters to all the members of the House of Commons, as well as particularly forceful ones to the Prime Minister, the Home Secretary and the Attorney-General, but received no more than a few polite acknowledgements. He wrote to Hooley, told him that he had decided to punish H.B. a little, and that he might have to be dismissed from the High School, that is the House of Commons. Hooley sent the letter on to Bottomley, who replied through his secretary, Holland, that a certain unnamed man 'should have a sea voyage to regain his health' and that he would be prepared to offer financial assistance for that purpose.

Bigland advertised in the *Daily Mail* asking for Victory Bond Club members to write to him, but none of them would assist in forming an association to expose Bottomley. He then decided upon a more drastic step. In acknowledgement of his debt to Bigland, Bottomley had in 1918 offered to arrange for him to become a prizewinner in the War Stock Combination. Bigland bought 135 tickets in the combination, and in the course of time his sister, Mrs. Saunders, won a prize of £1,000, which she received in the form of two £500 Treasury bonds. During the election of General Townshend at the Wrekin a telegram from Bigland was received at Bottomley's headquarters. The opening was an allusion to a recent article of Bottomley's:

And I heard a Voice from Heaven saying unto me, Confess! The spirit of William Lotinga is urging me on to unmask England's Greatest Living Humbug, the man that takes the name of the Lord to cover up his terrible sins. I shall come to Wellington, hand you back your war bond, and give myself up to justice to clear my conscience.

After the telegram came Bigland, clamouring to return money that was not rightfully his. At an interview with Bottomley, when the latter was accompanied by two husky throwers-out, Bigland tamely retracted his accusations and after his departure even wrote a letter of apology. 'I came there to do you a great wrong,' he wrote. 'I failed. You won.'

Such recantations, apologies, and returns to the attack, with letters signed 'Yours fraternally, alias Mad Jack', show clearly enough the ambivalent nature of Bigland's feelings for Bottomley. Had he been wooed he might still have become a faithful member of the stable: but instead of being wooed he was humiliated. At his interview with Bottomley he had not been quite foolish enough to hand over the two bonds. Now he tried again to expose Bottomley by using them. He telephoned Scotland Yard and said that at a certain time a man would be trying to sell a Treasury bond at a money-changers in the Strand, and that they would be well advised to inquire whether he was the lawful owner. He then visited the Strand money-changer and was found there by a detective. When Bigland refused to give his name or to give any information about the bond he was arrested, charged at Bow Street, and remanded for seven days. On being charged he said that he wished to subpoena Bottomley, and at the next hearing Bottomley was in court. The police who may be excused if they thought they were dealing with a lunatic, said that they had no evidence to offer; and to his astonishment and chagrin, Bigland was discharged.

'I don't want to be discharged,' he said.

'You are discharged,' said the magistrate.

'I do not wish to be discharged. I am representing 50,000 of Bottomley's Bond Club subscribers who have been defrauded. . . .'

The magistrate repeated 'You are discharged,' and a protesting Bigland was shown out of the dock.

After the ludicrous failure of this attempt to obtain publicity Bigland took at last the effective and damaging step of issuing a four-page pamphlet about Bottomley's activities. It was headed:

THE DOWNFALL OF HORATIO BOTTOMLEY, M.P.

*

HIS LATEST AND GREATEST SWINDLE

*

How he gulled POOR subscribers to invest
One-Pound Notes in his

'GREAT VICTORY WAR BOND CLUB'

The four closely-printed pages contained nothing that
is new to a reader of this book. Bigland called Bottomley
'one of the greatest crooks ever born of woman', said that
the Victory Bond scheme was a swindle and that there had
never been an honest draw for prizes, and added one or
two touches that must be called characteristic:

> I, a poor, uneducated species of humanity, in turn a cross-
> ing sweeper, boot black, and match seller, am urged on by
> some mystic power to cross swords with the great and only
> Horatio Bottomley. . . . You know that, like David, I have
> righteousness on my side.

Bigland hit on the ingenious idea of wearing a black
mask while he sold the pamphlets at a penny each. They
sold quickly, and he realized that he had found a way of
hitting at Bottomley. With three friends, all wearing
masks, he sold tens of thousands of pamphlets throughout
Lancashire, Yorkshire, Leicestershire and Nottinghamshire; visited the Trades Union Congress at Cardiff and
offered £100 to any Labour M.P. who would table a
question regarding Victory Bonds in the House of Commons;
finished his provincial tour, printed another 250,000 pamphlets in Birmingham and had them sold in London. In
London the sale was enormous, and well organized. Sandwichmen paraded with them outside Bottomley's favourite
eating- and drinking-places, like Romano's and the Horseshoe Hotel; they were sold outside the *John Bull* offices and
the King Street flat. They combined with the articles in
Truth to swell the spate of people asking for the return of
their money. Bottomley decided that he must act. He consulted Sir Ernest Wild, who, unaware of the pamphlet's
full effect, advised him to ignore it. Houston gave the same
advice. Bottomley scowled and jeered at his friends, then
said he had made up his mind. He got into a taxi with
Sir Ernest Wild and Charles Pilley, and drove to Bow
Street to take out a warrant against Bigland.

Reuben the Daring was delighted. He telephoned to the Birmingham police to say that he was going away for the week-end but would present himself for arrest at 11 o'clock on Monday morning. Then he sent a telegram to Bottomley:

> Congratulations. Please temper Justice with Mercy in your powerful position. Hope Charlie Chaplin won't be annoyed at taking some of his limelight. What a play! Selling pamphlets. Yours sincerely, Reuben Bigland of Birmingham, the man who dared call you a common swindler.

In due course Bigland gave himself up, was brought before the magistrate, Sir Chartres Biron, and remanded for a week. Bail was assessed at two sureties of £100 each. Bottomley's position as plaintiff was, as he was aware, a most delicate one. It was open to him to charge Bigland simply with writing and publishing a criminal libel. Bigland would then have pleaded justification, and the magistrate must have sent the case for trial. The libel had been so badly drawn that at the trial, it is thought by many competent lawyers, Bottomley would certainly have obtained a verdict. This course had the disadvantage, however, that in attempting to justify the libel, Bigland could have dragged in so much damaging material that Bottomley's political career might have been finished. He therefore took the more daring step of charging Bigland also with trying to obtain money by menaces; he hoped to concentrate attention entirely on this charge, obtain a verdict on it, and thus discredit anything Bigland said on other subjects. To prove these charges he had to go into the box himself and submit himself to cross-examination; and in the event this proved disastrous for him.

'Mr. Bottomley drove up to Bow Street in a taxi-cab at 10.15 and was accorded a rousing reception,' *The Times* recorded. The novelist A. E. W. Mason, who had a place in court, was surprised to discover that his chauffeur was one of the demonstrators, and more surprised to learn that he received five shillings for the work. Wild opened by reading the libel and then put Bottomley in the box. Dressed in a smart morning coat with a buttonhole of violets he looked out on the court through a kind of framework of packets of paid cheques. He gave evidence well and firmly: the accusations of demanding money by menaces against Bigland related to his visit at the time of the election at the Wrekin (the witnesses to this were Perkins, and two of Houston's election agents), and the blackmail related to Bigland's visit to King Street in connexion with the water conversion scheme, where it was more or less a case of Bottomley's word against Bigland's.

The cross-examination in connexion with the bond schemes occupied more than two days. It was perhaps less severe than Bottomley had feared, but it was bad enough. He was asked for books, and said they were in Paris. He was reminded that a notice to produce papers had been served on him and replied airily that he never took any notice of communications bearing the signature of Carter and Bell (who were acting for Bigland). 'They abuse the process of the court and have been reprimanded for it many times.' He denied indignantly that the books had been removed to Paris so that the subscribers should be unable to get hold of them. At one point he threatened to report Bigland's counsel, Comyns Carr, to the Bar Council. Several times he asked in vain for protection against the harshness of his cross-examination. Biron was not sympathetic to him. When the magistrate asked for the number of subscribers to the Victory Bond Club, and pressed the question, Bottomley accused him of cross-examination from the Bench. Biron rebuked him and Wild apologized for the phrase.

BOTTOMLEY: I used it advisedly.

BIRON: I think, Sir Ernest, you had better try to keep Mr. Bottomley in reasonable order.

BOTTOMLEY: It is a very trying position. I have enough to
do to fight Mr. Bigland.

Later Biron told Wild to make Bottomley obey his ruling
and said 'He does not know how to conduct himself in
court.' Bottomley complained that the bias he found from
the Bench was intolerable, and before the case had ended
bitter interchanges had also occurred between Biron and
Wild, when the latter wished to reply to some of Comyns
Carr's statements, and had the request refused. Wild complained that he had been insulted, threatened to leave the
court, and said that 'Throughout this trial it has been a
matter of common knowledge throughout the profession
and outside that this has not been a fair or proper hearing.'

It was the cross-examination on the blackmail charge
that was really damaging. Bigland suggested that Bottomley
had offered £200 to one of Bigland's sureties if he would
repudiate his bail. He suggested also that attempts had
been made by Houston and Hooley offering £10,000 and
£20,000 respectively, to induce Bigland to drop the case;
further, that Elias had been authorized by Bottomley to
approach Bigland 'and suggest an arrangement by which
the defendant should apologize and make certain statements, handed to him in writing by Mr. Elias, and that if
this were done to tell Bigland the case would not be pressed
against him.' Bottomley denied all this indignantly, and
appealed to Sir Chartres Biron to protect him from such
allegations.

Unfortunately this story was contradicted by Elias. Sir
Chartres Biron seems to be making no overstatement when,
in his memoirs, he says that Wild made an incredible
blunder in calling him. For Elias, in cross-examination,
confirmed Comyns Carr's suggestion. He agreed that he
had wanted to arrange a settlement, in the interests of
John Bull and Odhams Press; that he had talked to
Houston and to Bottomley and had then talked to Bigland.

The suggestion made was that Bigland should change his plea to 'Guilty', and that he should then ask Bottomley questions about four matters mentioned in his leaflet, which Bottomley, ready primed, would answer convincingly. Elias had given Bigland a note with the details of these four matters. 'Who wrote the note?' asked the magistrate, and Elias replied 'Mr. Bottomley.' Was Elias really so innocent that he did not realize that his answer in effect convicted Bottomley of perjury?

At the end of the case Bigland was committed for trial on the libel charge at the Old Bailey. He was also committed to the Shropshire Assizes on the charge of inciting people to extort money from Bottomley. The charge of attempting to obtain money by menaces was dismissed. Elias, as Biron said, had given his evidence with curious frankness, considering the nature of some of it. After this evidence, the magistrate said, he could not believe Bottomley upon oath.

From the time that he failed to discredit Bigland at Bow Street, Bottomley was doomed. The contrast in his life between appearance and reality was never more notable than in the months that passed between Bigland's committal for trial at the Old Bailey on the charge of criminal libel and Bottomley's own trial at the Old Bailey for fraud. On the surface his life as a public man continued. The members of the Independent Parliamentary Group still followed him loyally, and the group was still potentially a powerful political influence. He still made speeches marked by a high moral tone, and by the assumption that one day he would be Prime Minister. Hundreds of thousands of people still believed that he had behaved as a great patriot during the war. To these people he addressed his Christmas message in *Sunday Illustrated*:

> Look at my poor self. What a year I have had! . . . I suppose there is no man in Britain today so immersed as I am

in the waters of tribulation. But what is my motto? 'Always be merry and bright.' *Nil desperandum*. 'Clouds will be sunshine tomorrow.' Let it be the attitude of all of us this Christmastide. Where is the enemy? Let us forgive him. And the friend? Let us embrace him. That is the true Christmas spirit.

Behind this figure, a combination of Pecksniff and Cheeryble, there could be discerned more clearly with each passing day another: a man turning and twisting like a rat in a farmyard, with no hope of ultimate escape. This second figure was for brief periods lulled to a feeling of security by the fact that the first seemed still so popular and influential: surely the readers of *John Bull* would not permit the disgrace of Horatio Bottomley? Friends were dismayed by the fact that it was impossible to induce him to consider his position seriously for any length of time. It was, one of them said, as though something in his mind had snapped. He would suddenly go off for a couple of days' racing or pay a prolonged visit to one of his mistresses, in an attempt to convince himself that his way of life was permanently fixed. It was true that there was little he could do to interfere with the course of events. The Bond Clubs were in the hands of the Receivers and investigation of their affairs was proving wonderfully difficult. Intermittently he made attempts to get the Shropshire case against Bigland heard first. At the Old Bailey he would again have to face cross-examination, whereas in the Shropshire case he was not directly involved. He believed also that Bigland could have no defence in the Shropshire case against the evidence of Perkins and the other witnesses, and thought that the evidence could be restricted to the question of incitement. For the Old Bailey case, on the other hand, Bigland had prepared an enormously lengthy and most damaging plea of justification.

The attempt to obtain the hearing of the Shropshire

case before that at the Old Bailey failed. 'Trained to the hour, so to speak, and as eager for the fray as a greyhound is to slip its leash,' Bigland surrendered to his bail on the morning of the 23rd of January 1922. He found some difficulty in obtaining admission to the court, until he said: 'The play cannot very well go on without me. I'm Bigland!' He was let in, and entered the dock. 'Here you stand, Reuben Bigland,' he thought, 'with the eyes of the world upon you.' He asked for a glass of water and waited happily in the dock ready to read in his booming voice the fifty-seven Pleas of Justification.

Once again he was disappointed. Sir Edward Marshall Hall, who appeared for Bottomley, asked for an adjournment on the ground that he required access to the documents and books of the Victory Bond Club. This request was refused. Marshall Hall then said that the prosecution did not propose to help Bigland by allowing him to read his Pleas of Justification, and would offer no evidence. Bigland, to his evident chagrin, was discharged. 'From that dock I crept, once more, a depressed man. *Bottomley had cheated me again.*'

By thus abandoning the Old Bailey prosecution Bottomley achieved his aim of getting the Shropshire case heard without first exposing himself to cross-examination: but he did so at heavy cost to his personal reputation. It was felt by many who had hitherto believed in his integrity, that a man who employed such a stratagem to avoid entering the witness box must have something to hide. His friend and fellow M.P. Christopher Lowther wrote that Bottomley's followers in the House were seriously alarmed by the situation. 'I beg you most earnestly to let me know what is the worst that has to be faced and how you will counteract that fellow's allegations.' Bottomley's only public platform now was the *Sunday Illustrated*, and by way of answer to Lowther in this he published an article: 'Secret history of the Bigland case. Why I Allowed the Defendant to Go.' He explained that the prosecution at the Old Bailey had been hopelessly hampered by lack of access to the Bond Club accounts and warned his readers that 'The story is not yet complete. There is to be another chapter to it—at the Shropshire Assizes in the middle of February.' Posters about this article were widely distributed in Shropshire, and Bottomley was fined for contempt of court on account of it. Bigland was fined at the same time for issuing a circular pleading for funds. Bottomley took the opportunity to make a long, dramatic speech with the idea of restoring a little of his damaged credit. 'I am giving you fellows some splendid copy,' he said to the reporters.

The Shropshire Assizes took place at Shrewsbury, and Bigland's case was taken by Mr. Justice Darling. Bottomley was optimistic, not only because Darling's judgments had so often proved favourable to him, but because he thought he had weathered the worst of the storm. The worst had been the unusual step taken by *The Times*, when it published in full Bigland's Plea of Justification. But public recollection is short, as he had so often proved, and this unfriendly action by *The Times* would be forgotten. His anxiety was not for a verdict against Bigland so much as to smother the whole affair, and he regarded the Shrewsbury case as one which might end triumphantly, and at the most could do him little harm. In thinking this Bottomley underestimated Bigland's hatred, and his desire for self-advertisement. Elias was staying at the same Shrewsbury hotel as Bigland, and when Bigland was leaving for the court on the first day of the hearing, he shouted across: 'Good luck, Bigland! good luck! and I mean it.' This, as Bigland said, was an amazing thing to happen and he attributed it to 'The voice of conscience speaking,' because 'Elias knew as well as I did that Bottomley had framed up this case; that some of the witnesses were going to commit

wilful perjury to put me away.' If the incident occurred—
and it seems an unlikely invention—it throws a little more
light upon the relations of Elias and Bottomley. It is
obvious that Elias dissociated himself as much as possible
from the knowledge of the fraudulent competitions run by
Bottomley in *John Bull*. Certainly he did not participate in
such schemes: but he can hardly have closed eyes and ears
to certain aspects of the way in which they were run. For
many years Bottomley was as indispensable to Odhams as
Odhams was to Bottomley, but the close association which
was forced on him must have been in some ways almost
intolerable to a man of Elias' careful and orderly tempera-
ment. He must have felt a relief from anxiety when it
became possible for Odhams to buy Bottomley out of
John Bull: and although he cannot consciously have desired
Bottomley's downfall, a certain reluctant admiration for
Bigland's persistence may have moved him to speak that
good luck message.

The case lasted for two days. On the first day Perkins
and the other witnesses, both members of Houston's
election staff, told how Bigland had come up to them at
the time of General Townshend's election and said he had
come to get £50,000 from Bottomley and that if he did not
get it he would flood the constituency with pamphlets.
'Tell Bottomley this will lose the election, but you can get
it squared,' was Perkins' account of Bigland's suggestion
to him, and the other witnesses gave similar evidence.
Bottomley, dwarfish in a great fur-collared coat, was exul-
tant. 'After today's evidence Bigland is good for eighteen
months' he said to Houston. By a typically adroit move
Bottomley omitted his own name and the names of
Houston and Elias, from the indictment. They had all
given evidence at the Bow Street hearings, and what they
had said was on the depositions. By removing the names
from the indictment, all three of them avoided further

cross-examination. Comyns Carr protested vigorously. 'This is a case in which a man is on trial for his liberty, and not a game of chess.' With his customary facetiousness Darling said: 'If it were I could not play.' He added that if these witnesses were not called by the prosecution they would expose themselves to comment which he had no doubt would be made.

Then Bigland went into the box, and did what Bottomley had never imagined he might do: exposed himself as a crook in order to incriminate Bottomley. His hour had come at last, and he enjoyed it to the full. Large, expansive, beaming, he stood in the witness box and explained how he had come to be known at Hull as Telephone Jack. He made gestures to signify the ringing of a telephone bell, the receiving of messages, and then the shouting through a partly-curved hand or a megaphone. This went down well: Bigland was delighted. He went on to tell in full the story of the third prize promised him in the War Stock Combination, for the money owed him 'and for services rendered'. What were these services? Bigland described the action brought by Barrett against *John Bull* and his own part in getting and keeping Duos out of the way. He had tried to make all this public before, he pointed out, even to the point of deliberately arranging his own arrest, but he had been discharged against his will. 'And when you got to the Old Bailey you were again discharged against your will?' Mr. Justice Darling asked. Bigland agreed. 'You have had no sort of luck,' the judge said pleasantly. Bigland went on to say that Bottomley's action against the printer Greaney was a bogus case arranged in advance. 'Mr. Bottomley arranged with Greaney that I was to print a libellous, scurrilous pamphlet containing extracts of the doings of Bottomley and then the latter was to sue Greaney for damages. The case came before Your Lordship and a jury, and Mr. Bottomley got £500 damages.'

There was laughter, in which Darling gallantly joined. Why had Bottomley sued Greaney instead of the author of the pamphlet, C. H. Norman? he asked. Bigland explained that Bottomley wanted no defence to the action, and no doubt Norman would have defended it militantly. He had paid Greaney £100 to act as figurehead, and had settled his costs. 'Greaney agreed to put in a nominal defence so that really Bottomley would only have to address the jury as to damages.' There was more laughter, and Darling got a laugh also when he said resignedly: 'I suppose I summed up in his favour.'

Bigland elaborated the farcical aspect of his theme. 'Mr. Greaney was so upset at the way Mr. Bottomley conducted the case against him that I had to take him out of court, otherwise there would have been a scene in court, because Mr. Bottomley did not carry out his plans according to what he told us. Greaney thought there would be little said, but Mr. Bottomley's beautiful and eloquent address to the jury was in such a style that Mr. Greaney was very distressed, and I had to get him out of court. I took him out just before Your Lordship summed up.'

Bottomley sat through Bigland's evidence with a face that showed nothing of what he felt. At times he nodded his head, laughed, or made semi-audible remarks to the semi-circle of solicitors who surrounded him. At last Comyns Carr objected to these attempts to prejudice the jury on the part of a man 'who has not the courage to go into the witness box himself', and Bottomley received a stinging rebuke from the judge. At the end of it there was no doubt at all that if he wanted to obtain a verdict he must go into the witness box himself, and submit to cross-examination. He did not go into the box, and the final speeches, by Cecil Whiteley, K.C., for Bottomley and by Comyns Carr for Bigland were in the nature of a formality. Darling summed up ruthlessly:

Bigland's story has been supported by documents and not contradicted in one single particular, not by one word, from the man who can contradict it. . . . Not only that, but from the beginning of this case until now, the man who could have contradicted the defendant at one hundred different points has used every kind of artifice to keep himself out of the witness box.

The jury, after an absence of three minutes, returned a verdict of 'Not Guilty'.

On the way back to London Bottomley stopped with his friends in Birmingham to look at Sir Josiah Mason's Orphanage. In the train from Birmingham to London he wrote a letter to the Public Prosecutor asking what steps he proposed to take in view of Bigland's statements. Within forty-eight hours he had received a preliminary summons charging him with fraudulently converting money belonging to the shareholders of the Victory Bond Club.

A week later Bottomley's name was removed from the masthead of *Sunday Illustrated*, and he announced the suspension of all his political and journalistic activities 'to enable me to give my undivided attention to the work of vindicating my character'.

This was a task now altogether beyond his power, nor indeed did he seriously attempt it. During the weeks in which the hearings of the charges against him went on at Bow Street he dismayed his friends by his evident lack of any plan to defeat the carefully-organized attack against him. It would all come right at the trial, he told them—if it ever came to a trial: there was not a jury in England that would convict Horatio Bottomley. That it would come to a trial became daily more evident, and to this he seemed almost indifferent. He invited an accountant down to The Dicker to investigate his financial position, offered him champagne, declined to discuss business, went down

248

to the stables to see some horses fed, reluctantly returned to the study when summoned by the accountant, there caressed two dogs, and fell asleep. In another, but similarly wild mood, he went to visit Odhams' business manager, Cook, at his home. He was shortly to become Prime Minister, he said, and would need a personal secretary. The post would carry with it a title. Would Cook be interested? Finding that he would not, Bottomley asked if Cook owned the house he lived in. 'If so, have you the title deeds handy?' Before Cook could reply he sat down at the piano and began to pick out 'Hark, the Herald Angels Sing' one-handed. 'No title deeds? You are being difficult tonight, Cook,' Bottomley said sadly, and left in his Daimler. There was an element of mockery, and self-mockery, in such discussions, but they certainly did not help to solve his financial or other difficulties.

At the end of the long Bow Street hearings when he was committed for trial at the Old Bailey, he made a florid statement which prefigured the nature of his defence. He referred to himself as a 'public man who, for good or evil, commands a large following among the people, and who during the tragedy of Armageddon—and I speak from the depths of my soul—became conscious of a new awakening, and putting all the sordid things of the past aside, consecrated his whole being to the service of his country and of the men who fought and fell in its cause.' He arrived in court with this statement already printed for the use of press correspondents. They duly used it: but the Bottomley who said these things was no longer a great patriot and the editor of *John Bull*, but simply a man using his oratorical tricks, too obviously, in the attempt to keep out of prison.

His trial at the Old Bailey began on the 19th of May 1922, and lasted for eight days. By contrast with the strange and farcical incidents associated with the various prosecutions of Bigland it was undramatic. Bottomley, brisk and smiling, arrived in court to the accompaniment of the usual loud applause. His best hope lay in the rich confusion of the Bond Clubs' affairs, in the customary disappearance of any useful books—and of course in his own oratorical power to sway the jury. The prosecution's task was that of making the financial complications clear enough for a jury to understand, and to pronounce a verdict on them.

The Crown had instructed Travers Humphreys, K.C., who was a chartered accountant as well as a lawyer, to conduct the case. H. D. Roome and Vernon Gattie appeared with him and Sir Archibald Bodkin, the Director of Public Prosecutions, was in court during much of the case. With beautiful lucidity Humphreys outlined the various schemes which had merged into each other. Then he traced the disposal of the money, not through the clubs' books, but through various Bottomley banking accounts. With £80,000 of the money obtained from the war stock nomination Bottomley had bought National War Bonds, not for the benefit of subscribers but for himself. With £10,000 of it he had paid a debt outstanding since 1912. Another £7,500 in bonds had been handed direct to the liquidator of the John Bull Investment Trust. Later it was possible to show the use of the £100,000 allotment letter in buying the *National News* and *Sunday Evening Telegram*. At another time Bottomley had found himself short of money for a racing trip, and simply took it from the Bond Clubs in the same way that he had been accustomed to dip his hand into the petty cash at *John Bull*.

It was holiday time. Mr. Bottomley was going over to Ostend, and at that place he had a number of race-horses. Mr. Bottomley wanted some money, which certainly was not in his account until the trust fund money was paid in, to pay for the upkeep of those horses.

Bottomley angrily interjected 'Rubbish', but Humphreys went on patiently with his laborious task. Five hundred pounds for champagne, two thousand for debentures in Plumpton race-course, three thousand paid for a lease—they could all be traced back. The purchase of *The Deutschland* from *John Bull* for £15,000 had been made with a cheque drawn on the Victory Bond Club. More than £3,000 had gone to finance the British United Penworks which made John Bull pens, £5,000 had been paid to the manager of Bottomley's racing stable.

Then came the witnesses. Some 85,000 people had written claiming back their money since the clubs went into the hands of the Receiver; Travers Humphreys called a selection of them, including an out-of-work boilermaker, a widow, a builder and some domestic servants.

Bottomley opened the defence by asking dramatically whether he was entitled to call 100,000 members of the clubs to prove that they had had their money back? He used this number by way of contrast with the pitifully few prosecution witnesses. Mr. Justice Salter, who was hearing the case, justified his legal name of 'drysalter' by merely answering that he would listen to any evidence put before him. Then Bottomley made a passionate denunciation of those who were persecuting an innocent man:

> You have got to find that Horatio Bottomley, editor of *John Bull*, member of Parliament, the man who wrote and spoke throughout the war with the sole object of inspiring the troops and keeping up the morale of the country, who went out to the front to do his best to cheer the lads—you have got to find that that man intended to steal their money. God forbid!

He burst into tears, and it was agreed by many people in court that the speech was a very moving one. He went on to paint a picture of himself and his relations with the clubs which certainly resembled very little that of Humphreys: so greatly can two artists differ in the interpretation of a theme. The government, he said, had appealed to M.P.s and public men to popularize Victory Bonds; and although he was very busy at the time he had instantly responded—taking, as the original advertisements had pointed out, absolutely no remuneration for his services. It was true that, with the object of testing the market, he had borrowed on one £100,000 block of bonds; but, so far from his being in debt to the Bond Clubs, there could be no doubt at all that they owed him something like £50,000.

All this was not exactly convincing perhaps, but it was in a way persuasive. The effectiveness of this opening, however, was totally destroyed during his seven hours in the witness-box, when under Travers Humphreys' questioning he was forced to admit having received some £27,000 for his wartime lectures. Perhaps the deepest shock for his more innocent supporters during the whole trial was the discovery that the great patriotic orator had received nearly £27,000 for his work.

On the afternoon of Friday, May the 26th, Bottomley made his final speech in his own defence. It lasted for an hour and a half, and was yet another display of emotional fireworks. They were trying him as a public man, he said, for something dearer than his life—his honour.

> My honour and my life are one.
> Take honour from me, and my life is done.

He had endured so far because he could not comprehend the possibility of a verdict against him. Friends had asked what he would do if things went wrong. 'Things would not go wrong. If they did go wrong, it would be the most appalling error of justice the world had ever known. . . . You will never convict me. The jury is not yet born who would convict me of these charges.' Pointing to the sword of the figure of Justice brooding over the court, he said: 'That sword would drop from its scabbard if you gave a verdict of guilty against me.'

This address, like Bottomley's opening, had a visible effect upon the jury: but this, by an unlucky chance for him, was Friday afternoon, and there was the week-end to pass before the closing speech for the prosecution and the summing up. This must have been an agonizing week-end for him. He spent Friday evening watching the fight between Bombardier Billy Wells and Goddard at the Crystal Palace, and was then driven down to The Dicker. Here, in the company of several followers, including Houston, Cox and his race-horse trainer Jimmy Hare, he spent a drunken week-end. Asked what he thought would happen on Monday he said that he expected a sentence of three years. Poor Mrs. Bottomley, quite unable to fathom the depths and dangers of the situation (after all Horace had been in trouble so often before, and had always got out of it) wandered vaguely about the house. On Sunday night he went back to London and dined with Peggy Primrose. He gave her the impression that he expected acquittal. He was being prosecuted under a recent Act of Parliament, the Larceny Act, 1916, which defined fraudulent conversion as a misdemeanour punishable with a maximum sentence of seven years penal servitude.

On Monday Travers Humphreys made his final speech, cool, clear and reasonable like his handling of the whole case. 'I will now go, my lord, to the place where accused persons always go,' Bottomley said to Salter. At the end of Humphreys' speech he went to the dock and, head resting on hands, listened to a summing up that went utterly against him. At lunch-time Salter had not finished. Bottomley lunched with friends in a small room at the

Old Bailey. After lunch he was thoroughly searched, and was relieved of his money, his watch and chain, and of several Derby tickets which he had bought in a moment of optimism. Salter's summing up can have left Bottomley no hope that he would see the Derby. On the prosecution's side were facts, the judge said, on the side of the defendant were statements lacking documents, receipts, or bills. 'If the mere assertions of the defendant are to be accepted as sufficient in a case of this kind it is difficult to see how any trust funds can ever be protected.'

The jury were out for only twenty-eight minutes before returning a verdict of guilty. Bottomley stood gripping the edge of the dock, his face flushed, as the judge passed sentence:

> Your crime is aggravated by your high position, the number and poverty of your victims, by the trust which they reposed in you and which you abused. It is aggravated by the magnitude of your frauds, and by the callous effrontery with which they were committed and sought to be defended. I can see no mitigation. The sentence of the court upon you is that you be kept in penal servitude for seven years.

His face still more flushed, Bottomley said: 'I was under the impression, my lord, that it was sometimes put to an accused person, 'Have you anything to say before sentence be passed upon you.'

'It is not customary in cases of misdemeanour.' Salter replied.

'Had it been so, my lord, I should have had something rather offensive to say about your summing up.'

Now the warders, prison governor and prison doctor all closed in on him, holding his arms tightly to his side as he was removed below. In spite of the fact that he had been searched they were afraid that he might somehow attempt to commit suicide. Later they all drove away with him in a taxi-cab. A note in *The Times* on their departure indicates that the Bottomley era was already over. 'Mr. Bottomley passed on his way to prison without sound or sign of popular recognition.'

Chapter XIX

PRISON

'I am in better health and spirits than I have been for twenty years.'—HORATIO BOTTOMLEY, *on his release from prison.*

So it was all over. With the judge's words the great Horatio Bottomley, spokesman of the man in the street and future Prime Minister, suddenly disappeared, and was replaced by an old man wearing a coarse nightshirt blazoned with broad arrows. This old man had been changed quite suddenly, by legal decision, from an important figure in the world to a convicted felon. After his conviction it became obvious to men who had believed in him and praised him a month ago that he had all along been guilty of a shocking practical joke on respectable people. The nest of such a man, it was believed, must be well feathered, and these respectable people with notable unanimity refused to contribute to a fund that had been started for his appeal. This supposition, though natural, was wrong. Bottomley had managed to preserve The Dicker inviolate, but he had salted away no private fortune. He really was as poor, almost, as many of his victims.

His respectable and aristocratic friends were shocked: by the people he had most generally robbed and tricked he was mourned. Dicker at this time was a village where no one smiled. The people who lived there were worried about their own futures, but they were also grieved by the fate

256

of the man who had been, as a cowman said, 'a little King in these parts'; and who had treated most of them with a kindness and generosity unusual in kings. The blinds of The Dicker were drawn close; within, the large ornately-furnished apartments seemed suddenly dead. In the railway siding stood an empty van marked 'Dicker Stud'. Later, under his third bankruptcy, twenty of his horses were sold for less than £2,000. It was not only at The Dicker that people remained faithful to the tribute of the common man. A leader in the *Daily News* noted with puzzlement the sympathy that existed for him and found reasons for it in 'his unquestionable personality, and the impudence which, carried to such heights as he carried it, is a sort of courage'. The *New Statesman* also, in a surprisingly friendly article, observed that his name remained a household word to many thousands of people who had never heard of J. L. Garvin, and said that he really was John Bull as well as being a humbug.

On his first night in Wormwood Scrubs he was brought for supper four thick slices of bread and margarine and a tin containing a light brown mixture, with 'such a film on it as would have cheered the heart of a prospector for petroleum oil'. He refused this, said that he would go to bed and asked where he should put his denture. 'What's the matter with the sputum pot?' asked the warder. Within a few days he was in the prison hospital, where he made friends with the cat. He suffered badly from insomnia and was in low spirits. When he had been in prison three weeks Houston paid him a visit, and was shocked by his appearance. The prison authorities had found it difficult to fit a man so short and fat, and Bottomley's trousers were several inches too long. His short tunic had been buttoned tightly to hide the broad arrows on his shirt. A forage cap looked ridiculous on his head. His face was grey and his eyes heavy and lustreless. They discussed the question of raising funds for the appeal, and Bottomley's intention to attend the House of Commons on the day of the motion for his expulsion. As they talked, he cheered up a little.

'Before I go round with the hat in the House of Commons,' Houston said, 'I should like to know what you did with the £2,000 you collected for the purpose of your own defence at the trial. You acted as your own counsel and the solicitors' costs could not possibly have absorbed all that money.'

'Houston,' Bottomley replied, 'I marked my own brief.'

His appeal, on which he had set some hope, came on and was dismissed and the appearance in the House of Commons which had been expected of him was never made. Instead he wrote a letter which, in the fragment of it quoted here, seems to have true feeling mixed with its fustian:

> I desire, first of all, to express my deep sorrow for having brought this slur on the House of Commons, which I have loved as I have loved my King and Country, and to be a member of which was the dream of my youth. . . . Meanwhile I must submit to the cruel fate that has overtaken me. . . . My expulsion from the House of Commons is a punishment greater and more enduring than any sentence of any Court of Law. . . . But I have myself to blame, and all I can do is to ask Members of the House to judge me as they knew me . . . it is entirely due to my own fault, that I am the victim of an appalling error of justice.
>
> I beg, therefore, . . . to bid the House a respectful and affectionate farewell.

The letter was read, and in a hard silence Austen Chamberlain, Leader of the House, moved Bottomley's expulsion. One voice only found a word to say. It belonged not to a member of the Independent Parliamentary Group nor to one of those members who had often eaten and drunk with him, but to a stranger. Colonel John Ward, Independent Labour M.P. for Stoke-on-Trent, said that he had waited vainly to hear the Leader of the House say that he moved the motion with regret. Bottomley, Ward said, had never spoken two words to him, but 'remembering the remarkable position he occupied in the country, I cannot allow him to be expelled from the House without expressing my personal regret at the necessity.'

So he was expelled, and was swallowed by the routine of prison life. Or not quite swallowed. Occasionally news about him emerged. He was looking particularly well; he had complained of lack of appetite and of sleep; he had discouraged a monster petition that was being organized for his release; with typical inaccuracy he looked forward to the first Labour Government in seven to ten years' time under Ramsay MacDonald who, he had now discovered, 'stands as Parliamentarian head and shoulder above all his colleagues'. Once the man himself appeared in the Bankruptcy Court, haggard but lively. He corrected the Official Receiver about odd sixpences in matters involving thousands of pounds, made people laugh, and never once lost his temper; it was a successful performance.

Shortly after this *Lloyds Sunday News* announced that Bottomley was writing his life story for them, and a similar announcement was made in the *News of the World*. The articles had been sold to both papers by Bottomley's agent; and when this was discovered, the disputed right of publication became the subject of a court injunction in favour of the first buyer, *Lloyds*. The articles began to appear, with certain extracts from the manuscript reproduced in his handwriting. Their appearance, naturally enough, provoked further questions about the way in which Bottomley had managed to write them and got them out of prison. Two warders were dismissed from the prison service for being privy to the smuggling out of the articles: but there is a story that Bottomley handed these papers to a distinguished friend who visited him, and who passed them on in the belief that they were notes relating to the bankruptcy proceedings.

Most of his time at Wormwood Scrubs was spent in making mailbags; and this occupation is referred to in one of the best-known of all Bottomley stories. The story takes various forms, but its essential details do not vary. A prison visitor, a Home Office inspector or a personal friend, passing by his cell, saw him stitching at these mailbags and said: 'Ah, Bottomley, sewing?'

'No,' Bottomley replied. 'Reaping.'

There are good reasons for believing that this story, in spite of its apocryphal sound, is true; and certainly true is another story which shows his quickness of wit. In the Scrubs with Bottomley was an old acquaintance who had been sentenced for a number of frauds on bookmakers. When Bottomley saw this man mowing the prison grass he remarked: 'Still on the Turf, I see.'

He was not always so bright, or so cheerful. Hooley, who had received a three years sentence for fraud early in 1922 saw Bottomley pacing the exercise yard looking utterly dejected. 'Buck up, B,' he shouted, but Bottomley merely grunted and went on walking up and down.

After fourteen months at Wormwood Scrubs he was removed to Maidstone. There he was put into the book-binding shop and worked, among other things, at repairing old library books. The financier Gerard Lee Bevan was also serving a seven years sentence at Maidstone, and he was working as a compositor in the same department. Bevan, who was inclined to be snobbish about his education and social position, was at first reluctant to speak to Bottomley. 'When he found that I had a smattering of French and German and Latin, had read history, studied Theology and even possessed a superficial knowledge of the classics, he became almost friendly,' Bottomley observes. Also in Maidstone at this time was Jim Phelan, later to become well known as a novelist and short story writer, who found Bottomley disagreeably hypocritical and intensely vain. By the formalities of prison etiquette, however, which demands that only men sentenced for similar crimes shall talk together, Phelan and Bottomley had little contact.

When he had been in prison for two years some extraordinary allegations appeared in the *Daily Herald* about the tender treatment he had received at Wormwood Scrubs and was still receiving at Maidstone. It was said that at the Scrubs season tickets had been issued to certain visitors who could come and see him at any time, that in his fourteen months there he had received nearly 700 visits, and that only half-jestingly he called his cell his editorial sanctum. At Maidstone he was said to be called at six o'clock with a cup of tea, to be given grilled fish and mutton chops and to have a valet who washed his back and laced his shoes. He was said to arrive at the printers' shop two hours later than everybody else, at ten o'clock. There, he was accommodated in an armchair with plenty of cushions placed on a slightly raised platform so that the soles of his shoes did not touch the concrete floor.

This very circumstantial story was said to be written by a fellow-prisoner of Bottomley's, since released; it was denied, not altogether convincingly, and it does seem likely that Bottomley's age and former position gained him some privileges. The *Daily Herald* stories were followed by a fresh crop of rumours. He was ill, he was dying, he was on a milk diet, he was to be sent to Parkhurst, he was as slim and straight as a young man of twenty-five. Then there was silence. The months changed into years, and in the world outside prison many things happened about which he would have had a good deal to say. The first Labour

Government came and went. (Its Prime Minister, Ramsay MacDonald, wrote a letter of congratulation to Reuben Bigland for his part in 'unmasking one of the greatest scoundrels this country has ever known'.) The General Strike was called, and failed. The pattern of current feeling moved further and further away from the patriotic fervour through which he had had his great success. In the sudden development of many forms of amusement the man in Maidstone prison was, by a rising generation, forgotten.

Their elders, however, remembered him. The villagers at Dicker talked of having a brass band to greet him, and of towing his carriage home. 'We have a slogan down here: when old Bott comes back he won't have to walk home,' one of them said. The actual release came as a surprise to the villagers, and to Bottomley. On a Friday morning nine days before he was due to be released, he was called to the governor's office, told that he would be discharged that day and that he must go straight to The Dicker. The night staff were not allowed to go off duty, and no telephone messages in or out of the prison were accepted until he was clear. He reached The Dicker at almost nine o'clock at night, and the official secret had been so well kept that Mrs. Bottomley did not expect him. He had been in prison for five years and two months.

The Government had achieved their object of preventing any immediate demonstration after his release. On the following day, however, the local grocer drove to Hailsham to arrange for the Hailsham prize band to play outside The Dicker. They did so: a Union Jack was hoisted at the house and Bottomley's racing colours were displayed in the field opposite. There were hundreds of telegrams, many callers. A crowd gathered outside the house, and called for three cheers for Mr. Bottomley. When he came out, white-haired, lined and much thinner but smiling, they began to sing:

> *Then welcome home to Bottomley,*
> *Deny it if you can;*
> *He played his part; he's right at heart—*
> *And every inch a man.*

Within a few days of his release Bottomley's story of
his prison life was appearing in the *Weekly Dispatch*.
Bernard Falk who was at that time editor of the paper,
suggested that the display line in the advertisement hoardings should be 'I Have Paid.' Bottomley insisted on the
addition of the word 'but', so that the line read: 'I HAVE
PAID, BUT——.' The end of the quotation, which was
supplied in Bottomley's story, was 'I did not owe the debt.'
The ingenious amendment made Falk confident that
Bottomley had not lost his journalistic touch, but he was
somewhat shaken when the first article proved to be
written entirely in verse. It was called 'A Ballad of
Maidstone Gaol' by 'Convict 13', which was Bottomley's
prison number:

> *'13' upon his coat and cap*
> *The man identifies*
> *(A number now, and once a name!)*
> *At work or exercise.*
>
> *A First Offender (legal slang),*
> *His coat and cap are starred;*
> *His photograph and finger-prints*
> *Are filed at Scotland Yard.*
>
> *In felon's den—in convict garb;*
> *His sentence, seven years—*
> *Perchance a sigh, but ne'er a sob;*
> *The wound too deep for tears.*

Quite plainly this was not up to Oscar Wilde, and Falk
tactfully suggested that the verses should be spread over
several instalments. An argument ensued which horrified

Randal Charlton, who was with Bottomley at the time. 'Really, Falk, you must not talk like that to Mr. Bottomley,' he said. At last Bottomley agreed to Falk's suggestion, and the poem was interspersed among accounts of his prison experiences.

Bottomley had two or three distinct motives in writing these memoirs of prison life. He seems to have been genuinely distressed by the callousness and petty inhumanity with which prisoners were treated, and his straightforward account of such things is interesting. He thought that every Member of Parliament should serve three years' penal servitude before expressing any opinion about prison life, and much of what he said was in effect a plea for more generous treatment of the prisoners still serving their sentences at Maidstone. He suggested that every Briton should have a certificate of citizenship, and that this should be endorsed after he had been convicted of an offence. Junior and Senior Penal Workshops and Factories, in which useful work might be done, should take the place of prisons, and they should have married and single quarters. The small remainder of utterly intractable prisoners should, he suggested, be put into a modified Broadmoor. He was concerned also to rehabilitate himself by building the fiction that he had been unjustly convicted. He had mentioned this in his farewell message to Parliament, and had stressed it cleverly in the title of this series of articles. His real crime, he said, was tampering with the Lottery Acts; and he claimed to have noticed 'a marked change in the demeanour of the jury' after Mr. Justice Salter's summing-up. Another step in this move towards rehabilitation was taken when he held a meeting in the Queen's Hall. The great stroke at this meeting was to be the appearance of the foreman of the jury at his trial; this foreman, by Bottomley's account, would say that the jury had been horrified by the severity of the sentence. The foreman, however, did not appear. Bottomley gave an account of his prison life and recited 'A Ballad of Maidstone Gaol'. It was feared that this recitation might be followed by a demonstration against him on the part of disgruntled holders of Victory Bonds, and to drown their protests it was arranged that the Queen's Hall organist should start *fortissimo* with Rachmaninoff's Prelude in C sharp minor. No hostile demonstration took place, but the meeting was a shadow of the triumphs of his heyday. The organist's fee, like the charge for hiring the hall, was paid by friends who never received the money.

The failure of the Queen's Hall meeting he regarded as a minor setback. He was paid £12,500 for the *Weekly Dispatch* articles and to all appearance lived as well as ever. He felt himself to be a young man again, at the height of his powers. Within a few weeks of leaving prison he made it known that he would be starting a new periodical: a periodical which, with his name and influence behind it, would quickly supersede *John Bull*.

Chapter XX

AN OLD MAN SHUFFLING

For Man lives by his head;
He needs a larger size;
You try it for yourself. Your head
Won't feed a pair of lice.
 Why, for this existence
 There's no man who's smart enough,
 Life's too short for learning
 Every trick and bluff.
  BERT BRECHT, *trans. Christopher Isherwood.*

IN THE GRAND offices at Grosvenor Gardens secretaries and typists were flitting about busily when Charles Pilley entered. He gave his name and a few moments later heard Bottomley's voice, warm and rich: 'Come along, Pilley, I'm just the same as ever. Don't be afraid.' Pilley went in and listened while Bottomley, beaming, told him about the new publication. It was to be called *John Blunt*, and in appearance would be modelled on the old *John Bull*. There could be no doubt that with his name on the cover he would recapture his old public in its entirety. And he was employing the old people on the staff. Theodore Dahle, Randal Charlton, and A. G. Hales; Walter Moore, who had written the 'Imaginary Interviews' and 'In the Barber's Chair' features for *John Bull*; Hugh Cargill, for a long time advertising manager of that periodical; cartoonists J. T. Browne and W. F. Thomas. Would Pilley join them? Pilley, who had succeeded Bottomley as editor of *John Bull* and had held that position for eighteen months, was delighted to do so. An immense advertising campaign was carried out to publicize the first issue of *John Blunt*. Large posters were displayed up and down the country with the name *John Blunt* and a lithograph of Bottomley, fierce-eyed, gentle-faced, iron-jawed, a man who had conquered grief and sorrow.

Sandwichmen marched through the London streets with these posters; a parade of them moving continuously outside Elias's office must have made that little man thoughtful. After Bottomley's imprisonment the sales of *John Bull* had dropped from something near 2,000,000 to 300,000. Elias had refused to accept the opinion of experts that the periodical must be given up. Instead he had refurbished it, with an almost completely new set of contributors. Several of these contributors were famous men who had been opposed to Bottomley in the past. They included Asquith, Earl Haig, A. G. Gardiner, Arnold Bennett and the *Daily Herald* cartoonist Will Dyson. This blood transfusion— which amounted almost to a complete replacement of one type of blood by another— had been remarkably successful, but Elias did not underestimate the threat presented to him by the new paper, or the strength of Bottomley's personal feeling against Odhams, which drove him to the length of buying a few shares so that he could attend shareholders' meetings and ask questions about the accounts. This harassing tactic was of little importance: but in reply to *John Blunt* Elias strengthened *John Bull's* editorial appeal and enlarged its publicity campaign. It is natural to ask where the money came from that enabled Bottomley to start again on such a lavish scale. Some of it was provided by moneylenders, who had made a great deal of money out of Bottomley in the past and were prepared to take a chance on his return to power. Much more was obtained by putting pressure on friends and enemies to support him. He made an attempt to blackmail Lord Birkenhead which was wholly unsuccessful; but people of less strong character contributed sums of money to the paper's funds to keep their names out of its columns.

The first issue of *John Blunt* appeared in June 1928. It was a failure almost from the start, and the reasons for its failure are interesting. It contained, by design, much that was familiar. The cover showed a drawing of Bottomley, flanked by two descriptions of him as 'Tribune of the Man-in-the-Street' and 'Champion of the Bottom Dog'. Here was that old column of scandal and gossip, 'The World, the Flesh and the Devil'; here were the Open Letters—the first one addressed to 'His Majesty King George' and signed by 'Your Faithful Liege, Horatio Bottomley':

> And now, Sir, in launching this new member of the Fourth Estate, I plight my troth to your person and your House.

Here were A. G. Hales saying 'God Send Us a Man,' Pilley writing about 'Prudes on the Prowl,' Walter Moore putting Dr. Voronoff into the Barber's Chair, and the editor referring to his old uncle George Jacob Holyoake. It was all familiar: so familiar that it was old-fashioned. The journalistic approach favoured by Bottomley was in the tradition of ham acting; it was full of breast-beating and rhetorical gesture; its humour was vulgar in a down-to-earth way; its exposures of current scandals were made always in a scandalized moral tone. In the late nineteen-twenties such a journalistic approach had been superseded by a slick, hard brightness; vulgarity was offhand rather than outspoken; a moral tone seemed ridiculous. The acting technique of Sir Frank Benson had been replaced by that of Noel Coward.

All this Bottomley never realized: nor, had he realized it, would he have been capable of adapting himself to the new style. He was delighted when the pastor of Chesham United

268

Free Church said that the paper was 'A masterpiece of popular expression' and advised him to 'Strike the *high* note in *your* way, give the Devil "paddywhack", and never lose your faith in God.' Commendation in such terms, however, meant that the paper had no appeal at all for young readers; and older ones showed little inclination to enter his 'Co-operative Compound Coupon Competition,' to become members of his Hire Purchasers' Association, or to take up the £50,000 worth of one shilling Ordinary shares which he offered to them. Publication of his poems, *Songs of the Cell*, was said to have brought a 'phenomenal' number of orders from readers, but within a short time the volume was being given away to anybody who sent a two-penny stamp. His genius for picking sporting losers was emphasized once more by the appointment of Phil Scott, the British heavyweight boxer known as 'the horizontal champion', as boxing editor. The John Blunt League, founded 'to work for clean politics, irrespective of party', was never anything more than a joke, although it served as an excuse for Bottomley to publish his list of candidates who should be supported in the 1929 General Election. Among these were Herbert Morrison, rather oddly recommended as 'one of the best-educated members of the Labour Party', J. H. Thomas, Sir Harry Brittain, Winston Churchill, J. D. Cassels, Norman Birkett and his old enemy Comyns Carr (handsomely called 'one of the ablest men at the Bar, and destined for legal office').

Almost everything Bottomley did with *John Blunt* was wrong, and even the most devoted members of his staff realized before the death of the paper that during the years in prison his mental powers had greatly deteriorated. He had become quite unable to brook contradiction or even argument; he suggested ideas that seemed obviously ridiculous even to those disposed to believe that every utterance of his was inspired, he was unable to retain his concentration and rambled aimlessly at times from one subject to another. In the midst of a discussion on increasing circulation he would break off to say 'You mark my words, you will see myself and Gerard Bevan in the Government yet.' Even Randal Charlton can hardly have believed that he would ever be asked to enter any conceivable Government now.

One of his most foolish actions at this time was to bring an action against his former secretary, Houston, in respect of some newspaper articles. Bottomley took strong exception to statements in these articles that he had obtained money by blackmail, and he had brought the action, he said perfectly seriously, to vindicate his good name. In the course of this action a great deal of mud which might have settled for ever was stirred up again, and although Bottomley eventually obtained a verdict for £1,500 against Houston he was unable to get the money.

In September 1929 it was announced that he was to make a tour of the Empire. He would visit the British Dominions and study trade questions and political relations. During his absence *John Blunt* would be issued monthly, and special plant and machinery would be laid down capable of printing the million copies which would be needed on his return. After the publication of one monthly issue no more was heard of *John Blunt*. His Empire tour turned into a series of lectures in South Africa, which failed so wretchedly that he cut them short and returned home. He had already attempted unsuccessfully to give lectures in England about his prison experiences. In several towns he had been refused the use of halls; at Portsmouth a group of naval officers broke up the meeting; elsewhere he saw empty seats and only a few aging friendly faces. His audience was gone.

Now he suffered nothing but misfortune. Eliza Bottomley died, as puzzled perhaps by the troubles that had assailed her later years as she had been astonished by the golden times of the past. Bottomley and his daughter Florence were at her bedside. Soon afterwards he was taken through the Bankruptcy Court again. He spoke vaguely of political influences that had been at work against him. He had been guaranteed £100,000, he said, from a lecture tour in Canada, Australia and the United States. Somebody had stopped the tour, somebody was working against him all the time. As a result of this bankruptcy he lost The Dicker.

Now what could he do and where could he go? He was cared for by Peggy Primrose in her flat off the Tottenham Court Road; in the daytime he shuffled about Fleet Street, a poor broken old man, vainly trying to interest editors in articles about sweepstakes or pieces that told how he had, for the twentieth time, found God. He lived partly on the small sums provided for his support by a forgiving Elias, and a few other friends: mostly he depended on Peggy Primrose, who had visited him often in prison and afterwards became his inseparable companion. It was she who obtained for him a three weeks' engagement at the Windmill. He was billed as 'Revudeville in Excelsis: Horatio Bottomley': but when he walked slowly to the middle of the stage in his dinner jacket and cast a sad patient look at his puzzled audience he can hardly have seemed to them anything 'in excelsis'. He told a few stories about the people he had known in the past, but it was a past remote as the Ice Age to many of his hearers. What had they to do with long-dead judges, distant legal tricks and triumphs; what even with the war, which had been over now for fourteen years? Horatio Bottomley was to most of them only a slightly ridiculous name. They listened politely, without finding him comic or even pathetic; they simply thought him dull. They did not realize that they were watching a court jester whose privileges had been taken away.

After a few days at the Windmill he collapsed, and was taken to Middlesex Hospital. He was expected to die, but almost miraculously recovered. Soon after he came out of hospital he applied for an old-age pension on the ground that he was a man who had deserved well of his country. The news that he made such an application provoked the last appearance of the erratic, farcical Reuben Bigland in Bottomley's career. Through a newspaper Bigland offered Bottomley £1 a week for life and a cottage 'in Shakespeare's country'. Bottomley suggested that Bigland's conscience might be troubling him and said that he would consider the offer; finally he said that his self-respect would not permit him to accept it.

The old-age pension was granted to him, and then suddenly the grant was revoked: but when that news came to him Horatio Bottomley was past worrying about old-age pensions. He had been admitted again to Middlesex Hospital and there, in a public ward, was slowly dying. His last audible words were a demand for milk. 'Nurse,' he said, 'I want some milk. I must have milk. I will have milk.' Soon afterwards he lapsed into a coma, from which he did not emerge. Peggy Primrose was at the bedside when, on the 26th of May 1933, he died.

He was cremated at Golders Green Cemetery, and the ceremony was conducted by his friend Basil Bourchier. At the moment of death he became again respectable, a man with whom acquaintanceship might be acknowledged or even friendship claimed. Hundreds of letters and telegrams arrived at the cemetery. He had been, Bourchier said, like David a man after God's own heart: and the preacher added a reference to the running of the Derby on the following day which was not precisely felicitous and yet had its own appropriateness: 'When tomorrow at three o'clock the Great Race runs, Horatio Bottomley, I say in God's name, is assured of a place.'

Few of those most closely associated with Bottomley met comfortable deaths. When his world crumbled, theirs crumbled with it; they had no existence apart from him, and his imprisonment literally meant ruin for them. Harrison, the People's Perkins, was found dead by bailiffs on the 17th of December 1935 in his room at Median Road, Hackney. He had been dead for two weeks. In a corner of the room was a gold-mounted malacca cane marked 'From H.B.' from which he had never been parted in the extremes of poverty. A little later Houston died, friendless, in one small dirty room in East London. For a few weeks before his death Houston received money from Bigland and also from Elias, but it came too late to save him. Half a dozen other members of the stable, barely mentioned in this book, committed suicide or were found dead of starvation. Past association with Bottomley clung to them like a bad smell when they tried to get other jobs: and it is hard to think of any job for which service with him had fitted them. Tommy Cox, lucky as always, died soon after the trial and the prison sentence.

This disease of poverty affected Peggy Primrose. For years after Bottomley's death she lacked money to claim his ashes. At last in 1937 she did so, and scattered all that remained of Horatio Bottomley upon the Sussex downs.

For a biographer the most interesting characters are those whose inner lives, like that of Carlyle, present some kind of ethical conflict; whose conduct, like that of Poe, can be traced to a deep childhood injury; or who pursue a bitter theoretical logic to its practical end, like Rimbaud. Most statesmen and politicians show instead a mask to the world. The mask is labelled in the popular legend: Dizzy the Dandy, the Grand Old Man, Mr. Wait and See, the Fiery Little Welsh Lawyer, Old Sealed Lips. Tear off the label, try to distinguish the real from the legendary, to trace in action the springs of motive, and you make a strange discovery: behind the public face there is no private one. Politicians, in general, are like actors: in any important sense their lives are played in public.

So Horatio Bottomley seems a series of public attitudes rather than a person. The company promoter, bland and smiling, triumphing over angry shareholders; the well-paid recruiting agent, arms outspread, tears in his eyes; the lay lawyer yearning with sincerity; the Cockney wit and champagne guzzler. All this blended to make a wonderfully rich public personality, but behind the public personality there was, in any serious sense, no character at all.

He can be seen clearly in two lights: as an egoist whose need for public notice was so overwhelming that it drove him to fantastically reckless actions; and as a supremely skilful exploiter of mass emotion over a period of some thirty years. His career was punctuated by utterly reckless actions, actions which could never have been taken by a merely shrewd man. His disastrously foolish attack on the Prudential is inexplicable if we simply think of him as a rogue. It brought him almost to ruin, yet it is unlikely that he ever regretted the attack or thought that he had made a mistake. Part of his power over men and women came from his need to prove that Horatio Bottomley was equal to the Prudential; that Horatio Bottomley was equal to anybody or anything.

He needed to prove also that the greatest lay lawyer in England was above the law: and throughout his life the plans he made for hoodwinking shareholders and accountants were in some ways skilful and subtle, and in other ways remarkably careless. It was necessary for him to place difficulties in his own way so that he might overcome them. Probably the most important moments in his life were those in which he was able to triumph over awkward questions about the failure to publish accounts with such

274

answers as: 'He was appealed to by Mr. Snow as to where the £700,000 had gone. He could only say, in all sincerity and honesty, he had not the remotest idea.' To succeed by pure audacity through the skill of his own tongue in defiance of logic or figures—that was what he valued. In the Victory Bond Club dealings he covered his tracks most skilfully in many respects: but he also handed over £7,500 in War Stock which he had just bought with Victory Bond money direct to the Official Receiver in settlement of a debt. In his final speech Bottomley did the best he could with this incident by saying that it was so nearly incredible that it could not possibly have happened.

> Clumsy thief that I am, it never occurred to me this was a dangerous quarter to take stolen property to. As a rule a man who has stolen a £5 note does not go and ask a policeman to change it for him. . . . Members of the Jury, are you going to believe that I am such a clumsy thief as to take £7,500 of stolen bonds to a high official of the Court of Justice and of the Board of Trade?

Unfortunately for him Travers Humphreys was able to show conclusively that Bottomley had used the money in just this way: and the truth is that he really was the kind of man who would ask a policeman to change a stolen £5 note for him. Wartime success caused his egoism to expand very rapidly, almost to the point of megalomania. Before the war he was much less negligent over details, and before the war also he would never have permitted such a man as Bigland to destroy him. There is a notable difference between his handling of Lotinga and of Bigland.

His own character made it impossible that his political ambitions should ever be realized. The Independent Parliamentary Group might have become a real political force, but not under his leadership. His talents decreased, as his ego expanded, with success. He had no capacity for any kind of administrative work; his idea of politics was a succession of vote-catching phrases and impractical ideas.

Side by side with this maniacal recklessness went his wonderful instinctive feeling for time and place and person. He knew exactly the kind of person who would be amused by his offer to accept a kick on the bottom in exchange, as it were, for the loss of some thousands of pounds' worth of shares. His audacity was boundless, but it was judiciously used. There is a story that once when he had a property for sale he said that he would start by putting his cards on the table. He had paid £17,000 for it. 'But, my dear Horatio, I know that you only paid £3,000,' said the prospective purchaser. Bottomley was unperturbed. 'Quite right. First trick to you,' he said, and began to bargain on a more realistic basis. It is a good story: but the point, really, is not Bottomley's imperturbability, but the fact that he had judged the nature of his purchaser well enough to know that he would not be offended by the discovery of an attempt to cheat him. He had remarkable tact and sensibility of a certain kind. When he came out of prison Lord Birkenhead asked him to lunch. The occasion was an awkward one, until Lady Birkenhead began to talk about the discomfort of the chairs at a charity party she had recently attended, and Bottomley remarked: 'No one knows better than I do, how hard a seat can become.' The unmentionable had been mentioned, and thereafter all was well. Perhaps no man during the twentieth century has possessed to so great a degree the quality of being all things to all people. Clergymen loved him for his sincerity, politicians for his forthrightness, old people for his generosity, children for his kindliness. He possessed all these qualities, or at least he was able to display them: but he displayed directly contrary ones too. He had no character, but simply displayed the characteristics expected by the people with whom he was in conversation.

Nothing that he wrote is of the slightest literary interest, but it should not be supposed that he lacked capacity as a journalist. On the contrary: he knew by instinct what the public, *his* public, wanted to read, and he gave it to them. Whether he actually wrote many of the words that appeared beneath his name is irrelevant. During the war years he was more than a man, he was a climate of opinion; the ghosts who wrote for him articulated his feelings. Whether they were in any sense his own feelings, or simply the feelings dictated by the necessities of place and time, can never now be discovered: and it is certain that he did not trouble himself with such fine distinctions. He was content to exercise his charm upon everybody he met: to be loved by those he swindled, admired by those he laughed at, respected by those he puckishly deceived. If we find some kind of consistency in him it is that, in any company and at any time, he was consistently vulgar. Perhaps that was the secret of his success. Perhaps, as Whistler long ago suggested, it is a touch of vulgarity that makes the whole world kin.

INDEX

F 21